NATIONALITY AND EMPIRE

NATIONALITY AND EMPIRE

A RUNNING STUDY OF SOME CURRENT INDIAN PROBLEMS

BY

BIPIN CHANDRA PAL

GYAN

Published by

Gyan Publishing House
5, Ansari Road
Daryaganj, New Delhi-110002
Phone: 011-47034999, 9811692060
E-mail: books@gyanbooks.com

Distribution Network
gyanbooks.com
India, USA, Canada, UK, Australia, France

ISBN: 978-81-212-8240-6 (PB)
First Published, 1916

2nd Impression 2023

Printed at: Gyan Press, Delhi.

NATIONALITY AND EMPIRE
Author: BIPIN CHANDRA PAL

Bipin Chandra Pal

NATIONALITY AND EMPIRE

A RUNNING STUDY OF SOME CURRENT INDIAN PROBLEMS

BY

BIPIN CHANDRA PAL

CALCUTTA & SIMLA
THACKER, SPINK & CO

1916

PREFACE.

THIS is not a systematic treatise but simply a collection of various articles published from time to time in some of the Indian Reviews. The first article, which presents the fundamental sociological and political generalisations, in the light of which the modern problem of Nationality and Empire will, in my opinion, have to be ultimately solved, was published in "Modern Review" (Calcutta) in 1910. The other articles in which an attempt has been made to apply these principles to the consideration of the most pressing problems before the people and the Government of India at this moment, were published in the "Hindu Review" (Calcutta) during 1913-14. In a collection like this it is impossible to avoid repetition of certain fundamental ideas or ideals, which run through the whole series as their regulative idea. The ideal of Federal Internationalism or Imperial Federation runs, it will be found, through every presentation of the different aspects of the Indian problem, considered here; and the supreme value which I attach to it, as the only effective solution of modern national and international problems, if accepted as correct by the reader, will, I hope, be found to be a sufficient justification for this repetition. The articles collected in this volume were written before the present world-war; but the events of the last eighteen months, instead of calling for any reconsideration or amendment of the conclusions presented here, seem, on the contrary, to considerably strengthen and verify them.

CONTENTS.

...... But you have been a good physician for me. You found and you dared to *use* the right remedy—the *only* one that could help me.

...... Yes, at the last extremity of danger we physicians dare so much.—But now you will come to me again, will you not, Ellida?

...... Yes, my dear, faithful Wangel—now I will come to you again. Now I can, for now I come to you *in freedom*—of my own will—and *on my own responsibility.*

(IBSEN.)

ओं

श्री श्रीगुरवे नमः।

INTRODUCTION.

I have tried to present a view of Indian Nationalism in these pages which may seem rather new and strange even to many of my own Nationalist friends. They are familiar with my earlier writings and speeches in which the emphasis was unmistakably more on the ideal of independence than on that of Federation. National independence is still what people understand, Imperial Federation is to most people a more or less meaningless term. The conditions of the years 1901-1908 or 1909 were not favourable for the appreciation of this federal ideal. The controversies of that time raged around the question of "Absolute National Autonomy" or "Colonial Self-Government" as a true and practicable ideal for modern India. The Nationalist school proclaimed the former, while the old Congress school pressed the latter upon the attention of the country as the more reasonable and practical. All the literature of Indian Nationalism practically grew out of this controversy.

But controversial literature of this kind can rarely bring out the full and complete positive values of any thought or ideal. In my Madras-speeches, I tried to expose the hollowness of the ideal of Colonial Self-Government; and consequently there are statements and arguments in them which lend themselves to the interpretation that I positively advocated then the ideal of absolute and isolated sovereign independence as the only true objective of all Nationalist endeavour in India. Those who are not acquainted with the history and psychology of those speeches, who did not know or would not remember that those speeches were really a reply to Mr. Gokhale's speeches in Calcutta (Congress of 1906), Allahabad and Lucknow (February 1907), naturally took the arguments which I urged against Mr. Gokhale's position, as representing the whole view of my own ideal also. Mr. Gokhale had, for instance, declared that though he would put no limit to the political aspirations of his countrymen, still he urged them to accept the ideal of Colonial Self-Government as the most practicable under existing conditions; because this is what British statesmen and the British people would understand and sympathise with. I tried to show up the utter impossibility of this colonial relation between India and Great Britain. But this was read by many people, including Sir Valentine Chirol who devotes one whole chapter of his book on "The Indian Unrest" (1911), to the consideration of my Madras-speeches—as urging the absolute severance of the British connection as a necessary condition of the realisation of the Nationalist Ideal in India.

But in *New India*, which was started in 1901 and finally ceased publication in December 1907, and which is universally regarded as the earliest exponent of the new Nationalist thought in this country, I had distinctly urged that though we certainly objected to the perpetuation of the British subjection, we did not object to the continuance of the British connection; and even in one of my Madras-speeches I did not hesitate to declare that "I was an Imperialist of Imperialists, but it must be a *right sort of empire*." In fact, in the very height of the raging passions of the Swadeshi and Boycott agitation, on the first anniversary of the Bengal Partition, October 16th, 1906, which we proclaimed as our "Nation-Day," I wrote in the columns of the *Bandê-Mātaram*:—

> We dedicate this day to that Patriotism which finds its fulfilment in Humanity. We dedicate it also to that Humanity which is the only eternal revelation of God to man.
>
> Blessed is the perfected life of the individual. Blessed is that larger and diviner life of the nation wherein the individual finds his highest fulfilment, and blessed, thrice blessed, is that Universal Life of Humanity wherein is the fulfilment and fruition of all national life and aspirations.

I have only tried to work up *this* Nationalist Ideal, which finds its highest fulfilment and fruition in Universal Humanity, in the following pages; and to present it in its practical aspects as affecting our existing relations (*i*) with the different communities and cultures represented in our own composite populations, and (*ii*) with the great British people with whom we have been placed by our past historic evolution in such close and vital contact. What may at first sight appear new in these pages is, therefore, really not new at all, but only a fresh and fuller presentation of the old, old ideal.

In 1909, in discussing "The Real Problem in India" in a London periodical (*Swarāj*, April 1), I wrote:—

> The Empire-Idea is a great idea, but the Federal-Idea is greater. It reconciles the absolute autonomy of its members with the perfected unity of the whole. And India is the meeting place not of fluid tribal organisations, ... but of

> perfected and fully developed nationalities......and the growing Indian Nation will be of a new type of nationhood, the real Federated Nation.

I frankly confess that this Federal-Ideal, not only in relation to the different communities and provincialities of India but comprising within itself the different units of the existing British Empire, was not revealed in the earlier years of our Nationalist agitation. The time was not yet ripe for it. To proclaim this ideal in 1905 or 1908 would have been suicidal to the Nationalist cause. Those were years of protest and self-assertion. That protest and self-assertion was absolutely needed (*i*) to awaken a new self-consciousness in the people, and (*ii*) to bring home to the British rulers of the country the supreme need of working up a reasonable reconciliation with the Nationalist Ideal. The general course of present-day world-politics also had not then commenced to reveal all their fearful possibilities—a revelation that has brought home to us also the supreme need of this reconciliation in our own interest as well.

I was privileged to observe these world-currents standing almost at their very centre in Europe, during the years 1908 to 1911. I was privileged to come in close, though exactly not personal, contact with some of the very men who have made new South Africa and who manœuvred the last revolution in Turkey. I came in personal contact with the leaders of Egyptian Nationalism, and watched at close quarters the forces behind the Home Rule Movement in Ireland. I saw even one or two prominent Chinese and Japanese publicists. And all these helped to reveal to me the full grandeur and meaning of

Federal Imperialism as both the highest and the most practical Ideal for the Indian Nationalists. This is how I was led to declare, in course of an address to my friends in London, on the eve of my return to India, in 1911, that

> If God were to appear before me with the gift of absolute but isolated sovereign independence for India in his right hand, and of an equal co-partnership with Great Britain and her Colonies in the present association called the British Empire, in his left hand, I would unhesitatingly say, "Father, give us the gift in your left hand."

And I made my position as clear as I could in an interview with the late Mr. W. T. Stead, which he subsequently published in the *Review of Reviews* (October 1911), from which I quote the following :—

> "I" (says Mr. Stead) "said to Mr. Pal: If that is what you have tried to teach us, what have we succeeded in teaching you?" "I will be quite frank with you" said Mr. Pal. "I have learned a great deal in these three years, but one thing more than all else stands out before my mind. I am more deeply impressed than ever I was, with the immense influence which might be wielded in the future history of the world by Britain and India acting together. Such co-operation must be, of course, based upon a recognition of the right of India to be treated as a free and equal partner and not as a dependant in the Empire. Let us suppose that the British government in India were to be reconstituted on a basis which would give the freest possible scope of self-fulfilment to India and continue the association now known as the British Empire. It would be a federal constitution, the freedom of the federated parts being realised in and through the unity of the federated whole. Such a partnership between Great Britain and India......would be preferable to isolated independence for India............I have been led to this by reflecting upon the great problems which threaten to convulse the world in the near future. These problems are three in number. There is first the problem of the White against the coloured races........The second

> question is that of Pan-Islamism........The third question is that of the Mongolian Confederacy........ These three problems are among questions which have no mercy for the peace of nations. Yet in all three it seems to me that Britain and India united will be able to exercise a far more potent influence for the avoidance of war and the arrangement of some *modus vivendi* than could be done by Britain alone or India alone. It is in the combination of Britain and India that my hope of the future lies. I object to call it an Empire. I would rather call it a co-operative partnership."

This book contains a presentation of this ideal of co-partnership which seems to me to be the only rational and practical policy for ensuring the integrity of the present British Empire, reconciling the legitimate demands of Indian Nationalism with the reasonable requirements of British Imperialism.

Few people, however, seem to understand the real significance of this large and true empire-idea, which alone can furnish a basis for this co-operative partnership between India on the one side and Great Britain and her colonies on the other. Least of all it seems to be understood by those who so loudly claim to be "Imperialists" in modern politics. To them Imperialism means the political and military domination of a central suzerain authority over extensive territories and diverse races of peoples. This false view of the imperial relation is responsible for the opposition of many British Radicals to it. This is equally responsible for the deterGined opposition offered to the empire-ideal by nationalist politicians among the "dependent" nations of our time. Many of my own Nationalist friends have evidently been influenced by this false idea of Imperialism in misunderstanding the position which I took up since my return home from England in 1911.

In the following pages, I have tried, so far as it lay in me, to dissipate this false and mischievous view of the empire-idea.

The true empire-idea is not, in fact, a political but essentially a social idea. The superior value of the Empire consists not even in its so-called mission of civilisation and progress upon which the modern European and American Imperialists openly seek to justify their conquest and exploitation of non-European lands, but in the fact that it offers the largest formula of human fellowship, so far discovered by our social movements and speculations, and that it is, therefore, the largest vehicle and instrument of that Universal Humanity towards which social evolution is always moving as its ultimate ideal-end. Man has always been a social being, a living limb of some social organism; even as we know some species of animals to have been always gregarious. In the earliest stage, we see man as a member of his family, as we see his family also as a part and limb of some tribe. The family may thus be taken as the primary unit of man's social life. This family is composed of different individuals. These individuals have their individual tastes, inclinations, and interests, which have an inevitable tendency to more or less isolate them from one another. The common life of the family, however, seeks to reconcile all these conflicts of individual tastes and interests, and, thereby, prevents the full development of these isolating influences. "This is my family and I am a member of it;" this idea becomes, in this way, a very effective formula of human association, binds and keeps individual men and women together, by providing adequate fields for mutual help and co-operation, and the due satisfaction of their primary instincts of love and affection. From the family to the tribe, which binds many families together by various ties of common habitat, common ancestry, common traditions, common customs and sacraments, and a common language and culture, however primitive these may be—man reached a larger formula of human fellowship and a higher stage of social evolution. As in the common life of the family there is an attempt to reconcile conflicting individual inclinations and interests, so in the larger life of the tribe there is an attempt to reconcile all actual and possible conflicts of family-interests. It is through this reconciliation that both the family and the tribe become vehicles of a higher and higher social fellowship. Nation which includes many tribes, offers similarly a larger ground of human fellowship, and works a higher social synthesis. And the Empire, being a combination of many nations, offers a still larger formula of human association, and a wider basis of international fellowship and co-operation. This is the real superior moral value of the empire-idea. This Imperialism offers, therefore, an essentially higher ideal than Nationalism.

All moral relations, however, have an element of freedom at their very root and constitution. Physical compulsion does not create, but really destroys, the true ethical value of all duty. The real ethical value of the family life consists, therefore, in the free choice and determination of the various adult members of the family, to live its common life and bear their respective share of the common obligations of that life. This choice, again, is influenced, though perhaps unconsciously only, by the fact that the common life of the family offers greater assurance of personal comfort, peace, and happiness, and a wider field for the self-realisation of the different members of the family, than what can be secured by the isolated life of the individual. It is peculiarly so in the earlier stages of social evolution, when man is almost perpetually engaged in conquering wild nature and wilder beasts about him, and is in a constant state of war with other human groups in his neighbourhood. In the earliest stage of social evolution, the numerous social functions that are now discharged by separate classes and professions had to be performed by each family, practically for itself. Each family, then, had to kill its own game or grow its own food, build its own hut, weave its own clothing, make its own weapons of war, and delegate its own representatives for the discharge of the common obligations of the tribe to which it belonged. Food and shelter, raiment and nursing, education and protection, whatever the individual wanted for his own life and happiness, he had to receive from the collective life and endeavour of his family and from nowhere else. And his primary instincts of self-preservation thus, unconsciously determined his choice to live in the family, bear its common burdens, and participate in its common privileges. But though it worked unconsciously this was really an act of free choice on his part. Originally our relations with our community or our nation, like our relations with our family, are not the result of our free choice and determination, it is true. We are born inside a certain community or within a certain nation, even as we are born in a certain family, without the exercise of any free choice. But the continuance of these relations depend *really*, though not always *formally*, upon our free will and choice ; we are subjected here to no sort of actual physical compulsion. Indeed, such physical compulsion would be needed only when we willed to repudiate our communal or national obligations ; and we would wish to repudiate them only when the common life of our community or our nation failed to appeal to our primary instincts of self-preservation or to provide adequate vehicles for, or sufficient scope and play to, our natural hankering for peace and happiness and the freest and fullest realisation of our social, or civic, or religious ideals. Freedom, thus, is the very soul and essence of all human fellowship and co-operation. Where this freedom is absent, either in feeling or in fact, there the real moral value of these relations is also lost. And it is just here, in the very primary need and condition of the moral life, that the profound ethical significance of the principle of self-government in the administration of the common affairs, whether of a community, or a church, or a state, actually lies.

But it is a curious thing in connection with the expansion and evolution of human freedom, that it is always restricted in some direction while reaching out to higher and higher forms of expansion and activity in other directions. The freedom of individual passions and appetites is restricted by the common life of the family, though through accepting these very restrictions, the individual attains a much larger freedom than what he could ever have hoped to get amidst the fierce conflicts and competitions of his isolated individual life and pursuits. Similarly, the primitive freedom of the tribal life has oftentimes to be lost in the process which forces many tribes into the larger unity of national life. At first, this apparent loss of the older and narrower freedom of the tribal life may be felt as a wrong and a deprivation; but in course of time, when the tribal fusion is compete and real community of interests and activities is established between the different units of the new national life, this loss is more than amply compensated by the new rights and privileges earned by the tribes in the larger life and freedom of the nation into which they are incorporated. Similarly when one or more alien nations are forced into subjection to some central suzerain authority, the loss of national freedom resulting from this new relation is resented as a grievous wrong and injustice. And as the new relation is forced upon these nations generally through conquest, and, therefore, against their will, it is undoubtedly a wrong and an injustice. But these are gradually more than amply compensated by the larger life and activities which the new association opens up to the conquered peoples. And the real ethical value of the imperial relation commences to develop in proportion as the dependent nationalities recognise these compensations and accept the new obligations, freely and willingly, as necessary conditions of their own highest good. As long as this is not done, so long the real empire is not formed; and so long the imperial obligations do not receive conscious ethical sanction. The true empire-idea demands, therefore, that the obligations of the imperial relations and the restrictions which these impose upon national independence, must be acceptable to the different national units composing the empire, as necessary for their own highest self-fulfilment, and be accepted by them, therefore, as their own free and considered choice. For it is only when this condition is fulfilled that the empire is able to truly offer a larger formula and field of human fellowship and international cooperation. Territorial possessions may have been originally acquired by force of arms, but the fundamental wrong of the rule of the sword is never righted except through the larger life and freedom that it ultimately secures for the conquered. The ethical value and justification of the empire-idea must, therefore, be measured by the help that it is able to render to the expansion of human freedom *and* human fellowship.

The family, the tribe, the race, the nation—these form the ascending series of social evolution. In this series each succeeding term is larger and more complex than each and all the preceding terms. Each succeeding stage is reached also by simultaneously restricting and expanding the freedom enjoyed by the social units in the preceding stage. The individual sacrifices his individual freedom in gaining the larger freedom of the family. The family sacrifices, similarly, its older and narrower freedom in entering into the larger and more regulated freedom of the tribal life. Tribes have to do the same while claiming the larger freedom of national existence and autonomy; and nations have, necessarily, to give up the glory of their isolated national independence in entering into the larger and more secure freedom of the empire. Man has, thus, both individually and collectively, to always lay down his freedom to gain it. Every human association encroaches upon our freedom, and even by encroaching upon it, it enlarges its bounds and increases its quality and strength.

And this result is achieved through the identification of the smaller units and interests with the larger unity and life of these new associations. Every new human association, thus, actually expands our self. This self expands itself always through the cultivation of what may be called the sense of own-ness. The sense that "this is *my* family and I *am* of this family," identifies my self with them and thus expands it, and by this dual process of identification and expansion, it at once restricts my freedom, so far as it is not in harmony with the larger life and interests of my family, and enlarges it also so far as it includes in its range and authority the collective field of activity and the collective rights of that family. Similarly, by expanding our self from the family to the tribe, from the tribe to the nation, from the nation to the empire, we identify it with larger and larger units, and through this identification, we at once restrict and expand the limits of our freedom. The imperial relation thus enlarges our self and helps it to cover much wider ground than the mere national relation; and in so doing while restricting our lower and narrower freedom, it expands the range and improves the quality of the new freedom, which we reach as members of this larger and more complex human association. This is exactly why in being members of a real imperial whole nations, though apparently sacrificing their isolated sovereign independence, really gain assurance of a much larger freedom than what as isolated sovereign states they could ever hope to secure. This is why I hold that National Autonomy inside an Imperial or International Federation is far more preferable even *ideally* than isolated national independence.

And this is why I cannot see any necessary conflict or antithesis between Nationalism and Imperialism; but on the contrary believe that no Nationalist propaganda has any moral worth or significance which does not work towards its own fulfilment in the larger life of some Federal Empire, which is the next higher step in the process of our advancement towards that Universal Humanity, which is the Ideal-End of all Social Evolution.

Presented in these general and abstract terms, the superiority of the empire-idea over the nation-idea will not perhaps be denied. What the Indian Nationalists will feel inclined to deny is the practical value and reference of this higher empire-idea to the stern actualities of their present life and relations. The British Empire, to which India belongs now, is not as yet a Federal Empire. It is composed of a number of self-governing States, a few minor Crown Colonies, and a great Dependency. There is no uniform relation between the central suzerain authority of the Empire and its various parts; no unity of policy or purpose; no vital community of interests between the parts themselves, or between them and the whole of which they are parts. The whole structure is inorganic and arbitrary. The relation between Great Britain and her Colonies is voluntary, based partly upon selfish and partly upon sentimental considerations. The relation between Great Britain and India is entirely different. The trends of Britain's Indian policy have so far been different from those of her Colonial policy. While British statesmen have been avowedly willing to consolidate their colonial relations by building up an Imperial Federation composed of the Mother Country and her Colonies, even the very best and broadest of them have openly declared the practical impossibility of any except a personal, which means an autocratic, rule in India. While the development of self-government has been the avowed object of their colonial policy, the establishment of good government has been the central aim of their Indian policy. And these actualities of their political life and lot weigh powerfully with the Indian Nationalists in leading them to reject the imperial idea as a mere idle fancy in Indian politics. They cannot lead themselves to believe that Great Britain will ever consent to accept the swarthy Hindu or Moslem as co-partners in her world-wide imperial concern.

That she will not *easily* do so need not be denied. The Britisher is not free from the colour antipathy which is characteristic of the European. And this is, perhaps, the greatest difficulty in the way of building up a real Federation of the British Empire; for to do so would mean the concession of equal rights and freedom to the Indian and the Egyptian with the British, the Irish, the Canadian, the Australian, and the other white peoples of the Empire. But, however strong this colour-sense may be, the British people, at any rate, have not allowed it to interfere with the pursuit of their political or commercial interests, when these required any association or comradeship with non-white peoples. The British, thus, of all the European peoples, were the first to enter into an open alliance with Japan, and freely accept that Asiatic Power into the comity of the White States. In Africa, America, Australia and New Zealand, the British have preserved the colour-bar far more rigidly than they have done here in India; not because the Indian climate dulls the colour-conceit of the Britisher, but because the Indian conditions make it impossible for him to maintain it without submitting to serious loss economically and otherwise. Their capacity to submit to unpleasant necessity with exceeding good grace and make a virtue of it, is one of the secrets of the marvellous success in life of the British people. They are a notoriously practical people, which means, in plain English, that their conduct in life is influenced far more by considerations of material gain or loss than by abstract idealism or gushing emotionalism. Even their prejudices have at their back some practical considerations. And the question whether India and Egypt will or will not be accepted as co-partners with Great Britain and her self-governing Dominions in the British Empire will be determined by these practical considerations only. As long as it is possible to keep India as a Dependency, and Egypt as a Protectorate, Great Britain will try to keep these countries in their present dependent position in the Empire. But the moment the trends of world-politics on the one side, and the course of public thought and agitation in these countries on the other, indicate the risks of continuing this policy, Great Britain will not hesitate for a moment to throw all her colour-conceit and race-pride to the winds, and assuming an attitude of noble generosity, concede to the Indian and Egyptian all the rights of imperial citizenship. Those who have studied British character know, or at least ought to know, this much.

And it is in this psychology of the British character on the one side and in the general trends of both British and world-politics on the other, that the force of my argument for the inevitable evolution of a true federal relation between India and Egypt and Great Britain and her self-governing Dominions lies. The internal evolution of imperial policy tends towards it. The external tendencies of world-politics also seem to be irresistably driving British policy towards some sort of a reconciliation between Indian and Egyptian nationalism and British Imperialism. The self-governing Dominions are becoming increasingly eager to secure their rightful place in the council and constitution of the Empire. At present they have no voice in the initiation or administration of imperial policy. The foreign relations of the Colonies are controlled by the British Cabinet and the British Parliament. Neither of these have any direct responsibility to the colonial peoples. So long the colonies had no call for determining their foreign relations; for they stood, practically, isolated from the main currents of world-politics. But the sudden emergence of Japan into a great Eastern Sea-Power has created a new menace to the old isolation of the Australian Colonies. Canada, similarly, is coming into closer contact with American politics, which also has started, however tentatively it may be, upon a course of imperial expansion. In the South African Union racial problems are likely to arise sooner or later, and they may create foreign complications, unless satisfactorily solved betimes. And in view of all these new developments, the Colonies will not consent to leave the absolute control of their foreign policy to the Mother Country alone for any length of time. They are keenly conscious already of their vital interests in the world-movements about them, and are building up their own militias and navies for safeguarding their special interests. Some of them, Canada for instance, have already commenced to move independently of Great Britain, in entering into special trade-relations with their neighbouring nations and forming commercial treaties with foreign States directly and without any regard for the special trade-interests of either the Mother Country or of the other members of her family. And all these are clear proofs of the loosening of the old bonds that bound Great Britain to her Self-Governing Colonies, and that held, thus, the different parts of what the *Times* calls her Self-Governing Empire, together. And unless new bonds are forged, the break-up of this Empire will be absolutely inevitable. The Colonies do not desire this rupture. But they are demanding with increasing insistance the institution of a representative Council of the Empire, which will strengthen the present relations between Great Britain and the so-called British Colonies by giving them a definite constitutional basis. This demand was openly pressed at the Conference of Colonial Premiers held in London in the summer of 1911, when New Zealand brought a specific Resolution for the organisation of a Council of Empire composed of the representatives of the United Kingdom, the Self-Governing Colonies, and India. I forget, just now, if Egypt too was included in this scheme. This Resolution received considerable support from the colonial representatives, but was strongly opposed by Mr. Asquith who presided over the Conference, and was finally withdrawn. And the main ground of Mr. Asquith's opposition was that it would place the representatives of the United Kingdom in an absolute minority in the proposed Council of the Empire, and would practically transfer the supreme authority in imperial politics from Great Britain to her Colonies. Great Britain will have some day to submit to it. But she cannot do so now. And the main reason of her present inability to accept the position assigned to her by the Resolution of the New Zealand Government is, I think, India. India cannot, in her present state of helpless dependence, be provided with a seat in any Council of the Empire vested with real federal rights. The organisation of any Federal Council just now would mean the admission of the Colonials into a share of the sovereign rights and privileges now enjoyed by the British Crown and the British Parliament alone in regard to the Government of India. India would thus be made the common dumping ground of the British Colonies, a position that would be injurious to particularistic British interests, both political and commercial, and intolerable to India herself. India's sensibilities in this matter might not count forty years ago, when India was practically ignorant of England's imperial and colonial relations, and there was no keen sense of rivalry and conflict between Indian and British interests; but they cannot be safely ignored to-day. The thing is absolutely unthinkable, specially in view of the notorious ill-treatment to which Indians are subjected in some of the British Colonies. All these must have worked at the back of Mr. Asquith's mind when he opposed the New Zealand Resolution at the Colonial Conference of 1911.

But the present nebulous state of England's colonial relations cannot be indefinitely continued. Something will have to be done within the next decade or two, if not even earlier, to consolidate these relations and place the British Empire upon a sound and enduring constitutional basis. The attainment of what may be called the state of majority by the different colonies has made the building of a Federation an imperious necessity. Indeed, this federal idea is already in the air, visibly shaping the evolution of British politics in more than one direction. The scheme of Irish Home Rule has a distinct reference to it. No responsible Irish statesman ever seriously desired the complete severance of the British connection. It is generally admitted now that Mr. Redmond's demand for a Parliament in Dublin with an Executive in Ireland subject to the control of this Parliament and responsible for the administration of all purely Irish affairs, is not something new but only a reiteration of what Parnell wanted years ago. And Parnell failed, not because he wanted to break up the Union, but because British statesmanship felt no call to accept it in its own interest. That necessity has arisen now. And even leaders of Unionist thought did not hesitate to propose a coalition between the Unionists and the Irish Nationalists in 1909-10, as a counter-move against the Liberal attack on the House of Lords. The building up of an Imperial Federation can no longer be indefinitely delayed. Such delay might spell the disruption of the Empire. And to make ready against the day when the Colonies will have to be admitted into the Council of the Empire and given a voice in the determination of imperial policy, proportionately to their population and wealth, the Mother Country must reconstruct her political life and constitution upon a federal basis. For an Imperial Federation without a federal reconstitution of the different members of the United Kingdom itself will mean the certainty of the latter being more or less completely dominated in the Council of the Empire by the representatives of the Colonies. Irish Home Rule is needed thus, now, not as before, only for the settlement of the Irish unrest, but imperatively for the consolidation of the British Empire itself. Home Rule in Ireland will be followed by the establishment of similar autonomy in Scotland and Wales and finally in England itself. The establishment of Federal Home Rule all round is already on the Liberal "ticket," as they would say in America. But even this reconstitution of the United Kingdom upon a federal basis will not remove all objections against the admission of the Colonies into the Council of the Empire. India would still remain as a serious obstacle in the way. India is a Dependency of Great Britain, but not of the British Colonies. The Colonials have no voice in the control of India's internal or external affairs. To admit them into any sort of direct partnership in the Government of India would mean positive loss to the British people and might involve possible risk to the British Empire itself. The Colonials have not the qualifications to run the business of a large Dependency with a teeming population of alien peoples, owning a history and civilisation of their own, which in their own estimate at least, are in no way inferior to and are by all accounts immeasurably more ancient than those of Europe. Their dealings with Indian emigrants also have been so notoriously offensive that their presence in the Council of the Empire, from which representatives of India are excluded, would arouse public indignation in this country to a pitch which it would certainly be difficult and possibly impossible to control. The Colonies are not half so interested in India as Great Britain. They may live and grow without India, Great Britain cannot. Both her economic and political position is bound up vitally with her Indian connection. India really is to Great Britain the only actual British Empire. Great Britain cannot, therefore, ever dream of consolidating her relations with the Colonies without fully safeguarding her relations with India. She cannot afford to allow the Colonies to break away from her. She cannot afford to run the risks of being deprived of India either. How to keep India and the Colonies together, both bound to her and to one another as parts of one great organic whole—the British Empire—that is the supreme problem before British statesmanship just now. Upon the satisfactory solution of this problem lies, indeed, the future of the British Empire.

For the British Empire can endure only upon the fulfilment of two conditions. First, the consolidation of the present Colonial relations of Great Britain in and through the organisation of an Imperial Federation, and second, the admission of India as a co-partner of the Empire into this Federation, as an equal among equals. Upon no other condition can the British Empire be truly and permanently worked into a real federal unity. Upon no other condition, as far as human reason and imagination can foresee, can the British connection with India also be made permanent. The thing is simply unthinkable, first in view of the awakening self-consciousness of the different Indian races and communities, who have already commenced to shake off their old stupor and to rapidly move forward to occupy their rightful place as builders of a new nationality and history in India, and whose spirit of self-confidence and self-assertion is mainly responsible for the present Indian unrest; and second, in view of the general trends of contemporary politics and especially Asiatic politics, as manifested in the rejuvenescence of China on the one side, and the revival of Islam as a new force in world-history on the other. Both the Chinese rejuvenescence and the Pan-Islamic upheaval affect the possibilities of the present Indian situation very vitally. I have more than once referred to these two new influences in modern history, in these pages. Unless the problem of her Imperial Federation is satisfactorily solved by Great Britain within the next few years and India is incorporated into the Empire, not as a Dependency but as a valued and valuable ally and rightful co-partner, both the Chinese rejuvenescence and the Pan-Islamic ferment may lead to very serious complications affecting equally the future of Indian Nationalism and British Imperialism both. Whether India is or is not to be admitted into the coming Federation of the British Empire is, therefore, no longer an attractive intellectual problem in historical probabilities, but has come visibly within the very range of living, practical politics. Neither British nor Indian statesmanship can dismiss it as a vain speculation. The question really is no longer debatable; for British statesmanship *must*, in the interests of the British Empire itself, devise adequate means for the admission of India into the Imperial Federation as a rightful co-partner of the Empire, and as an equal among equals, in relation to its other partners. The motive force that is driving British policy towards this end is neither justice, nor generosity, but pure, even vulgar, self-interest. The moral sense of the British people may clothe it with the purple robes of justice. Their social speculations may enshrine it as a new and enlarged vehicle of universal humanity. Philosophy may proclaim its spiritual significance. And poetry may sing of its lofty idealism. But none of these things will alter the fact that this Federation, when, and if it is built up, will owe its existence absolutely to an intelligent estimate of the self-interests of the different nations composing it.

India is not ripe as yet to take up her rightful place in the present British Empire. She must be a self-governing unit first of all, before she can enter the commonwealth of the self-governing members of the British Empire. She is too big, however, and much too diversified, to form one unit. The problem of self-government in India can only be solved through the evolution of some sort of federalism. The only conceivable form of the Indian State is that of a Federal Union like that of the United States of America. In the various Indian provinces, with their respective provincial laws and administrations, we have an excellent nucleus of the "State-Governments" of India; while the Government of India overlooking these various Provincial Governments and Administrations and controlling directly all inter-provincial agencies and works—such as Post and Telegraph, and Railways, and the Army and the Foreign Office—has all the necessary powers and instruments of a Federal Government. The scaffolding and superstructure of a United States of India are there already, and the evolution of a truly federal constitution is very easy with all these materials ready at hand. And even as the development of a Federal Union among the different parts and provinces of the United Kingdom is being forced upon British statesmanship by the needs of the Empire, so the same needs have already commenced to force the idea of a federal constitution in India also, upon every thoughtful and far-seeing British statesman. Lord Hardinge, at any rate, has fully seized the situation and has become keenly conscious of this imperious need. And his Lordship's Despatch of August, 1911, is an open confession that without the establishment of a Federal Union in India, composed of its different autonomous provinces, worked simultaneously with the scheme of provincial federation in the United Kingdom, it would be impossible to organise a Federation of the British Empire in which the economic and political interest of Great Britain would be fully safeguarded against the greed of her own childern grown over-seas. For the time is coming when Great Britain in her own national interests will have to play off the Indian and the Egyptian against not only the South African Boer and the French Canadian, but equally against the British Australian and the New Zealander. And to be able to do so, she *must* admit both India and Egypt into the Federation of her Empire as equal co-partners with the other members of the Imperial Concern; and with a view to do this, she *must* suit her Indian and Egyptian policy to the demands of national autonomy in these countries. And *must* means necessity and no favour. It admits of no apology and leaves no room for generosity. This *must* is the solid basis of the reconciliation, in my political philosophy, of Indian Nationalism and British Imperialism.

But I press this Federal Imperial Ideal upon the attention of my countrymen not merely because it is ideally higher than isolated sovereign independence, but also because there is, humanly speaking, no other alternative before us for the attainment of national autonomy. Granting that sovereign independence is the highest national ideal, the question is, how is India to attain it in her present helpless condition? As long as we had to consider only Great Britain or any other European power, for the matter of that, as standing in our way, this was not perhaps absolutely inconceivable, and we might have thought it possible to attain this national independence by making the situation impossible for our present rulers. But the emergence of Japan into the rivalry of world-dominion, and the rejuvenescence of China on the one side, and the rise of Pan-Islamism on the other, have practically killed all chances of any isolated national autonomy for India. To hold our own against China or Japan, we must have a powerful navy and a large army equipped and organised according to the most up-to-date methods. And there is practically no possibility of our securing these, except through the continuance of the British connection, or through a long period of undisturbed national self-rule should this connection be severed. But neither China nor Japan will impose a self-denying ordinance upon them to help us to this essential period of undisturbed self-rule, and thus enable us to realise our ideal of isolated sovereignty. Nor will the Pan-Islamist refuse to exploit the helpless and disorganised State that must follow any violent break up of the British connection, in favour of a fresh Moslem domination in

India. All these are patent possibilities. They are more, almost absolute certainties. And a consideration of these forces upon us the ideal of Federal-Self-Rule in preference to that of isolated sovereign independence.

This is briefly the central thesis of this volume. This federalism is our only salvation. This is also the only means of preserving the integrity of the British Empire. Indian Nationalism and British Imperialism both demand, in their own interest, the pursuit of this ideal. Will not the larger statesmanship of both India and England join hands in the pursuit of an ideal which is so essential to the future of both these countries?

BHOWANIPORE,
Calcutta, 15*th January*, 1916. } BIPIN CHANDRA PAL.

CHAPTER I.

PROBLEM OF NATIONALITY AND EMPIRE.

NATIONALISM AND IMPERIALISM.

A Conference on "The Claims of Nationalities and Subject Races" was held in London in June 1910.

It was an international gathering, in which Finland and Georgia, Poland and Ireland, Egypt and India were all represented by recognised spokesmen of their respective peoples. The differentiation that the organisers made between what had hitherto been known as "subject races" and what they called now "dependent nationalities" marked, at the very outset, a very important advance in the general thought of the European peoples in regard to ancient countries like Egypt or India. In some sense this Conference sounded a counter-blast to Mr. Theodore Roosevelt's gospel of civilisation and the big stick. This is not, of course, the first time that liberal-minded and sympathetic members of the dominant European races have pleaded before their own people for a just and kindly treatment of alien peoples subject to their rule. There is an old organisation in England whose object is to watch over the moral and material interests of what are called the native races in Africa and elsewhere. But this and similar organisations of the kind never seem to have gone to the root of the problem which they have been trying to handle. They never questioned the claims of the dominant European powers to a higher civilisation, upon which they based their moral right to rule the less civilised races of the world. The government of these so-called native races by some civilised European nation has always been accepted as a good thing, both in the interests of these races themselves and in those of humanity at large. European domination over non-European races spells the participation by the latter in a higher civilisation and life. It means the substitution of peace and order for disorder and anarchy, the replacement of the rule of might by the law of right, the progress of the people from savagery to civilisation. This general moral plea had never before been examined, much less seriously questioned. The right of every people, whatever the state of their progress or the character of their culture, to freely live their own life and evolve their own destiny, without any let or hindrance from their stronger, and possibly more advanced neighbours, had never before been boldly asserted. All that the friends of so-called native races tried to do was to help make their lot a little easy and their yoke a bit light. Their claims to sympathetic rule and humane treatment had, thus, been strongly urged before ; but their absolute right to self-government and legitimate freedom of self-fulfilment had never been recognised. There was an implicit recognition of these fundamental principles in the work of this International Conference on the claims of nationalities and subject-races.

Races and Nationalities.

At the very outset, this Conference started with a clear differentiation between dependent nationalities like those of Ireland, Poland, Finland, Egypt or India, and what are known usually as subject races. This elementary differentiation is bound to clear up a good deal of confusion that still surrounds the problem of nationalities. There is a very wide difference between a race and a nation. In the first place, territorial unity is an essential condition of nationality, but not of raciality. A race may spread over different and distant territories, and occupy various parts of the globe, but a nation must be confined to a definite habitat. A race is essentially a homogeneous thing. It has a special physical structure, a special thought-structure, and a special social structure. This three-fold structural affinity is of the very essence of the race-idea. This structural affinity is observed among the different branches of the so-called Aryan family. It is equally seen among the different branches of the Mongolian family. It is observed among the different branches of the other races of mankind. A nation is, however, a more complex and heterogeneous thing. More than one race can go to the making of a nation. There is a good deal of racial intermixture in all the developed nationalities of the world. The growth of nationalities indicates a higher stage of social evolution and a more developed order of social life than is found in mere racial units. There may, therefore, be primitive races, but hardly any primitive nation. The tribe, the race, the nation, this may be regarded as an ascending series in social evolution. In this series, India or Egypt, Ireland or Finland, Poland or Georgia cannot be classed under the first or the second term. These are not tribes, nor races, but nations. This International Conference implicitly took its stand upon this essentially right conception of nationality.

NATIONALISM *vs.* IMPERIALISM.

Unfortunately, however, social philosophy is very imperfectly developed, so far, even in the West, and consequently this rudimentary conception of nationality was not fully worked out by the Conference and established as the highest generalisation of Sociology. There were some eminent professors and university lecturers on the platform of the Conference, but none of them threw any light upon the real problem before it. Professor Gilbert Murray, who was invited to deliver the opening address, and was naturally expected to present a philosophical statement of the problem and examine the root-idea upon which the Conference was got up, practically refused to do anything of the kind. In the absence of any really fruitful philosophical consideration of the problem before it, all that the Conference did was to voice forth the bitter cry of dependent and down-pressed nationalities. It entered a vigorous protest against the grasping pretensions of modern European imperialism, urged the claims of dependent nationalities to self-government, and condemned the attempt of the dominant powers to put down the legitimate aspirations and activities of these nationalities towards a self-dependent existence.

But when we condemn any wrong or injustice, we oftentimes forget that condemnation is no cure. This world is God's and an essentially moral thing at its soul and centre. Wrongs rule in this world not on their strength and authority, but on those of some right whose semblance they assume. Even modern imperialism is not a pure falsehood or an absolute wrong. Its falsehoods are mixed up with its truths and its wrongs with its rights. No new thought or idea can take its birth unless impelled by some great need, either of the intellectual or of the moral, either of the personal or of the social, life of man. Even errors and superstitions have some such organic need at their origin. And the right way to cure these is not simply to pass strongly-worded condemnation on them, but to examine the organic need that called them forth, to separate the right that is mixed up with the wrong in them, to point out their essential truth and thus to dissipate their untruth. If we want imperialism to be just, we must ourselves be first just to it. All imperialists are not moved by unworthy motives. There are men and women, as thoroughly honest as ourselves, who regard imperialism as beneficial to the best interests of humanity, and who lend their support to it, because of its beneficial or supposed beneficial influences. Professor Hobson pointed out this fact, in explaining the reason why imperialism commanded the allegiance of many honest and really well-meaning people. In so doing he made a fairly correct diagnosis of the case before him. Unfortunately, however, even Professor Hobson did not drive this psychology to its legitimate conclusion. But I am not at all surprised at it; for it is only a true philosophy of nationalism that could have given the learned professor the right key to the solution of the problem he so clearly raised.

Nation-idea and Empire-idea.

The greatest fascination of imperialism, to the modern mind, is that it makes for the unification of humanity to an extent and upon a measure that is impossible under any other known form of human organisation or association. As nations are larger than tribes, even so empires are larger than nations. Raciality is a higher synthesis than mere tribality. Nationality is a higher synthesis than raciality. And imperialism offers, similarly, a higher synthesis than nationalism. The empire-idea is essentially larger and broader than the nation-idea. It aims at the unification of widely separated territories, of widely divergent interests, of widely different cultures and characters, into one organic whole. As families combine into tribes, each family contributing its peculiar characteristics and possessions to the common life of other families, in and through the unity of the tribe-life; as, at a subsequent social synthesis, tribes combine to form races, which, though divided by space, controlled by different environments, evolving under divergent historic epochs, still pursue a common ideal-end, are moved mainly by a common regulative-idea, and, thus, make for a larger union of mankind than had been realised before; and, as at the next synthesis, different racial units combine to form a larger, more complex and yet more intimate unity, namely, that of the nation; so the unification of these national units into an imperial organisation or organism is really a higher and larger social synthesis than even what has been attained through the nation-idea. It is impossible to deny, therefore, that the empire-idea is positively larger, grander, nobler than the nation-idea. This is the fundamental truth of the concept empire. The family, the tribe, the race, the nation ; these are all old syntheses of social progress. The empire is a later synthesis, though not really a new, modern synthesis. From the family to the tribe, from the tribe to the nation, from the nation to the empire, from the empire to universal federation, this is the complete scheme of social evolution. And in this ascending social series each antecedent term must be judged and justified by each subsequent term. Families must be judged and justified by their capacity to develop into the larger life of the tribe ; tribes must be similarly judged and justified by their capacity to grow into the more complex and variegated life of the nation ; nations must be similarly judged and justified by their capacity to combine into the wider life of the empire ; and, finally, empires must be judged and justified by their capacity to work out the universal federation of mankind.

This is the correct rationale of imperialism. Its claims to the attention and allegiance of mankind are based essentially upon its promise to work out a larger unification of humanity than has as yet been realised. But what is the true character of this unification ? What is the real nature of the unity that humanity has been progressively seeking through the entire course of social evolution ? In the first place, it must be understood that unity is not homogeneity. All organic unity is a unity which does not destroy and deny all differentiations and diversities, but which realises itself in and through not only the maintenance of these diversities and differentiations but even more fully through their development and perfection. Our conception of unity is essentially different as much from the old pagan, as from also the mediæval Christian, idea of it. The pagan view was the denial of the legitimate freedom of the units in the interest of unity. The social philosophy of paganism regarded the individual human unit as a mere limb of the body politic, having really no end unto himself apart from the common ends of the State. Christianity was the first to enter a protest against the usurpation of the rights of the individual by the Society or the State in Europe. It was the first to proclaim in Europe the divine right of the human personality, to declare that man was himself an end unto himself. But the right to dominate the individual and usurp his legitimate freedom of self-development and self-fulfilment, which Christianity denied to pagan Society and the pagan State, it practically claimed for the Church, in the new philosophy of life which it propounded, even in a more aggravated form. The old usurpation of the fundamental rights of the human personality was thus continued by the new Church. This was the logical need of the subsequent Lutheran protest, even as the French Illumination, with its gospel of absolute individualism, was the logical sequence of the philosophy of Christian Protestantism.

A War of Half-truths.

All this was, what may be called, a war between half-truths. The pagan view of social unity was only a half truth. The Protestant Christian view of it, which culminated in the individualism of the French Illumination, was equally only another half-truth. The one denied the organic end of the individual, the other ignored the organic character of society. Neither therefore could really reconcile individuality with social unity, freedom with subjection. And the reason was that neither the old pagan view nor even the subsequent Christian view had a true conception of the nature of organic unity. This conception is the latest contribution made by modern thought and research to social philosophy. The modern conception is that society is an organism, but an organism composed of a number of smaller organisms, that have, as such, necessary ends unto themselves. But these individual ends are so arranged that they are interdependent upon one another and upon the collective ends of the social whole to which they belong. The social unity is thus what the philosophers would call, not unity but really totality, which is a much higher category. It is a federal unity, which means the freedom of the parts in the unity of the whole. In a federal organisation the whole realises itself only and always in and through the perfection, each in its own way, of its parts; and these different parts also reach out to and realise their own specific ends in and through the general life and progress of the whole. This is the very essence of the concept organism. As society is an organism, this must be the universal law and condition of social progress and the realisation of social unity. For society to usurp the legitimate freedom of movement and development of the individual is to commit suicide. For the individual to seek his own individual end without regard for the larger collective ends of society is to miss that very end itself.

This is a fundamental social conception. It is the universal law of social progress. Racial evolution, national evolution, and imperial evolution are all subject to this universal social law. Nations are composed of smaller units, each an organism in itself, but united through larger organic ends in the broader unit or unity of the national life. The ends of that life can never be realised by denying to the subordinate units their legitimate freedom of self-movement and self-development. A nation which seeks to do it kills itself. Empires similarly are composed of smaller organisations called nations, or popularly, states or dominions. These nations or states or dominions are themselves social organisms, larger than individuals or families or townships, but they have a specific end unto themselves, an end that is determined by the peculiarities of their special structure and environment. But they are united organically to the larger organism of the empire, and have, therefore, necessarily to seek their own specific ends and realise them only through the larger ends and the broader unity of the imperial whole. These larger imperial ends or this broader imperial unity can never be realised and perfected by denying to the subordinate national units their legitimate freedom of self-movement and self-development. An empire that seeks to do it kills itself. The cure of rampant imperialism must ultimately come through the recognition of the truth of this fundamental social principle. Modern imperialism is trading upon a mere half-truth. Its main strength comes from its pretensions to work up a larger unity of mankind than has as yet been realised.

We may deny the validity of these pretensions, but we cannot refuse to accept the grandeur of its ideals.

THE NATURE OF THE EMPIRE-IDEA.

The empire-idea offers a broader ground for the unification of humanity than the nation-idea, even as the nation-idea offers a broader basis of human fellowship than the unity of tribal or racial relations. This is the fundamental claim to superiority of the empire-idea. It is the claim, really, of a broader generalisation and a higher synthesis. The family, the tribe, the race, the nation, all these are, what may be called, social syntheses; each succeeding synthesis being broader and higher than the preceding ones. The social synthesis offered by the empire-idea is broader and higher than all the others. The first condition, therefore, of the realisation of the true empire-idea is a correct and clear understanding of the nature of this synthesis.

THE NATURE OF SOCIAL SYNTHESES.

Now, every synthesis is the fruit of some antecedent antithesis. It is essentially of the nature of a settlement of contending claims and a reconciliation of opposing interests. The value of a synthesis lies entirely in its capacity to work out this settlement and reconciliation. The family is a social synthesis; because it offers, through its larger and collective life, in which all the individual members of the family fully participate, a basis for the reconciliation of their divergent individual activities and interests. The failure to work out this reconciliation would inevitably break up the unity and solidarity of the family life and thus destroy its usefulness, for the simple reason that it would then cease to be a synthesis at all. The unity of the family-life endures only so long as its collective authority and interests are not identified with those of any particular member of the family. Of course, this collective life and authority must have some concrete vehicle for itself, and must use some member of the family for this purpose. But the detachment of the head of the family from the passions and prejudices of the individual members of it, and equally the almost absolute merging of his own individual ends and interests in the general ends and interests of the family, preserves the real value of the synthesis. It was this detachment of the head of the family, and his self-effacement in the interests of the common life of the family which he represented, that, joined to favourable economic causes, helped very materially to perpetuate the joint-family system in India. And it is the loss of this detachment, leading to an inevitable decline of the moral authority of the head of the family over the individual members of it, that, among other things, has been gradually bringing about the disruption of that old family system. Similarly, the tribe is a social synthesis, larger than the family, because it offers a ground of reconciliation to the rival claims and conflicting interests of different families included in the tribal unit. And this synthesis also endures so long as the collective life and authority of the tribe, though formally vested in particular individuals or families, yet really stands above them all, and, on account of this independence, or rather, more correctly speaking, transcendence, it is able to harmonise in itself the conflicting interests of the different families comprising the tribe. Whenever this collective life and authority of the tribe loses this character, whenever its representative or representatives identify this life and authority with the particularities either of their own or of any other individual's or family's life and interests, the social synthesis is really broken up, even though the social authority may be exercised through mere brute force, whether actual or potential. The real value of the next higher social synthesis, namely, that of the nation, also consists in the same fact—in its power to reconcile, in its larger life and ideals, the divergent and oftentimes conflicting activities and interests of individuals and families and tribes and races, who go to make up the collective life of the nation. And this synthesis also similarly endures only so long as the right and authority of the collective life of the nation, though necessarily vested in, or represented by, particular individuals, or even special families or classes, does not identify itself with any part or particularity of the nation. Such identification really means the usurpation of the right and authority of the whole by a part of it. And such usurpation inevitably breaks up the synthesis, though, here also, the exercise of the usurped authority may be long continued through sheer brute force. The empire-idea is also a social synthesis, much larger and higher no doubt than the other social syntheses, but as a synthesis it must fulfil these essential conditions. It must be a ground of reconciliation of divergent national ideals, different national geniuses, and conflicting national interests. It must mediate between different national units, and through this mediation knit them together into a larger social unity. And to do this the Empire cannot be in any way identified with any one particular nation or particular group of nations composing it. These nations, like all other nations in the combination, shall be *in* the Empire, but the Empire though perpetually present *in* them as a high regulative idea, shall, all the same, stand perpetually *above* them. The Empire shall hold together the different nations composing it by inspiring them with ideals and interests larger and higher than their isolated and smaller national ideals and interests, and by supplying them with common grounds of co-operating with one another for the realisation of national, as well as universal humanitarian, ends. It shall help their evolution this wise, but shall not impose the special ideals of any particular nation or groups of nations in the imperial family, over the others. Nor shall the collective life and authority of the Empire, in whomsoever it may be vested, in any way permit itself to be identified with any particular nation in the imperial family. Such identification would necessarily destroy the synthesis itself, make the representative of the Empire a party in the conflicts of national interests, and at once destroy his right and authority to mediate between these national units and reconcile their conflicting interests.

A Terminological Usurpation.

An empire is a much larger unit than a nation ; and the smaller can never hold the larger. Nay more. The family, the tribe, the race, the nation, the empire, all these are distinct social categories ; and one cannot, therefore, be converted into the other. None of these can by mere physical or numerical expansion develop into another. A family might multiply to a hundred members, still it would be nothing more than a family; a very large family, no doubt, but never a tribe. Similarly a tribe might contain a hundred thousand or even a million individuals, but it would still be a tribe, as much as the smallest tribe, but never a race. So with races and nations also. A nation might multiply itself to any extent, might expand its territorial possessions to any length, but it would still be a nation and not an empire. Even the possession of sovereign authority over many nations would not convert a nation into an empire. When a nation assumes the name of an empire on these grounds, it only adds what may be called a terminological usurpation to its already-achieved territorial usurpations. That is all.

The Actual and the Ideal Empire.

The imperialism with which we are familiar in history, whether ancient or modern, has been universally of this type, though ancient Indian legends and political philosophy do suggest the recognition of a different ideal. The acquisition of political sovereignty over immense tracts and diverse peoples has been regarded as a sufficiently sound title to the name of empire. Even this imperialism has undoubtedly been a great factor in the evolution of human society and civilisation. It was, perhaps, the only type that could be realised in early times. Even this extension of political sovereignty hepled, in those days, the unification of humanity. I would not belittle the contribution of the old and imperfect imperial idea to the progress of the race. But this type of imperialism has practically done its work. In any case, even if it may yet claim to be able to help the evolution of primitive races, it is an absolute anachronism in relation to advanced nationalities having a long course of historic evolution and a distinctive type of culture and civilisation behind them. The older imperialism was needed for the unification of tribes and races into national units. This old synthesis was, perhaps, the only possible form of synthesis in those primitive times. But what the modern world wants is not a mere administrative unity but a complete social synthesis. It wants a larger and more organic formula of association than what the old-world imperialism could offer. The new empire-idea, which is undoubtedly superior to the nation-idea, is not a mere political theory or ideal but essentially a social synthesis. Its superiority lies in the fact that it offers a much larger field and formula of human fellowship and human association than any other social organisation.

The Nationalities Conference in Caxton Hall, while raising its protest against the spirit of rampant imperialism, failed however to prove the failure of that imperialism to serve its own legitimate end, namely, to further the cause of human fellowship and international co-operation in the pursuit of common humanitarian interests. It is, indeed, exceedingly doubtful whether any movement or organisation guided by the members of the dominant white races, however sincere their motives and strong their enthusiasm for humanity, can offer a real and effective criticism against this imperialism. The ultimate notion at the back of this imperialism is the superiority of the civilisation of the white races. It is a notion shared in with the imperialists by even the most cosmopolitan of the white peoples. And consequently the appeal of the opponents of imperialism is based upon what the practical politicians and working statesmen of the modern world dismiss as "considerations of abstract justice." The real solution of the problem, the true cure of the evils, of imperialism will come from a new philosophy of history and human society. We are moving towards that philosophy. The organic conception of society, the special contribution of the culture of the nineteenth century to the study of social phenomena, has laid the foundations of that philosophy. The truth of it is being increasingly realised in the internal movements of the dominant nations of the world. It is this conception that is gradually helping the replacement of the old individualistic social philosophy of the eighteenth and the nineteenth centuries by modern collectivism or socialism.

The Real Solution: True Internationalism.

Society is an organic whole, the strong and the weak, the healthy and the sick, the learned and the ignorant, the rich and the poor, the virtuous and the sinful—all are organic parts of this social whole. And in the face of their organic interdependence upon one another, it is absolutely impossible for any individual member or any class or caste of any society to realise their own special ends without a similar realisation by other individuals or classes or castes of their own ends. Individual possessions are absolutely valueless except in a community that has attained a certain amount of economic progress and stability and can maintain a certain level of wealthy living. The preservation of personal health is dependent to a very large extent upon public hygiene and the general health of the community. Intellectual, æsthetic, and even high spiritual culture—all these demand a certain high level of intellectual and artistic and spiritual life in the community. And this organic interdependence between individual and individual, and class and class, and between individuals and classes and the society to which they belong, demands that for the collective ends of that society, upon the realisation of which really depends the realisation of all particular ends of the individuals and classes of that society—this organic interdependence demands that the members of every society must work together—the strong imparting his strength to the weak, the rich giving out of his wealth to the poor, the learned freely communicating his learning to the ignorant, the good dedicating all his own goodness to uplift the vicious and the criminal, and in thus helping each other and bearing each other's burdens, every individual member of society shall in his own interest help forward the interest of other individuals and thereby promote the realisation of the collective ends of the society to which all individuals belong. This organic conception of society really supplies the basis and the philosophy of modern collectivism. And the expansion of this organic conception from the society to universal humanity, will furnish a working basis for that broad internationalism which alone will be able to correct and cure the errors and evils of modern imperialism.

Wanted a Corrected View of Human History.

But something more also will be needed, and that is a corrected view of human history and social evolution.

In Europe, from the time of Hegel downwards, the history of civilisation has been conceived "as a single line of progress, which, in realising the successive stages of the Absolute Idea, flows continuously from one race or nation to another, each representing a single phase of the Absolute, a single moment in the dialectic process. This punctual conception of races and epochs, and this lineal view of development, are essentially false." European sociologists have hitherto measured and adjudged different races and cultures by an abstract and arbitrary standard derived from the history of European civilisation. And they have given to non-European culture and civilisation only a subsidiary and provisional place in their sociological scheme, "as if they were either monstrous or defective forms of life, or only primitive ancestral forms, the earlier steps of the series, that have found their completion in European society and civilisation." But, as Dr. Brajendranath Seal pointed out in his Introduction to "Vaishnavism and Christianity," more than ten years ago, "with the ethnological material at our disposal, it is a gross and stupid blunder to link on Chinese, Hindu, Semitic, Greek, Roman, Gothic, Teutonic cultures in one line of filiation, in one logical (if not chronological) series. No race or civilisation with a continuous history represents a single point or moment. In fact, even Chinese civilisation, like the Chinese language, has had a development of its own; and though in all this race-history the Chinese race-consciousness has subsisted, it has still been a differentiation of the homogeneous, a development of a coherent heterogeneity out of an incoherent homogeneity. Hindu culture, too, has passed through most of the stages observed in the growth of the Hebraic-Graeco-Romano-Gothic civilisation. The same may be said of Arabic or Mahomedan culture. To conceive these statically, to reduce each living procession to a punctual moment in a single line is to miss their meaning and purpose."

"Universal Humanity," he adds, "is not to be figured as the crest of an advancing wave, occupying but one place at any moment and leaving all behind a dead level. Universal Humanity is immanent everywhere and at every moment—I will not say, a circle of which the centre is everywhere and the circumference nowhere—but at any rate generically present in each race-consciousness though each race may not have reflected the perfect type or pattern. From the statical point of view, Universal Humanity, though present in each race, is diversely embodied, reflected in specific modes and forms. The ideal of Humanity is not completely unfolded in any, for each race potentially contains the fullness of the ideal but actually renders a few phases only, some expressing lower or fewer, others higher or more numerous ones. To trace the outlines of this universal ideal we must collate and compare the fragmentary imperfect reflections, not at all in eclectic fashion, but as we seek to discover a real species or genus among individual variations and modes."

It is this conception of social evolution and universal history, when it is properly worked out and applied to the study of the different world-cultures, that will alone be able to offer a solution of the problem which this Nationalities Conference was trying to tackle.

London : July 1910.

CHAPTER II.

HINDU NATIONALISM: WHAT IT STANDS FOR.

THE EAST AND THE WEST.

One of the most striking achievements of the Nineteenth Century has been, it seems to me, to make the world at once smaller and larger than what it ever was before. Modern science has helped to practically annihilate the ancient distances both of space and time; while modern historic movements, following so closely upon the advance of modern industry and the expansion of modern commerce, has enormously enlarged the field of human associations, overriding the old and narrow limits of the communal or the national life, and has, thereby, made the world much larger than that in which our forefathers lived. Commerce in commodities has opened up the highways of a higher commerce in spiritualities. Exchange of goods has slowly and imperceptibly been leading up to the exchange of thoughts and ideas between the most distant and divergent peoples of the world. As a result, modern humanity is passing through strange and mighty transformations such as, perhaps, the world had never yet seen or known. And the confusion seems to many people almost chaotic.

To work some sort of a practically permanent order out of this conflict and confusion is a universal problem to-day. It faces all the peoples of the earth. The West, no less than the East, is passing through the travails of this transition. The West may be restlessly kicking about, while the East may still be cosily lying in bed ; but both are equally in the dark. Neither really knows the way out. Neither, therefore, can legitimately claim to lead the other. All that they can do to render mutual help is to open out their respective Book of Experience, and, in the spirit of the earnest inquirer, compare notes with each other.

The Essence of the Hindu Race-Consciousness.

As Hindus, we are necessarily identified with a particular culture and civilisation ; and quite naturally we have a pardonable partiality for our own ideals and institutions. But at the same time we know this also that we shall be faithless to the very spirit of this Hindu culture itself, if we fail to respect natural differences of view-points, or tolerate the inevitable conflicts of ideas due to these differences.

The spiritual genius of our race has always recognised the fundamental Unity that underlies all forms and classes of diversities and differences. A passion for this Unity has characterised the entire course of our past evolution. Some moved by this passion have negated the actualities of man's sense-life upon which our consciousness of differences and diversities is based, and have sought to dismiss both the demands of the natural and the obligations of the social life as illusory. Others have conceded a kind of conditional truth and relative reality to our natural and social life and activities, accepting them as mere moments in the evolution of the consciousness of the Ultimate Unity, or as varied manifestations, for purposes of his own sport or *leela*, of the Supreme Reality. But never have we lost sight of that Ultimate Unity where all the diversities of the natural and all the conflicts of the mental or the social life are explained, justified, and reconciled. In the Hindu's philosophy there are endless appearances but One Reality. In the Hindu's pantheon there are countless gods but only One Supreme Lord or Isvara. In the Hindu's social economy there are numerous castes, but one organic Social Whole of which these castes, the highest as well as the lowest, however mutually exclusive they may be, are mere limbs and organs. And the Hindu's view of other races, other communities, other religions, and other cultures, is that these, like his own race or community or his own religion or culture, are all parts, moments, or manifestations of that One Supreme Unity which fulfils and realises itself through these endless differences and diversities.

Even as advocates of Hindu culture and Hindu civilisation, we can not, therefore, consistently with the teachings of Hinduism itself, refuse to admit that our culture and civilisation represent only a part of universal human culture and civilisation, and at their best, have so far rendered only a few notes of that universal humanity which includes all the different races and cultures of the world.

For we hold that God has left no country or people without witnesses unto His Spirit or proofs of His Providence; and that the Universal is present behind the Particular everywhere. Universal Humanity is the regulative idea in all historic evolutions. Particular culture-histories are therefore only parts of the history of universal culture and have consequently a close kinship with one another. Their unity is necessary and basal. Their divergences, however wide and vital, are due either to differences of race-consciousness—which is the element of permanence in racial evolution—or of physical environments or historic associations or to differences in the stages of evolution in which these severally stand.

Hindu Nationalism means, therefore, neither selfish conflict with, nor proud isolation from, the other nations of the world.

Mazzini's View of Nationality.

Nationality has been defined by Joseph Mazzini as "the *individuality* of a people." The Hindu's monistic instincts would, perhaps, prefer to describe it as the *personality* of a people. For the idea of individuality is associated with the European doctrine of Rights, which implies inevitable isolation and conflict. The authors of the French Illumination seemed to have realised this limitation of their doctrine of individuality, and consequently they sought to remedy, if not to entirely remove it, by adding to their dogmas of Equality and Liberty, a third dogma, that of Fraternity. But this Fraternity of the French Revolution had no organic and necessary relation to its other two dogmas of Liberty and Equality. It did not logically follow from them; but was evidently added on to them, in an arbitrary way, to save certain vital aspects of the social life. And, consequently, while the dogmas of Liberty and Equality created endless conflicts and confusion, that of Fraternity, though meant to act as a corrective against these, failed to furnish the modern world with either any formula of reconciliation or any inspiration for unity. Mazzini himself clearly realised all this; and he, therefore, called upon his own compatriots, as well as the nations of Europe generally, to get rid of "the incubus of the French Revolution." But brought up in the dualistic and legalistic atmosphere of Latin Christianity, even Mazzini failed to fully reach out to that higher Philosophy of Nationalism, which could offer a true and effective antidote against the isolating and disrupting tendencies of the popular European gospel of Equality and Freedom.

European Nationalism.

The philosophy of nationalism in Europe is still associated with the individualistic inspirations of the French Revolution. And as enthusiasm for the gospel of individualism has developed certain anti-social tendencies in every European country, tendencies that passing through various phases, some harmless, some harmful, but all inherently revolutionary, have culminated in the modern schools of philosophical anarchism, like those of William Morris, Neitzche and others; so the enthusiasm for nationality has developed all over Europe unmistakable anti-humanitarian tendencies, converting Christian love into patriotic jealousy, and encouraging the practical annihilation of the weaker or younger members of the great human family, in the name of humanity and civilisation. And the popular European concept, individuality, carried to the domain of the national life, and seeking to convey the legitimate but particularistic claims of the different social units into which universal humanity is divided, has absolutely nothing in it to combat or correct these anti-humanitarian tendencies of the popular ideas and ideals concerning the character and it will be claims of nationalities in European thoughts and speculations.

THE HINDU CONCEPTION OF NATIONALITY.

Hindu culture took, however, a somewhat different view of what is called individuality in Europe. It is able to present, therefore, an ideal of nationality much superior to the popular European view of it. In fact, the corresponding Hindu idea is very imperfectly rendered by the European term individuality. The conceit of individuality is a universal fact of human experience. But while modern European culture has been trying, by all manner of means, to strengthen and develop this conceit, ancient Hindu culture put forth its highest efforts to cure, if not to altogether kill it. For the Hindu has always recognised the havoc that this conceit of individuality, as it exists in men and women in the natural state, causes both in their social relations and their spiritual life. It is this conceit which leads ordinary human beings, living more or less only the common life of their natural instincts and appetites, to regard themselves as standing practically apart from all other individuals about them, except those few who are connected with them by natural ties. And this sense of separateness impels them to pursue their own individual ends and interests as if these were in perpetual antagonism to the similar ends and interests of the other members of their social body. This conceit of individualism accentuates, thus, the conflicts of economic competition, and enfeebles the spirit of co-operation in the community, and sets up the doctrine of the survival of the fittest, in its crudest and least scientific sense, as the predominating principle of the evolution of human society, as it is, perhaps, to some extent, the law in certain parts of the lower animal kingdom.

Realising all these inevitable evils of the individualistic emphasis in the social life, Hindu culture never encouraged the cultivation of that type of individualism of which modern European culture seems to be so proud.

Hindu Socialism and Pagan Socialism.

It is notorious that what they call Pagan culture in Europe also gave no room for the growth of this individualism. Both in Greece and Rome, the individual was completely subordinated to the social whole to which he belonged. Society was the whole, individuals were parts thereof. Society was the body, individuals were mere limbs of it. And though parts and limbs may have their specific functions in the general life and activities of the body to which they belong, they have, really, no specific and organic ends of their own. So it was also with individuals ; they had no ends unto themselves. This was the social philosophy of Paganism. The Hindu view, while having some semblance to this Pagan view, is, however, fundamentally different from it. The preservation of the social order was the key-note of Pagan polity : the perfection of the individual is the key-note of Hindu polity. The difference between the two views is, thus, very wide and vital ; and we cannot as summarily dispose of this Hindu view as we have done the old Pagan view.

Hindu polity demands, no doubt, the absolute subjection of the individual to his social order ; but at the same time, it should be remembered, that in no other social polity, whether ancient or modern, have we any provision for what may be called a super-social state, wherein the individual, finally freed from all social obligations, has the fullest possible scope and freedom to live and grow as a law unto himself. To set up each individual upon the true law of his own being is, indeed, the ideal-end of the Hindu's social polity. *Through* subjection *to* freedom, this may be said to be the key-note of Hindu culture. Even the most galling restraints of the Hindu's religious or social life have this freedom as their ultimate end. And Hindu polity works upon the assumption that this end is reached by every individual who, faithfully discharging the obligations of his caste and order, enters in his ripe old age the order of the *Sannyasin.* This is the last of the four stages or orders of the ideal Hindu life, sought to be realised by Hindu polity. The *Sannyasin,* which is crudely rendered into English by the term " roving mendicant ", is a law unto himself. Cured of his natural conceit of self by the rigid laws and disciplines of the first three orders—that of the student, the householder, and the hermit—the *Sannyasin* is assumed to stand consciously identified with the Universal. Devoid of all self-regarding desires, his body placed through long and laborious physical and psycho-physical exercises and disciplines above the changes and conflicts of the physical world about him ; his intellect established in the eternal verities of Reason, undisturbed by fancy, falsehood, or doubt ; his emotions perpetually lost in the sense and enjoyment of the Universal as revealed in both the natural and the human kingdom; and his will freed from all individualistic impulses, the true *Sannyasin* stands really for the Universal in every department and aspect of his life, and can, consequently, be safely allowed to be a law unto himself. He is, therefore, no longer subjected to the rules and restrictions of caste, nor to any other social laws and regulations. The order of the *Sannyasin* may consequently be well called supersocial.

Nationality Defined.

This being the true Hindu conception regarding what is called the human individuality in Europe, personality, from Latin *persona*, meaning a mask, would perhaps be a better rendering of our idea of it. The function of a mask is to create a difference in appearance, where there is, in truth, no difference in substance. Personality implies therefore, not *isolation* but only *differentiation*; and the difference that the concept personality implies is a difference which only breaks up uniformity in appearance or organisation but in no way destroys, or even disturbs, the fundamental unity of being.

I would therefore describe Nationality rather as the *Personality* of a People, than, following Mazzini's lead, define it as their Individuality.

The Real Value of Nationalism.

Indeed, the real value of the ideal of nationality consists in the fact that it offers a much larger and broader formula of human associations than the idea of either the tribe or the race. As the family is larger than the individual, and the tribe is larger than the family, and the race is larger than the tribe, so is the nation much larger than the race. And in this ascending series each subsequent term represents a higher category of social life and evolution than the antecedent term. And consequently, the family life offers a much narrower field for the development of the human faculties than the life and activities of the tribe, and the comparatively simpler and more limited needs of the tribal life, offer a much narrower scope to our powers and possibilities than the larger and more complex life of the nation. And it is just here that the higher value of the Nation-Idea truly lies.

The Ideal-end of Social Evolution.

The development and perfection of the human personality is, indeed, the one ever-present idea, as well as the ultimate ideal-end, of this social evolution. This personality realises and perfects itself, not through individualistic isolation but through larger and larger social associations. And these social associations continually expand the range of human interests beyond and above the narrow range of the individual's own life and activities. As a mere individual, man is but little removed from the lowest animal kingdom, is a mere isolated biological unit, not simply "cribbed, cabined, and confined" within the narrow limits of his individual life, but is inevitably in a state of latent or open war with other individuals of his class, ever ready to kill, or be killed by them. But as a member of his family he is no longer a mere unit, but an integral part of an organised unity—a larger whole; and is able, thus, to fully and freely participate in the powers and possibilities of that whole. The corporate life of the family, as the price of the protection which it offers to the individual, does not really hamper or contract, but distinctly helps and expands the individual's life and evolution. Indeed, the very disciplines which it imposes upon the individual in the interests of the life of his family, though sometimes in apparent conflict with the free play of individual passions and appetites, do effectively strengthen and truly expand his personality even by chastening it. Similarly, the demand of the tribal life and authority that both individuals and families shall always subordinate their particularistic interests to the larger interests of their tribe, does in no way crush or cripple, but on the contrary, distinctly enlarges and strengthens this human personality. And the complexer and the more organised and varied life of the nation, helps a much larger development of the individual than can possibly be done by either his family or his tribal life. And thus, by subordinating his individual instincts and interests, tastes and appetites, to the requirements, first of his family, then of his tribe, then of his nation, man finds even his own individual life and interests ennobled and enlarged ; and through this very subjection to the authority of these larger corporations, he gradually reaches out to a much fuller and more perfect freedom than what he could ever dream of attaining, amidst the perpetual conflicts and competitions, for even the very barest necessaries of life, of mere individual existence in this world.

The European Dogma of Freedom Needs Reconsideration.

In fact, modern social philosophy, with its organic conception of the social life, demands a fundamental reconsideration of the gospel of human freedom preached by the European Illumination of the Eighteenth Century. Indeed, the idea of freedom as it has gradually developed in Europe, ever since old Paganism was replaced by Christianity with its essentially individualistic ethical implications and emphasis, is hardly in keeping with the new social philosophy of our age. Freedom, independence, liberty, are all fundamentally negative concepts. They all indicate *absence* of restraint, regulation and subjection. Consequently, Europe has not as yet discovered any really rational test by which to distinguish what is freedom from what is license, or what is liberty from what is libertinism. Practically, like the popular distinction between orthodoxy and heterodoxy, that between freedom and license is more or less a question of individual opinions and associations. As my "doxy" is orthodoxy, and yours, when opposed to mine, is heterodoxy; so my "dom" is freedom, and yours, when it opposes mine, or does not suit me, is license. There is as yet, in European thought and culture, no universal standard to which we might both submit our different ideas and ideals of freedom and test which are true and which are false. In practical life, owing to the lack of any Supreme Court of Reason to which the claims to freedom either of individual members of society or of different classes in the community, or of different nations in the world, could be submitted,—physical force, whether open or veiled, stands as the only arbiter of these disputes. And the cause of orderly progress in different countries, or of peace between different nations, will never be really secured or advanced without a radical change in the present European conception of freedom.

THE HINDU CONCEPT—SWADHEENATA.

Our own concept corresponding to that which is called freedom or independence or liberty in Europe, is different. For, unlike that of the European, the Hindu's conception of freedom is not negative but a positive something. The corresponding term in our language is not अनधीनता (*Anadheenatā*) not-subjection, which would be a literal rendering of the English word independence, but स्वाधीनता (*Swadheenatā*) or self-subjection which is a positive concept. It does not mean absence of restraint or regulation or dependence, but *self*-restraint, *self*-regulation, and *self*-dependence. In fact our स्वाधीनता (*Swadheenatā*) means a good deal more than what even the terms self-restraint, self-regulation, or self-dependence would convey in English. For the *self* in Hindu thought, even in the individual, is a synonym for the Universal. स्वाधीनता (*Swadheenatā*) means therefore in our thought, really and truly, subjection to the Universal. The complete identification of the individual with the Universal, in every conscious relation of his life, is, thus, with us, an absolute condition-precedent of the attainment of स्वाधीनता (*Swadheenatā*) or freedom, as it would be called in English.

The conscious identification of the individual with the Universal is both the form and the norm of the Hindu Gospel of स्वाधीनता (*Swadheenatā*) or Swarāj. This word Swarāj, recently introduced into our current political literature by Mr. Dadabhai Naoroji, though evidently borrowed from the political records of the Mahratta Confederacy, belongs really to our ancient philosophical and theological literature. It occurs in the Upanishads, where it indicates the highest spiritual state, wherein the individual self stands in conscious union with the Universal or the Supreme-Self. When the self sees and knows whatever is as its own self, it attains swarāj —so says the Chhāndogya Upanishad. This state of swarāj was attained, we read in the Vedas, by the sage Bāmadeva, who, in the enthusiasm of his beatific union with the Universal, cried out—"I am the Sun, I was Manu."

The Metaphysical and the Practical Aspects of the Hindu's Sense of the Universal.

In spite of our excessive metaphysical emphasis, which no doubt led some people to deny the value of the practical and the social life as organs of the self-revelation of the Absolute, the Universal has always been the quest of our social economy also. While the *Nirgunam* or the Abstract Universal has been the last word almost of Hindu metaphysics, the *Sagunam* or the Concrete Universal has been the eternal quest of Hindu Art and the Hindu's social life and philosophy, as much as it is of the other cultures of the world; though the Hindu sought it, perhaps, more consciously than others. Reason may revel in the *Nirgunam* or the Abstract Universal; but our emotions and our will demand the *Sagunam* or the Concrete Universal for their play and fulfilment. And though the Reason, the Emotions, and the Will are not three entities but only three different aspects or modes of one and the same unity, and, consequently, each is implied in the others, yet our emotions and our will are, in a special sense, the bases and organs of our social life. The progressive self-revelation of the Absolute as the *Sagunam* or the Concrete Universal, is, therefore, the universal logic of all social life and evolution.

This social evolution proceeds from lower and simpler to higher and more complex stages, in proportion as the range and variety of man's relations with other human units and associations expand and increase. It is by means of these larger and larger associations that man progressively realises his own personality, and in the consequent development and perfection of his humanity, unveils the Divinity that is in him. For Humanity and Divinity are, indeed, one.

THE UNITY OF THE DIVINE AND THE HUMAN.

This unity is the key-note of Hindu thought. The Hindu alone, has, perhaps, among all the peoples of the earth, one single word to denote both Humanity and Divinity. That word is *Nārāyana*. *Nārāyana* is the In-Dweller in individual humans, indeed, in all beings, severally. *Nārāyana* is also the In-Dweller in the collective life of Humanity, the Director of all social and historic movements. The English concept, Humanity, even when spelled with a capital H, is really more or less of a mere abstraction like goodness or badness, for instance. It is an abstract noun, and not a substantive. Mazzini was the first, I think, to characterise Humanity as a Being, and he tried, no doubt, to indicate by this that Humanity was something more than a mere abstraction. This Humanity, he declared, has an aim, and therefore, a law, through submission to which, that aim is reached and realised. But though Mazzini posited this Humanity which he called a Being, as the logic of the national life, it is very doubtful if even his conception of Humanity reached the fulness and reality of our own concept *Nārāyana*. Christ, as Logos, is perhaps the nearest equivalent of our *Nārāyana* :—the Christ of the Christian dogma of the Trinity, where He is a Person, and not a mere Idea. Modern Christian consciousness is seeking to realise this Christ in and through the collective life of Humanity. But the essential dualism and legalism of Latin Christianity, which still so largely dominate Christian thought and culture, stand in the way of the fullest realisation by Western Christians, of the identity of Christ with Humanity. The political predominance of the Christian peoples in the modern world is perhaps a still stronger reason of the incapacity of the Christian nations of our time in this matter. And as long as the modern Christian consciousness has not been able to fully realise the identity of Christ with Humanity, not as an abstraction but as a Being, the true philosophy of modern nationalism, not as a disrupting but as a uniting and integrating force in history, will never, I am afraid, be reached, and, possibly, not even understood by Christendom.

Hindu Philosophy of Nationalism.

And we claim to understand this philosophy better, because, from of old, our holy men have known and revered every human individual, whatever his colour, creed, country or caste, as *Nārāyana* himself. Every human, the lowest socially as well as the highest, is uniformly saluted by the holiest of our holy men all over India, as *Nārāyana*. The collective life of the various tribes, races, and nations of the world, is equally regarded by the highest Hindu thought, as diverse vehicles and manifestations of *Nārāyana*. This *Nārāyana* or Humanity is the Whole, the different nations of the world are parts of that Whole. *Nārāyana* or Humanity is the Body, the different tribalities, racialities and nationalities are limbs of that Body. The whole is implied in the parts: the organism in the organs. *Nārāyana* or Universal Humanity is, therefore, logically implicit in every tribe, race, and nation. And the end and aim of the evolution of all these various social units must, therefore, be to make explicit this hidden life of *Nārāyana* in their own life and activities. To wound, to injure, or to hamper in any way, the freest self-fulfilment of the least of these social units, is really, therefore, to wound, to injure, and to obstruct the self-revelation and self-realisation, in and through the world process—of *Nārāyana* himself. On the other hand, to seek absolute social isolation from other races or peoples, under a false idea of superiority or independence—is also, equally, to impair and obstruct the fullest self-revelation of *Nārāyana* in history and humanity. If the one may be compared to murder, the other may well be called suicide: and both are equally a sin against *Nārāyana*.

This is the philosophy of nationalism, as it is understood by the highest Hindu thought. It is for this reason that we hold that Hindu Nationalism implies neither selfish conflicts with, nor arrogant isolation from, the other nations of the world.

Nationalism and Civilisation.

For, in fact, even nationality is not the last word of social or historic evolution. From the individual to the family, from the family to the tribe, from the tribe to the race, from raciality to nationality, which includes many races—this has been so far the ascending series in social or historic evolution. And the interests and obligations of the individual, gradually expanding from his own personal life, to the collective and corporate life of his family, from the life of his family to that of his tribe, from the life of his tribe to that of his nation—have so far helped the evolution and self-fulfilment of both the individual and the race. The necessary contraction of the self-regarding interests and activities of the individual with a view to co-ordinate these with the larger interests and activities of his family; then, in the next stage, the similar contraction of his family-interests with a view to co-ordinate them with the interests of his tribe; and then the contraction of all purely tribal or communal interests with a view to co-ordinate these with the larger interests of the nation—this has been the universal process of social evolution. It is through this process of the subordination of the smaller and more particularistic interests to the larger and more universal interests, that man has always been able to develop and perfect even his own individuality. It is, indeed, the one universal process of true civilisation, which means, as Matthew Arnold pointed out, "the humanisation of man in society." To give preference to individual interests over the interests of the family, or to give preference to the interests of the family over those of the tribe or the commune, or to give preference to mere communal interests, under any plea whatsoever, over the larger and more complex interests of the nation, is, therefore, really to go back to barbarism. The enemy of Nationalism is, therefore, a mortal enemy of Civilisation.

The Ethical and Spiritual Value of Social Evolution.

The value of these different terms or stages in the progressive series of social evolution, consists really in their capacity to offer wider and wider fields of human fellowship. The family represents a higher category in social evolution than the mere individual, because its corporate life and interests furnish a formula of human association which the individual could never find in himself. The tribe is a superior social category than the family for a similar reason; because it offers a larger formula of human fellowship than the family. And the nation stands highest in the series, because of the still wider formula and field of human association and fellowship that it offers.

The Trends of Modern Social Evolution.

But have we reached the highest stage of social evolution and the widest field of human fellowship even here? Can there be nothing higher than nationality? —which, offering a still wider field of human association, will advance the cause of universal humanity still further. The course of modern historic evolution seems unmistakably to be pointing to such a higher category. From nationalism to internationalism: this seems to be the growing cry of the history and culture of the twentieth century. And no nation, in our time, can with impunity refuse to accept the lead of modern historic evolution in this matter and oppose the advance of this internationalism.

Signs of the growth of this internationalism are distinctly visible in both the economic and the political movements of our time. Whatever may be said of the particular philosophy of life, upon which the present aggressive Socialist propaganda seems to be based, it can scarcely be denied that Socialism represents, to some extent, the most advanced thoughts and speculations of modern economics, and that it will largely shape the historic evolution of the Western world, if not of the East also, for the next hundred years. And in its attempt to organise and concentrate the forces of Labour in various European countries, with a view to successfully combat the politico-economic predominance of capitalism in modern industrial life, Socialism is rapidly developing a new and powerful form of internationalism in present-day economics and industry. Modern imperialism is also helping this new ideal in another direction, through the evolution of the modern colonial policy. The new type of empire is not autocratic, like the old type, but essentially democratic. It represents, in its most advanced form, not the subjection of extensive territories to one centralised and despotic governmental authority, but the union of many small sovereign States into one large organic and self-governing whole. The British Empire, so far as its self-governing Dominions are concerned, represents this coming type of empire. These Dominions, while owning general allegiance to Great Britain, are both in theory and in fact, really so many sovereign States. And this Self-Governing Empire of Great Britain, as distinguished from its other, the Dependent Empire, as the mighty statesmen of the *Times* newspaper love to call it—represents this coming type of political internationalism.

FEDERALISM—THE NEW NEED.

But even this is not a perfected type of true internationalism in politics. In fact a higher and more organised type of it is already evolving before our own eyes, within the British Empire itself. The different component parts of the self-governing empire of the British have not as yet evolved any vital and organic relations with either the Mother Country or with one another. They are just now hanging very loosely together. A few subtle sentiments, standing behind grosser considerations of material self-interests, are, at present, the only cement that holds Great Britain and her self-governing colonies together, and, consequently, the breaking up of this inorganic relation, though it will seriously inconvenience both the parties, may not necessarily and mortally affect either. In fact, the new ideal of internationalism, that has commenced to dawn upon the modern consciousness almost all the world over, is the real, though silent, force that is working behind the colonial policy of Great Britain on the one side, and the imperialist sentiments of her Dominions on the other. This ideal will demand more and more organised expression as it grows in the consciousness of these peoples. Indeed this demand is already vocal in more than one Dominion, some of whose statesmen are openly seeking to build up a real federal constitution for the British Empire.

And this is exactly the form in which the new spirit of internationalism will be bound gradually to concretise and incarnate itself, if it is at all to realise its promise. In fact federalism is only another name for organised internationalism. Freedom of the parts in the unity of the whole, is the very soul and essence of the federal idea. It is also the soul and essence of that internationalism towards which the modern world is visibly moving, as a higher stage of social evolution. Federal Imperialism—or, if any one should object to the term imperialism—as some people do, I know, even in England, on account of some of its ugly memories and associations—Federal Internationalism is most decidedly the coming Idea in current social evolution and modern world-politics. And the Nationalist Ideal will assuredly fail of its own purpose if, either through lack of strength or of wisdom, it cannot reach out gradually to this federal internationalism.

Nationalism and Federalism.

The different national units must, therefore, with a view to help the evolution of this federal internationalism and fully participate in all that it stands for, diligently cultivate both their strength and their wisdom. They must first be strong in themselves, physically, economically, and politically—in other words, they must improve their physique, increase their material resources, and develop their capacity for co-operation and combination in every department of life, always subordinating personal or family, or communal interests to the larger interests of the nation. And they must do it, for the simple reason that though the other and stronger nations of the world may be only too ready to exploit their weaker brethren, no one will care to fraternise on absolutely equal terms with the latter. And they must also at the same time, cultivate that superior wisdom which recognises the universal evidence of history that unless physical or economic or political strength of a people is constantly controlled by the vision of the ultimate ideal-ends of the national life, instead of helping, it perpetually hinders all real peaceful progress, and, almost invariably, first de-humanises the strong nation, and then destroys it.

FROM CONFLICT TO COMPROMISE.

Federal Internationalism being the immediate end of the evolution of all national units, the Nationalist ideal can never demand a *deliberate* breaking up of any relation into which any nation may have already entered either by consent or by conquest, or, as it has been the case with us, partly by consent and partly by conquest, in the course of its past history. All that the true Nationalist Ideal demands, in these cases, is the gradual evolution of all such existing relations towards the true federal type. Never seek to recklessly break away from the past is the very first article of the nationalist creed. And the "past" here means the entire time series, from the prehistoric beginnings of the nation's life up to the very latest phase or stage of its historic evolution. For, the one abiding idea running through the entire course of this evolution is to continually increase the range and complexity of the life and culture of the nation by leading or even forcing it into fresh associations with other national units and racial cultures. Conflicts may sometimes, indeed, they do very frequently, arise between the ideals and interests of the dependent nation on the one side, and the narrow and particularistic instincts and interests of the dominant nation that may have entered into vital historic or politico economic relations with it, on the other. But, however strange it may sound, it is proved by the universal testimony of history, that the inner objective of these conflicts has never been to destroy, but, on the contrary, always to develop, human fellowship and social unity. In primitive culture, tribes who first met to fight onę another for robbing one another's cattle or pasture or for adding to the number of their slaves, found it afterwards far more profitable to join their forces together for protection against other stronger tribes and to gradually assimilate their respective knowledge of the means both of production and defence, and thus to combine their primitive strength and culture with a view to form a larger and more powerful community. Races have done so in later stages of social and historic evolution, combining thereby to form nations. Thus the ultimate end even of temporary conflicts of particularistic human interests, however bitter these may seem to be at the time, is not necessarily to absolutely oppose or obstruct the growth of social unification, but, on the contrary, by their very antithesis, to promote and perfect it.

For, though conflicts between the competing interests of one people and another, placed, by force of historic conditions, in close and vital political or politico-economic relations with each other, may, under certain circumstances, be quite natural, it should never be forgotten, especially by the leaders of public opinion among both these peoples, that compromise is always rational. It is, indeed, the universal master-key of every social or international complication. And the objective of all statesmanly compromise should be not merely to work a temporary truce between rival social or political forces, but to establish a permanent reconciliation between them. The true nationalist ideal, therefore, while not flinching from any conflicts that may have to be faced for its legitimate realisation, and that may be calculated to call out all the latent strength and wisdom of the nation, must always strive, even in the midst of the most bitter struggles, for that ultimate reconciliation and synthesis which will enlarge and multiply the organic relations of the nation with other nations; and make it, in combination with these, a great power for good in the common life of universal humanity.

THE TRUE HINDU NATIONALISM.

And because of its very faith in the future of social unification, HINDU NATIONALISM stands for the higher ideal of Federal Internationalism as well; and for such conflicts and compromises also as may be reasonably calculated to develop this true federal idea in the existing relations of the Hindu People, with the other Indian communities on the one hand, and with Great Britain and the other component parts of the great Association known at present as the British Empire, on the other. HINDU NATIONALISM stands, therefore, not only for the furtherance of the cause of true freedom in India, by which I understand the fullest scope and opportunity for the utmost possible development and perfection of the special genius and character of our people, our culture and our civilisation—with the view to be able to bear our share of the work of universal humanity and to make our special contribution to the culture and character of the race—but also for the continuance of the British connection with us for the immense pessibilities of that federal internationalism which may be most easily secured for our nation through this connection.

Indian Nationalism and the British Connection.

Nationalism demands the fullest legitimate scope for the self-evolution and self-fulfilment of the nation, without let or hindrance from any other nation or nations engaged in the pursuit of their narrow and particularistic national ends and interests in their relations with the former. The realisation of the Nationalist Ideal is, therefore, inherently incompatible with the presence of any form of outside subjection. But we should not forget it that though there can be no subjection without connection, there can well be very intimate connection without such subjection. Connection implies, no doubt, some degree of control, but while in subjection this control is exercised by one party only over the other, in the kind of connection which the ideal of federal internationalism or imperialism implies, however intimate the connection may be, the necessary control is exercised mutually over one another by both or all the parties to the relation. And such control, making only and always for the good of all, can never be hurtful to either the sentiment of self-dependence of a people or to their real national interests.

In fact, some measure of control, and even restriction, is inevitable in every form of human association. The family everywhere exercises this kind of control over its individual members, the tribe over its component families or clans, the nation over its component communities, the State over every individual citizen—and it does not necessarily impair their legitimate freedom or hamper their rational growth and development. Why, then, should any control or restriction, that must follow the formation of any larger association than that of the nation, impair national freedom or hamper national self-fulfilment?

The continuance of the British connection with India in and through the gradual evolution of federalism, would, therefore, in no way conflict with the truest and the highest Nationalist Ideal. On the contrary, it would materially help the evolution of our national life towards the next higher social synthesis, namely, federal internationalism, in which every nationalist ideal must seek and find its meaning and end. It is along this line only that we must move, like the other nations of the world, to finally take our God-appointed place in the Universal Federation of Mankind, which will find progressively the largest and most perfect organ of the Life and Love of *Nārāyana* here below.

To sum up, then:—The Nationalist Movement in India, which, so far, is essentially a Hindu Movement, stands—

I. Ideally, for—1. Hindu Nationalism. 2. Federal Internationalism. 3. Universal Federation.

II. Practically, for—1. The Preservation of the distinctive genius and character of Hindu

Culture and Civilisation. 2. The Promotion of sympathetic and reverent study of other world-cultures, *e.g.*, Christian and Islam, represented in the composite life of modern India, and the Cultivation of the spirit of mutual understanding and helpful co-operation with them. 3. The Continuance of the British Connection through the gradual building up of a Federal Constitution for the present Association called the British Empire, a Federation in which India and Egypt shall be equal co-partners of Great Britain with Ireland and the British Colonies. 4. The Advancement of Universal Federation.

It stands, in a word—

FOR GOD, HUMANITY, AND THE MOTHER-LAND.

Calcutta, January, 1912.

CHAPTER III.

THE POSITIVE VALUE OF NATIONALISM.

HAS NATIONALISM ANY POSITIVE VALUE ?

THIS question has been raised by an esteemed English friend, well-known in London literary circles, and a frequent contributor to the premier British Magazines. In acknowledging the first number of the " Hindu Review " he wrote, a few weeks ago :—" I think I find myself in complete agreement with the principles you lay down in your introductory article, and you seem to me to adjust the balance admirably between the view which deprecates the national tradition in India and the view which fails to see the higher interests to which even nationalism is subordinate . . . Any criticism I might offer would not take the form of objection to anything in your pronouncement, but would simply express my feeling that the real difficulties arise when one comes to the concrete application of your principles. It is inevitable that the statement of policy with which a new journal opens should consist mainly of generalities. And yet so long as we are on the field of generalities, we have not come to close quarters with the problems. To say, for instance, that in any change a nation ought to be true to its own personality, to preserve continuity with its past, does not seem to me to take us very far in practice. Nationalism as a guide for practice seems to me very much like the principle of self-realisation in the sphere of individual conduct—to have a negative and restraining rather than a positive value. The principle of self-realisation does not tell the individual, which of all the potential and competing selves in him, he is to realise; it only tells him that one characteristic of the right line of conduct will be that it will correspond with his special temperament. It is a notice-board warning him off any line which is essentially uncongenial to his best self. Just so, the principle of nationalism does not tell the nation which elements in its present life it is to suppress and which it is to develop; it merely declares that one characteristic of the right course—whatever of all possible courses that may be—is that it will be in harmony with the nation's essential genius, and that any course which has not this characteristic is therefore wrong. And I rather think that both in the case of the individual and the nation, self-consciousness is rather a hinderance in dealing with the concrete problems of thought and conduct. A man, for instance, confronted with a new idea, ought rather to ask—'Is this true?' than 'Is it in conformity with my temperament for me to believe this?' If he, so far as in him lies, believes what is true and does what is good, his individuality will take care of itself. If a nation pursues the true and the good, there will be no danger of its specific personality being lost, any more than the distinctive individual note is lost in the work of an artist who strives to realise certain ideas with perhaps entire self-forgetfulness. This means that in practice, each problem of thought and conduct has to be treated on its own merits—'Is it true?' 'Is it good?'—and the individual and nation who answer these questions right will, in the very act, realise their best self, whether they do so consciously or not."

The Psychology of National Activities.

I am exceedingly thankful to my English friend for this criticism. The views expressed in it are held, I know, by a large body of educated people, not only in his but in our country also. A discussion of the issues raised by him will, therefore, be helpful to the study of the philosophy of nationalism. And the first thing that occurs to me, on reading this note, is that my correspondent seems to think here really in the abstract. Both his truth and his good have an air of abstraction about them. For, practically, neither individuals nor nations, as a rule, deliberately refuse to accept that which they know and believe to be true. Acceptance of any truth is an act of the intellect; and it follows immediately we know it as true. Avowal or public confession of it is another thing. We may or may not avow what we believe to be true, but we cannot help believing it, when it satisfies our reason. To *accept* a thing as good is also an act of the intellect, though *pursuing* it practically, *translating* it into life and conduct, is not an act of the intellect but of the will. And our will does not stand or act in isolation from our other faculties. Our will really follows the line of resultant of all the various and complex forces, intellectual and emotional, that act and react upon one another and struggle for mastery, immediately we are called upon to choose and select any particular course of action out of a number of rival and competing courses. Individuals may, and oftentimes do, follow a wrong course knowing it to be wrong. But I do not believe nations ever do it or, indeed, can do it. For real national movements are always automatic. The movements of masses whether of men or of matter are not really deliberative and conscious, like those of individuals, but are impulsive, automatic, and unconscious. Social movements are due to the action and interaction of social forces, and not to the deliberate and considered choice of the individuals who compose the social whole. It is no doubt conceivable that when we shall reach the millennium, and men shall be moved always and only "by reason, and not by gold," social movements may be determined by the considered choice of the members of the society. But in our present state, at any rate, nations and communities act, impulsively and unconsciously, by the collective force of their passing passions or fixed prejudices. Social activities are acts, not of considered and deliberate choice, but really of what may be called unconscious cerebration. Society accepts that only as true which is in perfect consonance with the sum total of its intellectual, moral, economic, political, and spiritual life and experience. New truths and ideas seeking acceptance from any nation or community must fit themselves into the general scheme and philosophy of life of that nation or community. This is how Christianity spread in Europe. Before it could be acceptable to the Greeko-Roman culture which ruled the dominant nations of Europe then, it had to adopt, as part of its own theology, the philosophy of Greece, and as part of its own ethics, the legalism of Rome. Our own Hinduism had to do the same thing in propagating itself among the other cultures of ancient India. And in view of these facts, how can we say that the value of nationalism is not positive, but rather negative? The warning-sign-board-position of nationalism would have been true to facts, if nations exercised conscious and considered choice in the determination of their courses of action. But they don't do it. They simply follow automatically the impulse of their own nature or personality; which means, in other words, the spirit of their nationalism, the genius of their social organism; and in so doing, automatically, preserve continuity with their own past. But my correspondent was perhaps thinking here not of the nation, but of its leaders, of those men of thought and action, who educate the nation's intellect, inspire the nation's ideals and emotions, and initiate, direct, and control the economic or political life of the nation by deliberately introducing new instruments, organisations, and vehicles of that life. And the question before them should not be, what is in consonance with the past, but what is required for the present life of the nation. Quite so. These men should always, and above all, ask themselves, in inculcating new ideas or initiating new organisations and activities—'are the ideas true?'—'are the organisations and activities good?' But even here, whether the ideas which they believe to be true will be accepted as such by their nation, will depend not on considerations of their abstract logic or reasonableness, but upon their affinities with the general intellectual life and traditions of their nation; and whether the nation will adopt their new organisations and activities, will be determined not by their abstract justice or general utility but by the actual, inner needs of the social organism itself. That which the social organism needs for its own self-preservation it accepts, irrespective of all considerations as to whether it is true or false, noble or ignoble. That which has no reference to this supreme need, it either indifferently brushes aside or violently throws out. No organism, neither animal nor social, affects pure superfluities. These are commonplace observations. The real practical difficulty does not arise in those cases where there is a slow and gradual assimilation of a new, and possibly higher, thought or civilisation by a lower culture. It arises only when there is a conflict of competing thoughts and cultures, both occupying an advanced and developed stage of evolution. It is, evidently, cases like these that my correspondent has here in his mind. But even here, can we reasonably say that the value of nationalism, in practice, is more negative than positive?

A Practical Question.

Take for instance, our own case in India. There is a very keen conflict of civilisations among us, just now. On the one hand, there is our own ancient culture with its special and specialised ideals and institutions. These ideals and institutions are the growth of ages. They are the fruits of our specific national genius or race-consciousness, stimulated and controlled by our natural environments on the one side, and our contacts and conflicts and associations with other nations and races during different epochs of our past history on the other. These ideals and institutions aim at certain results which have been the special quest of all our social endeavours. On the other hand, there is the new culture, which the British rulers of the country have brought to us with them. That too is the growth of ages. That also aims at certain results which have been the quest of all *their* social endeavours for countless ages. But the characters of these two cultures are different. In fact, it may even be said that the key-notes of these two civilisations are in more or less conflict with one another. Fellowship, for instance, as Bishop Carpenter pointed out many years ago, is the key-note of Hinduism. Legalism, on the other hand, is the key-note of Christianity. Collectivism or socialism, in the widest sense of the term, is the key-note of our social organisation. Individualism is the key-note of modern European social economy. Co-operation is the key-note of our economic life. Competition is the key-note of that of Europe. The way of renunciation has been our eternal way. That of assertion and appropriation has been the way of Europe. The conflict between our civilisation and this new civilisation from Europe, is undeniable. At the same time, it can hardly be denied that this new and imported culture is more attractive than our old, indigenous ideals. The former appeals oftentimes to those instincts and impulses which the latter had noted as lower and had tried to keep under the strictest control, if not to altogether suppress. The temptation before us to go after this new gilded god is, therefore, very great. There are higher elements in European culture, I know. Christianity has developed, after its own manner, as high and superior types of manhood as have been developed, after our own kind, among us. I admit all this. But still we cannot ignore the fact that the immediate appeal of the civilisation of Europe is to man's instincts and appetites more than to his reason and his spiritual life. And if we succumb to the temptation, it will mean a complete annihilation of the specific character of our culture. And if we lose that character our title to live as a nation among the other nations of the modern world will be gone. The question with us, as a nation is—are we to live or are we to die? It is not a question whether, as between our ideals and theirs, which is true and which is false; for neither is absolutely true nor absolutely false. Nor is it a question as to which of these cultures is good and which evil; for neither is absolutely good nor absolutely evil. There is a mixture of truths, half-truths and fancies and falsehoods, as much in our thoughts, speculations, philosophies and religions, as well in those of Europe. Some institutions are good, some indifferent, some evil, some bad here, as well as there. The most vital question therefore is, how to save our own culture and civilisation from being swamped by the imported ideals and institutions of this new and forceful civilisation that has come to us with the present rulers of our country.

Hindu Caste and European Class.

Let us take a very concrete case to illustrate what I mean. In India, among the Hindus, we have very rigid caste-divisions. Apparently, these divisions, based entirely and absolutely upon mere accidents of birth, are unjust. They are a distinct violation of the highest spiritual truth, that all men are made in the image of their maker, are children, so to say, of the same Father, and are therefore brothers. This brotherhood of man is a rudimentary principle of modern European social philosophy. To realise this universal fraternity is the ideal-end of every social, economic, or political endeavour in present-day Europe and America. This gospel appeals naturally to us also here in India. In the light of this ideal, we recognise the wrong and the ugliness of our ancient caste-exclusiveness. Our social reformers, from Keshub Chunder Sen downwards, have entered their protest against these caste-divisions. Some of us have openly repudiated these and broken away, consequently, from the old and orthodox community. But what is the result? With larger experience of life we find that social distinctions cannot be so easily and summarily eliminated from any conceivable social economy. There are these distinctions even in England and America, where there is nothing like our caste-system. Here, in India, we have caste-distinctions: there, in Europe and America, they have class-distinctions. Neither here nor there have we any real social equality. The ideal of human brotherhood is as yet an unrealised ideal as much in caste-ridden Hindustan as it is in class-divided Christendom. Yet in both the countries persistent attempts have been made from of old to realise it. The highest spirits both among Hindus and Christians have preached against these social inequalities, and have sought to override these distinctions in their own life and conduct. The Brahmin has sat at the feet of the Pariah and has acknowledged him as his Guru. The Pandit has always been taught to look upon the "untouchable" chandāla and the "sacred" Brahmin with the same eye. But notwithstanding all these, we have still these caste-divisions among us, as they have their own class-divisions in Christendom. At one time we thought that because there was no caste in England or America, the ideal of human brotherhood had been fairly, if not fully, realised there. We felt the inconvenience of our caste-rules, which interfered with the freedom of our individual movement and social intercourse. They interfered with our personal comforts. We could not drink water out of everybody's hands nor take food, however clean or inviting, that was not cooked by men of our own or of a superior caste. The Englishman or the American has not to suffer these inconveniences. They are not subject to these irksome restraints. They are absolutely free in the matter of eating and drinking. And all these at one time appealed very powerfully to us. All these personal comforts and conveniences, due to the absence of any strict social or socio-religious restrictions upon eating and drinking and even marriage among non-Hindus, added, I am sure, a good deal, however unconsciously to us it may be, to our enthusiasm for this and similar social reforms. The ideal of human brotherhood is, undoubtedly, a very noble and lofty ideal; it is a great spiritual truth. But its real spiritual appeal could only touch those whose spiritual life had been truly developed. To us, who were still living in the lower carnal plane, the appeal of this new gospel of human brotherhood and equality, was not to our higher spiritual, but only to our lower animal nature. Food-desire and sex-desire are declared by our sages and saints to be the strongest in all humans. Caste-restrictions interfered very seriously and at every step in our social life and activities, with the free and unrestricted play and fulfilment of these two common human appetites. The immediate effect of the gospel of human equality, as preached by the European Illumination which our British rulers brought to us, was to proclaim and procure our freedom from the unnatural and irksome restraints imposed by our castes upon these two the strongest of all our appetites. We idealised a lot, undoubtedly. Our protest against caste, whatever its inner and unconscious psychology, was not altogether carnal. There was a very large element of youthful idealism at the back of it. But still we were striving after a social utopia. We were longing for a social equality which does not exist anywhere in the world. We broke through caste, broke away from the old and orthodox communion, in search of a social arrangement where there shall be no distinction between man and man except that which is due to each individual's personal character or intellectual and moral and spiritual acquisitions. Honestly speaking, we have not found it yet: we do not, indeed, expect to find it ever: not at any rate along the road we took in breaking away from our old society. In place of the old divisions of caste, we have set up, even in our advanced and reformed community, new divisions of class, after the manner of England and America. Our old caste-divisions were based upon birth; these new class-distinctions are based upon money and official or professional rank. The man who had the blood of the Brahmin in him could claim special privileges in the old society, he could commit many wrongs with impunity. The person who owns a large balance in his bank can and does claim similar privileges and has his sins similarly condoned in the new and reformed community. Poverty was never a crime or disqualification in the social code of the old community, it is becoming—if it has not already become—so in the new community. And when one calmly thinks over these actualities and their serious moral and spiritual implications, one cannot gather up enough courage to claim that our present "reformed" condition is intrinsically better than our old state; or that the new social economy and arrangement carry us nearer to the ideal of human brotherhood and human equality than the old and orthodox arrangement did.

Irrelevant Issues.

The fact of the matter really is, that neither our caste-system nor their class-system is absolutely rational or good. My correspondent's questions—Is it true? Is it good?—cannot be answered without any reservation in the case of either of these two social systems. Nor is it easy to determine which of these is comparatively better. Neither our old theocratic social economy, nor their modern democratic social economy, embodies the highest social ideal. Both are equally imperfect. If one has some advantages in one direction, the other has similar advantages in another direction. Both are a mixture of truths and half-truths, of good and evil. Both are merely tentative and distinctly experimental. And, what is most significant of all, both have latent in them the same ultimate ideal-end, namely, to help gradually to bring out the God in man. Consequently, there is neither room nor need for either borrowing or lending in organic social evolution. For Humanity is one. This Humanity is the whole. The different nations are limbs and parts of this whole. But it is not a numerical, but an organic whole. Humanity is an organism. The different nations are its organs. The whole is implied in the parts: the organism in its organs. Humanity is implicit, therefore, in every racial or national unit, as much as in every individual human. Racial and national evolution has only one end and meaning, namely, to make explicit in the life and thought of each race or nation, the ideal of Humanity that is ever present and implicit in it. India has, therefore, no rational need to borrow anything from Europe, any more than Europe has any need to borrow anything from India. There is really no exchange or barter, strictly speaking, as a result of the contact of one civilisation with another. What actually happens is that they each stimulate in the other those elements that are more developed in the one and less developed in the other. The process is educative, not commercial. It is the universal process of all human intercourse. The company of bad people does not inject their evil into me, but only draws out the evil that lay latent within myself. Association with good and noble men and women does not actually communicate their goodness or nobility to me, but simply and really, stimulate and quicken the nobler and diviner elements of my own life and character. Those who have not the seeds of any particular evil in them never suffer, therefore, by being thrown into the company of people who have that particular evil fully developed in them. Similarly those who have not any particular type of goodness or virtue latent in them, remain absolutely unaffected by even the closest and most constant association with others who have that particular goodness or virtue fully developed in them. These are matters of very common experience. And all these show that there is really neither room nor need for any borrowing or lending in organic social or individual evolution. And it follows, as a matter of course, therefore, that the questions "Is it true?"—"Is it good?"—do not and cannot arise in the case of nations or races, forced by historic circumstances into any contact or conflict with other nations or races.

Individual and National Psychology.

These questions very frequently arise, in the case of individuals standing face to face with any new thought or ideal. But we should not forget that the psychology of the individual human unit is not exactly the same as that of nations and communities. Individual members of a nation or community may, and do largely and even effectively, influence the course of evolution of their nation or community. But they do it not directly but indirectly, by the force of thought or habit which their individual thinking and living cumulatively produce in the community. A nation very rarely makes any deliberate choice and consciously wills to accept or reject any particular idea or course of action. National impulses, like those of all complex organisms, are not the result of calm deliberation or considered selection, but are due to what may best be characterised as unconscious cerebration. A nation rarely or never weighs and balances the truth or untruth or the good or the evil of any thought or course that presents itself before it, but accepts or rejects it simply according to the law of its own inner affinities or repulsions; that which is in harmony with the sum total of its past and present life and experiences, and that which is most calculated to help it in its struggle for existence, it accepts readily and perhaps even greedily; that which is not of this character, it rejects automatically. This law of natural selection operates equally in social as in biological evolution. Individuals may and do influence the course of social evolution, but only slowly, indirectly, by creating new conditions, stimulating new thoughts, communicating to their community new and nobler ideals.

But even here, society uses its own selective powers. The collective social consciousness accepts and embraces only such of these new thoughts and ideas and ideals and inspirations as are in consonance with its own inner spirit and character, and rejects those that cannot so fit in with that spirit and character. And the moment we consider these facts, we find it impossible to accept my correspondent's position that the value of nationalism is more negative than positive.

Absolutism and Nationalism.

I can fully understand, however, my friend's position. In the first place, truth and right are to him absolute categories: what is true for one is, to him, true for all; what is true in one country must be true in every other country. And so also with right or goodness. This absolutism is the key-note of all credal systems. But with us, it is different. Truth, in the sense and of the class to which my correspondent refers, is a matter of intellectual conviction or what we call rational belief. And this truth is always relative. What is acceptable and convincing to one person is not necessarily acceptable to others. Our intellectual convictions are always regulated by our experience, training, and temperament. A thought or idea to be acceptable to me must fit in with the general scheme of my thinking and reasoning; must conform to the particular cast of my mind. It is, therefore, that what seems to be very good reason to one person, appears as utterly unreasonable to another. Faith really is not a matter of volition, but of cognition and emotion. And our faith always accommodates itself to the general scheme of our thought and the general habits and avocations of our life. Dogmas of ancient religions are progressively interpreted from age to age, and the injunctions of the prophets and teachers of the world have new meanings put upon them, with either additions or reservations, to accommodate them to the actual thought and life of their adherents and followers. The Gospel of Jesus Christ received, thus, new interpretations from the Greek and Roman converts to Christianity : and some of his best teachings are being dismissed and shelved to-day by the modern Christian, because they do not fit in with their social life and current ethical standards. "If a man take thy coat, let him have thy cloak also"—is an impossible, unpractical, harmful injunction to a competitive and individualistic civilisation and social economy, whose law is each man for himself and the d—l take the hindmost. We understand these diversities. We may vote a thing as lower, but cannot condemn it as sin. It is true and good for those who are in that particular stage of evolution. They must pass through it, must beat their music out, wear out the animal and the carnal that is still in them in this way. It is bad for those who stand on another plane, and are therefore under another law. Those who are in the law must be judged by the law : and not by another, either a higher or a lower law. This is the real ethics of evolution. This is what I have always understood by self-realisation as the ultimate and eternal ethical end. This self is neither an arithmetical combination, nor a mechanical compound ; but is an organism, very complicated and complex, with many contradictions and competitions within itself, but all harmonised and reconciled in its own unity. The self is a unit. It is a unity. It is an organic unity, which realises itself through almost endless variations and changes. What we call good, and what we call evil, are both moments in the evolution of this self. Its evil is not absolute. Evil is only imperfect or misplaced good; or it is even, sometimes, only good in the making. Like shine and shadow, good and evil go together, set off each other, counterpoise each other, and work together to help the evolution and realisation of the self. For every good, as Emerson says, there is a counterpoise of evil; and for every evil there is, somewhere, whether manifest or unmanifest, some compensating good, in the very make and being of every human individual. If, therefore, what another person regards as evil, be really acceptable to me, that is, if my nature takes it in, then I take it for granted that this so-called evil is a necessity of my real growth and evolution, and is good to me. For the real judge of what will and what will not truly do me harm is my nature—the sum total of my life and being—my self. And the self is as much subject to the law of natural selection, as any animal organism. What my self chooses for me is my highest and best choice. But in our present artificial state, this self is so overburdened with so many superimposed faiths and ordinances, customs and conventions, and is subjected constantly to so much outside temptations and fears, that it rarely can know its own mind and make its own true and honest choice. This is why we see, as my friend points out, the conflicts of so many competing selves in us. And here our duty is to free our self, first and foremost of all, of these outer bonds. This is Carlyle's Eternal Nay: Accept nothing, believe in nothing, submit to nothing—that comes from without, whether Church or Society. Make your mind, so far as may be, a clean slate. Shake off these outer shackles. Be free of all *sanskara* (संस्कार) or prepossessions, social, ethical, religious. This is the first step, in the knowledge of the self. The self that is revealed then to you, may not be very pure or noble or good, but it will at least be true and real; and once that truth and reality is found, and it is established upon its own proper state, then its self-evolution from lower to higher and higher stages will follow as a matter of course, and will be uninterrupted. "To thine own self be true: and thou canst not be false to others"—is the utterance of the highest wisdom.

The Practical Value of Nationalism in India.

As it is with individuals, so also with nations. Every nation must, first and foremost of all, be true to its own self. Its self may not be very pure or refined or noble. But whatever its state of progress, or stage of evolution, it must above all things, be true to the special laws of that state or stage. For upon its faithful fulfilment of that law only will depend every chance and possibility of its ascent to the next higher state or stage. "Faithful in few things, I shall make thee ruler over many things"—this is the law here also. And this is true nationalism. It is the loyalty of a nation to its own genius, its own nature, its own proper and true self. Like individuals, nations too are sometimes, if not frequently, tempted to be faithless to itself. These temptations appear when a nation comes in contact with another nation or other nations owning a different culture and civilisation, which, if accepted, may place them in a position of greater earthly vantage. These temptations have come to us, for instance, in India now. The whole structure of the civilisation of our rulers is based, as Lecky says, "upon the belief that it is a good thing to cultivate intellectual and material capacities even at the cost of certain moral evils which we are able accurately to foresee." The preference of material and intellectual ends over moral and spiritual ends, constitutes a prominent feature of the present phase of this civilisation with which our nation stands confronted to day. The representatives of this new civilisation hold political sovereignty over us. It is always natural for the subjects to follow their sovereign. We adopted many foreign things in imitation of our Moslem rulers. We are doing the same to-day. This is almost inevitable. In the next place, the natural leaning of our common carnal appetites is to give preference to material over moral and spiritual good. The emphasis of our mediæval civilisation was different. It gave preference to moral and spiritual acquisitions over earthly powers and enjoyments. That was the straight way. That of the new culture imported into our country now is much broader and easier and more tempting. Nationalism has, therefore, a very positive value to us. Loyalty to our national ideals and institutions means really our only chance of living as a distinct and individual nation. It constitutes our only title to grow as an individual nation among the nations of the modern world. It is a supremely practical problem to us. Its value is positive and not negative.

NATIONALISM AND TRADITIONALISM.

I think, however, that the kindly criticisms of my esteemed English correspondent are based upon a very common misconception. To a good many people, even among us, and especially in the ranks of both our social reformers and reactionaries, nationalism means only rank and hidebound conservatism. This unreasonable and rigid conservatism has often masqueraded as real nationalism; and the note of sober and rational progress has frequently been stifled in its name. The apprehensions of my correspondent and those who think and feel like him, are not entirely fanciful or unreal. But my complaint is that they do not seem to take due note of the fundamental difference between mere conservatism and real nationalism. Hidebound conservatism is, really, as different from true nationalism, as rampant jingoism is, for instance, different from real imperialism.

NATIONALISM AND EVOLUTION.

In fact, the entire philosophy of nationalism, as I have been taught to understand it, is based upon the Theory or Law of Evolution. And this nationalism cannot, therefore, be in any way identified with hidebound conservatism. This conservatism is averse to all change; but change is the very soul of the Law of Evolution. Indeed, this law offers the only rational synthesis between conservatism and advance, between order and progress. It cancels the fancied conflict between what was, and what is, and what must be. It works present changes without breaking continuity with the past. In truth, change has no meaning unless it works and appears in an object whose continuity is maintained unbroken through whatever changes it may pass through. To get ill, to be placed in bed and under proper treatment, to get convalescent and well, and to resume, with returning health and strength, the ordinary avocations of life—all these are characterised as changes only when they follow one another *in* the same individual, but not when they represent so many different conditions of as many different peoples. "I was a baby, I became a boy, I went to school, I became a man, I married and had children, I retired upon becoming old"—these are changes, because they have reference to one and the same individual, whose continuity is maintained unbroken through all these changes. They are all evolutions of one and the same person. This "I," this first person singular, this what we call "self"—persisted through all these changes. If with each one of these various changes, the continuity of this personal consciousness—the sense that I am I—were destroyed, then they would not be parts of an evolutionary series. Thus we find that the fundamental fact in evolution is that it allows and effects almost endless changes in an object or organism, without breaking up its continuity or destroying its unity. The Law of Evolution cancels thus, every conflict between change and permanence, between continuity and progress. Change and permanence are contradictions in formal and verbal logic. But Evolution cancels and reconciles these. And as the Philosophy of Nationalism is based upon this Law of Evolution, it leaves no room either for hidebound conservatism on the one hand or for rank revolution on the other. Both are at war with real national life and advancement.

The Postulates of Evolution.

The postulates of the Law or Theory of Evolution are mainly two: first heredity, second environment. Its one aim is to maintain the individuality or distinctiveness of the type, in and through all the changes of forms and habits that it may undergo in its attempt to adapt itself to its changing environments. But even combination of different original types to form a new type is neither impossible nor unknown. This is not possible, however, in all cases. It depends upon the affinities of the types that are sought to be crossed to produce a third type higher, perhaps, than both the parent types. But even in these hybrids the individuality of the original types are not entirely destroyed, but rather preserved, either accentuated or modified, in the new type produced from them. Nationalism does not, therefore, deny possibility of the birth of new national types, through the crossing, so to say, of two or more existing nationalities. But this crossing can be fruitful in the case of such national organisms only as have sufficient affinities between them, both in their original race-consciousness, and in their present stage of culture and civilisation. Where these affinities are absent, there any attempt at "crossing" either biologically by indiscriminate intermarriage, or sociologically by the enforced or imitative introduction of the organs and institutions of a higher religion or civilisation among a lower race, will be bound to lead to atavism and degeneration. And the nationalist principle that "a nation ought to be true to its own personality," and should seek always to "preserve continuity with its past," is based upon the need and desire of avoiding these evils ; and is not meant really, to maintain its absolute isolation from the other nations of the world.

The Birth and Growth of New Nations.

Indeed, such isolation is neither possible nor desirable. It is not possible, because of the inevitable movement of populations from thickly-populated to sparsely-populated territories, under pressure of economic needs and the consequent irruption of the members of different nationalities upon their neighbouring countries. It had been so in the past when we had no nations really, but only tribes ; and it is through these tribal and racial fusions and combinations that most of the great nations of our day originally grew. It is even so to day, when conquest or commerce, or both, have been leading to colonisation of distant tracts and territories by the more aggressive and expansive nations of the world. These colonisations always lead more or less to international crossing and combination. These are strongly resisted by the members of a higher civilisation when they are placed in intimate physical and geographical contact with those of a lower culture, and especially of a different colour ; as we find in Africa, which is being increasingly colonised by the European peoples. But in all these new settlements free and unrestricted miscegenation is allowed among the members of the different white nationalities. These combinations do not, however, destroy national differentiations, but simply create new national types, more developed perhaps, and surely more complex, than the older ones. We are thus seeing, before our very eyes, the birth and growth of new national types, with distinct individualities or personalities of their own, not only in the United States of America, but even in the British Dominions of Canada and South Africa. And the fact that these new combinations of the members of different nationalities with developed and distinctive notes and marks of their own, do not destroy national differentiations but instead of seeking self-fulfilment in any shapeless and formless and undifferentiated cosmopolitanism or internationalism, rather create new national organisms, proves the truth of the essential postulate of the Philosophy of Nationalism, namely, that every composite people either living together in one common territory, under one common State, or inheritors and workers of a common culture and civilisation, whether primitive and simple or advanced and complex, from time immemorial, or thrown recently into one another's company, as members of the same State, have or develop a distinct personality of their own. International admixture does not destroy the personality of a new nation, but, on the contrary, develops it and gives it a new shape and form, in which the older types are not entirely obliterated, nor from which the older spirit is absolutely eliminated, but where these are simply transformed and transmuted. The law of conservation of energy and transmutability of force is not absent even from social evolution. And all these prove, it seems to me, the positive value of nationalism as a principle and law of social evolution.

Calcutta, May 1913.

CHAPTER IV.

NATIONALISM AND POLITICS.

THE POLITICAL EMPHASIS OF INDIAN NATIONALISM.

VERY few people even among those who claim to be very staunch Nationalists in this country, seem to have as yet grasped the true meaning of Nationalism or to have imbibed its inner spirit. To many of us Nationalism is only a political cry. It had its origin in our political conflicts with the British Bureaucracy in the country, and has for its ultimate ideal some sort of political freedom. With the so-called "Moderates," Nationalism aims at the attainment of Colonial Self-Government, whatever that may mean. With a section at least of those who are called "Extremists" by their enemies, the ultimate goal of Nationalism is absolute political independence, howsoever it may have to be realised. And in this, there is absolutely no difference between Indian and European Nationalism. For in Europe Nationalism has so far had an exclusively political meaning. We hear of it only among what are called dependent or subject peoples. It had been the cry of Young Italy, in the last century, when "Italia" was under the heel of the Austrian oppressor. It has also been the cry of the Irish patriots smarting under a sense of political subjection to Great Britain. It is the bitter cry of the Poles and the Fins crushed under the weight of the Russian Autocracy. And it would serve no useful purpose to shut our eyes to the fact that many of us in India have caught this cry from these European peoples. This is why even among us also Nationalism has so far been practically a political propaganda. And it shows how, all our bitterest antagonism against European ideas and institutions notwithstanding, we are, whether we affect heterodoxy and cosmopolitanism or orthodoxy and conservatism—much too overwhelmingly under the spell of European thought and culture, to be able to take an independent and truly Indian view of any of our present-day problems, whether social or economic or political. This incapacity is entirely responsible for the almost exclusive political emphasis of Indian Nationalism, as this emphasis, in its turn, has led to all the criminal excesses that have tarnished the fair fame of this new and soul-stirring patriotic movement among us.

The History of Nationalism in Europe.

Mazzini has so far been the only prophet of Nationalism in Europe. As I have pointed out previously, his is the best definition of the term that we have so far had in European thought. Mazzini defines "Nationality" as "the Individuality of a People." And individuality is that which marks out different human units from one another. My individuality is that which impresses those who come in contact with me that I am unlike their other friends and acquaintances. I have the same physiological organs and the same psychological powers as other humans of my class, but still I am not absolutely like them. There are certain undeniable but inexplicable tricks of nature which impart a distinctness to my physical and mental life and activities, and thus separate me from others. This is a matter of very common experience. And as there are these subtle characteristics that differentiate one human from another, though they may both belong to the same race, speak the same language, profess the same religion, observe the same social code, may even claim a common parentage, and may have received the same training from their infancy onward; even so there are certain characteristics which are usually found to differentiate one nation or people from another. This differentiation between the collective life and character of different social units constitutes the very soul and essence of the Nation-idea. Mazzini seized this fact very correctly, and his definition of Nationality is so correct because it is based upon this fact of universal experience.

The Elements of National Differentiation in Europe.

But neither Mazzini nor any one else in Europe, so far as my limited knowledge goes, seems to have subjected this generalisation to any further analysis with a view to reach out to a still higher synthesis. Owing to the want of this higher synthesis, modern European sociologists have hardly been able to discover as yet the true postulates of their specific science. This explains, I think, the excessive biolcgical and anthropological emphasis of current sociological speculations in the West. In the study of historic evolution and social phenomena too much attention has been paid to what M. Taine calls environments and epochs and much too little to what may be called the original race-consciousness of different social groups. In seeking to explain the phenomena of racial differentiations, too much emphasis has been put on environments and associations, and too little on heredity. And the reason of it is also evident. For, racially all Europe has practically been one. They all belong to the same original stock. Their race-consciousness is the same. They have the same physical or physiological, the same social and economic, and the same mental structure. Difference of historic evolution or national character in Europe has thus been very largely the result of environments and epochs and not of original race-consciousness. And the fact that almost for the last two thousand years Europe has been under the influence of one and the same credal religion, has helped very much to still further level down real national differentiations among different European peoples. Culturally all Europe has for centuries past been practically one. The different nations of Europe have had for centuries past one common social economy, and one common economic structure. The course of social evolution has been practically the same in all the great European countries. Nationalism means, therefore, really very little of vital importance in Europe. Modern European thought hardly realises, therefore, the significance of the nationalist philosophy or recognises the need of any nationalist ideal or inspiration. It understands internationalism. It aspires after the highest cosmopolitan ideal. But it has not as yet clearly grasped the fact that as the universal cannot exist without the particular—viewed apart from the particular, the universal is only an abstraction, like Hegel's Pure Being which is equal to Pure Nothing; even so cosmopolitanism, unless based upon nationalism, is a mere abstraction, a fancy, a mode of thinking, and not a reality. And the very feeble emphasis that modern European thought has so far laid upon nationalism, and the consequent absence of any true and lofty philosophy of it in modern European speculations, is entirely due to the fact that in Europe, the different nations are practically one people. They all have the same thought-structure and the same social structure. They are all moved, practically, by the same worldly or other-worldly aspirations.

EUROPEAN NATIONALISM AND THE SPIRITUAL LIFE.

In Europe, Nationalism can never get rid, therefore, of its political incubus. It cannot, without a much deeper analysis of the social life and experience, be raised to the dignity of a philosophy or the sanctity of a religion. The isolation of the life and authority of the different European States, based upon their respective territorial demarcations, and the consequent conceit of separate political and economic interests, unreconciled, and under present conditions apparently unreconcilable with one another, and the conflicts and competitions arising out of this separatist sentiment—these are about the only things that mark the real difference between one European nation and another. Patriotism in Europe is, therefore, mainly a geographical virtue. It has only a supreme territorial reference. Its general aim and end is to procure the political independence of one's own country, and, with a view to enhance its political power or strengthen its economic and industrial position, to deprive the weaker nations of the world of their political independence, in the name of civilisation and humanity. This desire for political freedom for one's own people, and this longing for political ascendancy over other peoples, these have always been the most vital object of national ambitions in Europe. It is these meaner rivalries that have, for centuries past, been the actual contents of the nation-idea among European peoples. It is very natural, therefore, that nationalism should be a term of the political life only, in Europe. It has consequently but little moral inspiration or spiritual strength in it.

THE NATION-IDEA IN INDIA.

But our history and evolution have been somewhat different. We did not develop the nation-idea in the sense and in the way that Europe developed it. Our language has, in fact, no word corresponding to the English word nation. We are now using the word "*jāti*" जाति for nation. But "*jāti*" really means *genus*. We had, thus, the terms "*go jāti*" गोजाति and *manushya jāti* मनुष्यजाति which mean the genus cow and the genus man, but nothing like "*Engrez jāti*"—इंरेजजाति or "*Bhārateeya jāti*" or "*Hindu jāti*"—to indicate the English nation, the Indian nation, or the Hindu nation, in our old literature. And the reason of it is that our old social synthesis practically stopped with the race-idea. The individual, the family, the caste, the clan, and after the clan—universal humanity or the genus *homo*—these are practically all the terms of our social philosophy. We never had, therefore, this nationalist ideal or aspiration before. Sociologically race comes after clan as the formula of a higher synthesis and a broader human fellowship; and nation comes after race; for many races frequently combine to form a nation. But ethnic systems, like those, for instance, of the Hindus and the Hebrews, are inherently opposed to these racial fusions. The Hindu and the Hebrew have, therefore, persisted, almost to our own time, as distinct ethnic units. In fact the Hebrew has preserved his ethnic integrity perhaps even more successfully than the Hindu. There has not only been much greater miscegenation among the Hindus than among Hebrews; but through his Varnāsrama or caste-and-order scheme, the Hindu has developed a type of inter-ethnic or inter-racial union and association unknown to Hebrew history and culture. In one sense, therefore, we did develop a nation-idea and a national type of our own, even without the term nation. But it was not a political synthesis only.

The Evolution of European Nations.

In Europe, racial fusion took place, at first, mainly through the propagation of Christianity. Religious unity was the basis of inter-ethnic or inter-racial unification. The acceptance of a common creed, and submission to a common socio-religious discipline, organised in a uniform system of sacraments and ceremonies, absolutely binding upon all, irrespective of their race or colour or country or culture, helped to obliterate the old ethnic divisions in Europe. The old ethnic institutions of the Christian converts were either entirely destroyed or absolutely absorbed by the new creed and culture. Linguistic differences, geographical boundaries, and political isolation or independence—these are all that remained now to indicate the difference between the different Christian peoples of Europe. These have continued even to our own time as the principal notes or marks of national differentiation there. On the other hand, the influence of the credal ideal in their religious life, which demanded an absolute uniformity of beliefs and practices in the followers of Christ, developed an ideal of homogeneity in their national life. Unity of geographical or territorial habitat, unity of language, unity of social life and economy, as much as unity of religious beliefs came, thus, to be regarded as absolute conditions of national unity in Europe. And as there was already unity of religious and social life among the various nations of Europe, difference of geographical habitat and state-authority and organisation, became naturally the most vital elements of the national life and differentiation among them.

The Course of Evolution in India.

In India, among the Hindus, social evolution took a very different course. It developed a federal type almost from the very beginning. And the main reason why we have been able to preserve this type is that we never came under the dominating influence of any credal systems like Christianity, for instance. Buddhism too is credal, like Christianity and Islam. But Buddhism though born in India, did not entirely overthrow the old religion of the country, but was itself practically thrown out as a foreign body. Buddhism expanded but did not absorb Hinduism. It contributed new elements to Hinduism, but did not kill its original life as Christianity killed the life of Paganism in Europe. Christianity took in all the nobler elements of the old Pagan religions and having absorbed all their life and sap, threw them away like a sucked orange.

Buddhism could not do so in India, but, on the contrary, was sucked dry by the revived philosophy and culture of the older religion of the people and thrown out as useless afterwards. The expulsion of credal Buddhism from India had, thus, been the salvation of the integrity of Indian culture.

THE CULTURAL BASIS OF INDIAN NATIONALISM.

National differentiations among us, therefore, have not been based upon territorial demarcations only, or upon political or economic competitions and conflicts, but upon differences of culture. Under the Moslems we had, whether Hindus or Mahomedans, one common Government, but that did not destroy the integrity of Hindu culture. We took many things from our Mahommedan neighbours, and gave them also something of our own, but this interchange of ideas and institutions did not destroy our special character or our special culture. And that special character and culture is the very soul and essence of what we now understand as Nationalism. This is by no means a mere political idea or ideal. It is something that touches every department of our collective life and activity. It is organised in our domestic, our communal, our social, and our socio-economic institutions. In fact politics form, from some points of view, the least important factor of this nation-idea among us. The so-called free political institutions of Europe might, indeed, hinder, instead of helping the growth of our real national life ; while under conceivable conditions, mere political subjection might not be able to touch even the outermost fringe of that life.

BRITISH RULE AND INDIAN CULTURE.

Practically, England's rule in India has been very vitally affecting our national life and integrity. But that is because British rule means a good deal more than mere political sovereignty. This rule is organically bound up with a special system of economics, for instance. The British rulers are not satisfied with simply exercising political authority over us; they must, in pursuance of their own ideal of statecraft, develop our material resources also. The spirit of European capitalism has, thus, been wedded to the administrative policy of the British Government in India. And it is here that the real conflict between Indian Nationalism and British Administration arises. The capitalistic spirit of the British Government in India has inspired from the very beginning its economic policy, and has developed a kind of State-Socialism among us which is almost fatal to our real national life. This fact cannot be ignored, and its importance must not be sought to be minimised. But this danger will not be removed by any expansion of our so-called political rights and privileges. Such expansion will, necessarily, mean greater co-operation and closer partnership with the present capitalistic and socialistic administration in the country. It will not change the capitalistic character of the Government or alter its policy of state-socialism. This being so, the expansion of so-called political franchise may spell only an increased menace to the true nationalist ideal among us.

THE RIGHT NATIONALIST POLICY.

So far as our present political life is concerned, the only right policy and attitude of the Indian Nationalist must, to my mind, be what is called *laissez faire.* This policy is forced upon us by the conflict of civilisations between the rulers and the ruled in this country. In view of this conflict, it is essential that, for the preservation of the integrity of our own thought and culture and for securing to our people sufficient freedom to grow in their own way, following the trends of their own special history and evolution, without being overwhelmed by any alien influences—the activities of the Government should be restricted, as far as possible, to the discharge of their primary functions only. And in this the Government must have our whole-hearted support. The preservation of peace and order is the primary function of every State. The failure of any Government to efficiently discharge this function spells anarchy, and leads ultimately to the break-up of the social organisation. It means, practically, the re-barbarisation of humanity. There is absolutely no excuse, therefore, for any community to wantonly obstruct the discharge of this primary function by the Government under which they may have to live. No considerations regarding the character of their state-constitution—whether it is autocratic or democratic—or concerning the nationality of the person or persons in whom the State authority may be vested for the time being—whether they are foreigners or of the people—no considerations of this kind can absolve them of their paramount obligation to help their Government in the efficient discharge of this primary function. To deny this obligation is not Nationalism, but Anarchism. There are occasions when particular measures of a Government may have to be resolutely opposed. There are circumstances which, in the opinion of some political philosophers, even justify open revolt, provided it has the practical sanction of the *whole* nation. Political philosophy recognises all these in extreme cases. But no philosophy, except that of anarchism—which is the ultimate logic of every form of absolute individualism, such as dominated the social philosophy of Europe for the greater part of the eighteenth and the nineteenth centuries—has any plea or justification for any people to deliberately obstruct the discharge of the primary functions of the State by the Government established among them. And as no Government can exist anywhere unless it is generally acceptable to the people whom it rules—except where they are kept in absolute physical subjection by sheer force of superior numbers—any attempt on the part of a small minority to paralyse the machinery of the Administration by a campaign of secret assassinations or organised lawlessness, is not merely an attack on the Government, but upon Society itself. It is the worst conceivable form of tyranny; because it really means an attempt on the part of a small and impatient minority to force the majority of their people into a position which they are either unwilling or unprepared to face.

A Suicidal Propaganda.

In times of abnormal excitement even noble men sometimes lend themselves to ignoble acts, which they sincerely regret or repent afterwards. It happened among us also. The young men who started this campaign of terrorism in 1907-1908, and who are doing penance for their acts now in the Andamans, were only misguided, but not devoid of either intelligence or conscience. Theirs was an act of madness. They never incited neurotic youths by secret circulars to sacrifice their lives, while they themselves were safe out of harm's way. They did not cherish the fatuous folly of securing "independence" for their country by a campaign of secret assassinations. I knew one or two of those young men personally and intimately. I know they were as tender as a woman, incapable of causing wanton pain to man or beast. It was a passing frenzy that possessed their spirit. Those who are planning secret murders and organising so-called political dacoities, may appeal in their name but are not made of their stuff. They have caught a few catch-phrases and have learnt to copy a few impassioned exhortations, that is all. This, and their bitter hatred of the British Government and the British people, are their only stock-in-trade. And I have no hesitation in saying that these men, whatever their number, who from the safety of their hiding are trying to keep up this anarchical campaign in the country, when all parties are so sincerely anxious to discover some rational and peaceful settlement of the vital issues of our present and future political life, are the worst enemies of Indian Nationalism.

EUROPEAN INSPIRATION NOT INDIAN.

Both their ideal and their inspiration are European, and not Indian. Political independence, they declare, is their ideal-end. But this so-called political independence is a fundamentally foreign concept. It is, as I have often tried to point out, a negative something, an essentially anti-social idea. It is associated with the European doctrine of Rights, which, as Mazzini rightly declared, is a formula of resistance, and not a principle of reconciliation. Association, not isolation; co-operation, not competition; socialism, in the highest and truest sense of the term, and not merely what it is understood to mean by the followers of Marx—this socialism, and not individualism; duty, and not right—these are the rudimentary concepts of our social and political philosophy. These are the fundamental ideas of Indian Nationalism. Our "individuality" as a people is based upon these distinctive notes or marks of our thought and evolution. These are the primary factors of our differentiation from other nations of the world. Humanity needs these larger social concepts, to be able to work up the next higher social synthesis. They are our moral title to live as a nation. Europe is groping after these. For us to seek isolation in the name of independence; to seek selfish competitions with other nations, under pretence of furthering our national interests; to set up individualism in place of collectivism as the true social goal; or give preference to a narrow and selfish, a competing and fighting nationalism, over the broader, altruistic, humanitarian ideal of co-operative internationalism and universal federation—is really to strangle, with our own hands, that very Nationalism, to which so many of us are ever ready to swear deathless allegiance. If we are to preserve the distinctive character of our thought and culture, we must perpetually keep, AUTONOMY, as distinguished from INDEPENDENCE, as our ideal political end.

INDEPENDENCE *vs.* AUTONOMY.

In fact, Svaraj, the accepted political ideal of the Indian Nationalists, does not connote the same thing as what is called "independence" in English. The correct rendering of Svaraj is autonomy and not independence. Autonomy is a positive, while independence is a negative, concept. Independence means isolation. Autonomy implies no necessary severance of outside connections or associations. Nationalism implies that, collectively, we, the composite Indian community, are a distinct, and individual social organism; and as such, we have a distinct end unto ourselves and a specific law of our own National Being, through which we must seek to reach and realise that end. And because autonomy means the act and the power of living according to one's own law, it is a legitimate nationalist ideal. For nationality implies that we have a special character, a distinct individuality of our own; a law of our being, by submitting to which alone we can perfect and realise our collective life. It is just for this reason that national autonomy is an absolute condition-precedent of the pursuit and realisation of the nationalist ideal. And we must deprecate, by every means in our power, this spirit of bitter antagonism to the British Government and the British people, which some people seem to mistake for an ardent devotion to the nationalist cause, for the very simple and sufficient reason that it has an inevitable tendency to lower our own ideals, confuse our thought, blur our vision of the Mother, in a word to simultaneously denationalise and dehumanise us. For anger is not merely secret murder, it is also incipient insanity. And hatred ultimately, like every other evil in God's world, defeats its own purpose. Cherished and inveterate hatred, by a strange psychological law, leads to the possession of the hater by the inner spirit of the very thing or person he hates. This is being proved before our very eyes. Their bitter hatred of Europe is visibly Europeanising the inner soul of many of our people. This passionate antagonism towards the British Government inevitably leads to a constant contemplation of their evil-side. And no man can ever find his own good by fixing his mind constantly upon the evils that another may have in him. This insensate antipathy towards the British Government really leaves us little time to think out our own problems soberly or recognise our present duty correctly. The frenzied vision of the misguided Indian patriot must inevitably see only the brute in the British; and this vision of the brute in the British, by an unfailing psychological law, calls out not the God, but only the brute in him also. This conflict is, thus, brutalising both parties equally. Centuries of moral and spiritual disciplines had considerably laid the brute in us. But this political frenzy by calling out the brute in our rulers is, in its rebound upon us, rebrutalising our people also. It is striking at the very root of our "individuality" as a people. And it is just for these reasons that I hold that this bitter and unreasonable antipathy towards the British people is suicidal to the very spirit of Indian Nationalism, and should never, therefore, be indulged in or encouraged by those who are truly devoted to the nationalist cause in this country.

PRACTICAL CONSIDERATIONS: THE WORLD-SITUATION.

All this may require some culture to understand and appreciate. But a little reflection will show how this bitterness is a very serious menace even to that political freedom, which seems to have obsessed the minds of a good many of our young men. It is a very real danger to our political future. That future will no longer be settled by the issues of any conflict that may arise between India and England, but by the future developments of what may well be described as the present world-situation. We may ignore that situation, but let us not fancy that it will ignore us. Three terrible combinations threaten to come into conflict with one another in the coming century. A world-wide confederacy of the white races is gradually being formed in Europe and America. Imperial Federation on the one side and the new diplomatic idea of what is called "Peace-and-Arbitration-Treaties" on the other, are clear signs of it. The practical extinction of Turkey as a European Power, whatever immediate conflicts or complications may arise out of it, will gradually bring about a situation which will be settled in no other way, except through a treaty of peace and arbitration among the various Powers vitally interested in keeping the *status quo ante* in the Bosphorus. To try to solve this more-than-a-century old problem of the Bosphorus in any other way would set all Europe ablaze; and even after any possible all-European War, the settlement of it will have to come through some clear and friendly understanding between the European Powers, in reaching which they will very likely settle most of their other outstanding differences also. And this will pave the way to the ultimate evolution of a Pan-European Confederacy. Then, there is the possibility of a Pan-Islamic combination. The fall of Turkey will not, to my mind, destroy but rather on the contrary most effectually enhance the possibilities of this combination. To think that the fall of Turkey and the imminent partition of Persia will break the backbone of Pan-Islamism, is to take a very superficial view of the situation. The real strength of the Pan-Islamic sentiment, and its menace to world-peace; never lay in the political power of the Mahomedan States—in their navy or their army. In these matters, Islam can never hope to approach the European nations. The chief strength of Pan-Islamism lies in the so-called fanaticism of the Moslem populations of the world. The fall of Turkey and the partition of Persia, should it come about, will not allay but increase this danger a hundred-fold. In fact these petty and disorganised Mahomedan States are, from some points of view, not helps but rather a hindrance to the spread of Pan-Islamism. They have diverted people's thoughts from their own strength to that of the armies of these Moslem potentates. The dispersion of these armies, will intensify the sense of communal wrong among the Moslems and strengthen the determination of the *people* to avenge that wrong. Fanaticism is stronger than guns; and popular upheaval spread over wide latitudes more invincible than trained army corps. Nothing short of a Pan-European combination will be able to successfully face a world-wide Pan-Islamism, should it ever come into existence. Thirdly, there is the possibility of a Pan-Mongolian Confederacy also. And I want my Nationalist friends to calmly ponder over these political possibilities, and then see, which way the future of Indian autonomy and the possibilities of Indian Nationalism actually lie. Of these three possible combinations, Pan-Europeanism will affect our future least of all, as long as the present British connection continues. Pan-Islamism and Pan-Mongolianism offer, therefore, the greatest menace to India's future and to the realisation of the dream of the Indian Nationalist.

PAN-EUROPEANISM.

These three possibilities are before us. Most people, I think, would accept the first as even a probability. European politics, all the apparent international jealousies and enmities notwithstanding, is distinctly moving towards some sort of a Pan-European combination. Socialism is openly advocating a universal federation of labour, which means a federation of the European *people*, as distinguished from their present rulers—the aristocracy and the bourgeoisie. One of the professed aims of this federation of the world's workers is to prevent war. The idea of an organised international strike among the working populations of belligerent countries, with a view to force the hands of those who make these wars, is already openly discussed in the prominent organs of the Socialist Party both in Great Britain and the Continent of Europe. And it shows that the principle of arbitration will have to be adopted before long for the settlement of all international disputes among the nations of Europe. Treaties of arbitration and peace will, thus, be gradually formed with one another by the European powers ; and this will be the forerunner of a general European Confederacy not only with its authorised International Courts of Arbitratoin, but, by and by, also with the other organs and instruments of a wide and complex federal relationship. The present century will mark this new development in modern world-politics and world-civilisation.*

PAN-ISLAMISM AND PAN-MONGOLIANISM.

This Pan-European combination will be a very serious menace to the non-European world. It will be bound to come into serious conflict with both Pan-Islamism and Pan-Mongolianism. If Europe can settle her internal jealousies betimes, she will be able to dominate easily both the Islamic and the Mongolian world. Nothing will prevent in that case the parcelling out of the Moslem lands on the one side, and of China on the other. But that is not very likely. It will take, at least, as long a time for the European chancellories to forget their past jealousies and present rivalries, as it will take for China, now that she has awakened from the sleep of ages, to put her own house in order and organise her leviathan strength to hold her own against all the world. The same thing is likely to happen in the Islamic world also ; and the fall of Turkey in Europe will hasten this combination. It will not be an organised confederacy like that of China and Japan, but a far more dangerous, because more subtle, combination of the hearts of countless hordes who hold nothing so dear, neither land nor life, as their religion. And the real strength of this Pan-Islamic outburst will come from Egypt

* Even the present European war calls for no reconsideration of this prognosis of the present world-situation ; because, if anything, at the close of this war the need of a Pan-European Confederacy will be brought home to the different European States ruinously weakened by this struggle, more clearly and vitally than it would otherwise likely to be ; and already there is in the English Reviews some discussion of what is called the coming " United States of Europe."

and India, where it will be safe from the crushing weight of the Pan-European confederacy. England will not allow her European confederates to interfere with her own domestic affairs; such interference would break up the Confederation at once. She will have to settle this Pan-Islamic problem, so far as it may affect her own dominions, herself.

Our Real Danger.

And it is just here that our safety from this possible Pan-European Combination also lies. Because of the British connection, India will have nothing to fear from any possible combination of the European Powers. The same is also true of Egypt, though perhaps in a lesser degree. Our real menace will come not from Europe but from Asia, not from Pan-Europeanism but from Pan-Islamism and Pan-Mongolianism. These dangers are, however, common, both to India and Egypt and Great Britain. To provide against it, Great Britain will have to find and work out a satisfactory and permanent settlement of the Indian and the Egyptian problem, and we, on our part, will have also to come to some rational compromise with her. British statesmanship must recognise the urgent and absolute need of fully satisfying the demands of Indian and Egyptian Nationalism, and India and Egypt will have to frankly accept the British connection—which is different from British subjection—as a necessary condition of their national life and freedom. To wantonly seek to break up this connection, while it will only hurt Great Britain, may positively kill every chance and possibility of either Indian or Egyptian Nationalism ever realising itself.

OUR TRUE SAFETY.

Indian Nationalism, in any case, has, I think, really no fear of being permanently opposed or crippled by Great Britain. On the contrary, the British connection can alone offer it effective protection against both the Pan-Islamic and the Pan-Mongolian menace. As long as we had to consider Great Britain alone or any other European Power for the matter of that, while thinking of the future of Indian Nationalism, the problem was comparatively simple and easy. But now we have to think of China on the one hand, and of the new Pan-Islamic danger on the other. The sixty millions of Mahomedans in India, if inspired with Pan-Islamic aspirations, joined to the Islamic principalities and powers that stand both to our West and our North-West, may easily put an end to all our nationalist aspirations, almost at any moment, if the present British connection be severed. The four hundred millions of the Chinese Empire can, not only gain an easy footing in India, but once that footing is gained, they are the only people under the sun who can hold us down by sheer superior physical force. There is no other people who can do this. This awakening of China is, therefore, a very serious menace—in the present condition of our country, without an organised and trained army and a powerful navy of our own—to the maintenance of any isolated, though sovereign, independence of the Indian people. Even if we are able to gain it, we shall never be able to keep it, in the face of this Pan-Islamic and Pan-Mongolian menace. And when one considers these terrible possibilities of the world-situation as it is slowly evolving before one's eyes, one is forced to recognise the absolute need of keeping up the British connection in the interest of Indian Nationalism itself, for the very simple and sufficient reason that there is absolutely much greater chance of this Nationalism fully realising itself with rather than without this connection.

India and Britain: Community of Interests.

In fact as it is to the interest of Indian Nationalism to seek to perpetuate the British connection, so it is equally to the interest of British Imperialism itself to help and foster the spirit of Nationalism both in India and in Egypt, and to co-ordinate these great forces with those of Great Britain and her Dominions. For it should be clearly realised that the real strength of this new Pan-Islamic idea comes not half so much, if it comes at all, from its religious devotion as from the sense of the political servitude of Egyptian and Indian Mahomedans and of the political impotence of the so-called independent Moslem States. Indeed, the backbone of Pan-Islamism is not in Persia or Afghanistan, much less in Algeria or Abyssinia, but in India and Egypt. This sentiment is the strongest among Egyptian and Indian Moslems. And if the legitimate aspirations of these two sections of the Mahomedan world, to take their due share in present-day world-politics, can be reasonably satisfied within the British Empire, the Pan-Islamic menace may be reduced almost to a vanishing point. In her own interest, therefore, Great Britain will have, before long, to come to terms with Egyptian Nationalism on the one side, and cure the conceit of separate political interests and superior political claims of the Indian Mahomedans on the other, and lead the Indian Moslems to recognise that their future is absolutely bound up with that of the larger and composite Indian Nation. This is the only remedy against the Pan-Islamic menace so far as it affects Great Britain; and it affects Great Britain more seriously and intimately than any other European Power. Nationalism, both in India and Egypt, is the only antidote against Pan-Islamism so far as the British Empire is concerned. Lord Curzon did not understand it. Lord Minto could not realise it. But the far-sighted statesmanship of Lord Hardinge has clearly seized, it seems to me, this fundamental fact. And his lordship's policy has been largely shaped by a recognition of it. Nationalism is also the only protection of Great Britain's interests in India against any possible menace from China. The moment British policy in India makes its peace with the ideals and aspirations of the Indian Nationalists, the Chinese menace too will be reduced to a vanishing point. With the people of India at her back, Great Britain can defy the whole world; without their support she will be at the mercy of the weakest of her enemies. And to secure this support, British policy will have to make room for the fullest realisation of our nationalist ideal. Lord Hardinge understands it. The authorities at White Hall are also more or less conscious of it. The King's visit proves it. The repeal of the Partition of Bengal confirms it. This is the only reasonable meaning and interpretation of Lord Hardinge's memorable Despatch of August 1911. And in view of all this, it seems to me an act of suicidal folly on the part of any one who really cares for the future of Indian Nationalism, even as a mere political ideal, to keep up the old attitude of bitter and uncompromising opposition to the Government.

Indian Autonomy and British Imperialism.

In fact any bitter and unreasonable antagonism to the British connection will, it seems to me, be the greatest menace, under existing conditions, to our political future. For, the gradual evolution of some sort of self-rule in India is far more likely with the continuance of the British connection than without it. In the first place, we must not forget the fact that the present British rule in India, however autocratic and irresponsible it may just now be, is really based, not upon the superior physical strength of the rulers, but upon the sufferance of the ruled. The people of India have so far acquiesced in this rule, and it is therefore that it is with us. This fact is our greatest strength. It is our greatest strength because it makes the problem of national autonomy in British India an essentially psychological problem. We wish to be ruled by England; therefore England rules us so easily. This is the secret of the government of three hundred millions of people by about one hundred thousand Britishers, civil and military, officers and men, all told. How to maintain this quiet acquiescence of the people to their rule, has been the one ever-present thought in the minds of British statesmen. British statesmanship has, therefore, been always anxious at least to apparently reconcile British rule to the wishes and sentiments of the people. It was seen immediately after the Mutiny, in the spirit and wording of the Queen's Proclamation. It was seen during the Administration of Lord Ripon, who, coming after Lord Lytton who had somewhat estranged and irritated the educated middle classes, took every means in his power to rally them around his Government. We have seen it, more recently, in the "Reforms" of Lord Morley; and finally, in the repeal of the Bengal Partition. Irresponsible scribes may talk of the sword. Unimaginative administrators may prescribe repression. We are pretty familiar with all this folly. But responsible statesmen know that India was not won by the sword, is not ruled by the sword, and can never be kept by the sword. The idea is physically preposterous. The very talk of it only betrays the antics of the panic-struck bully. And it is upon the physical preposterousness of this idea, that our faith in the absolute certainty of an orderly, a peaceful, and evolutionary expansion of popular political freedom in India, is based. The imperious necessity which inspired the Queen's Proclamation in 1858; which, subsequently, led to the formulation of Lord Ripon's scheme of so-called Local Self-Government; which brought about the reform and expansion of Indian Legislatures, by Lord Cross's India Councils Act; which pushed Sir K. G. Gupta into the Secretary of State's Council and Mr. S. P. Sinha into the Executive Council of the Viceroy; which promoted Lord Morley's "Reforms" and led to the Repeal of the Bengal Partition—the imperious need which helped to bring about all these, will gradually bring about a real reconciliation between Indian Nationalism and British Imperialism. It will be bound to lead to a Federation of the British Empire, in which India and Egypt shall be equal co-partners with Great Britain and Ireland and the British Dominions over-seas—a Federation which will secure to all these Federated States absolute freedom of self-rule and self-evolution, without breaking up their federal relation of co-ordination and co-operation with the empire as a whole on the one side, and with its other parts on the other. This Imperial Federation is Britain's imperious necessity. It should be our considered ideal. Great Britain, to maintain her own position as a great world-empire, must do everything in her power to keep India to herself. And the only way to do it is to reconcile her own interests with those of the Indian people. India's desire for self-rule will have to be satisfied. And the only reconciliation between England and India is possible in a scheme of real Imperial Federation. For the freedom of the parts in the unity of the whole, is of the very essence of the Federal idea. Great Britain in her own larger self-interest will have to gradually work up this Federation. India, in her own interest, to secure her own national autonomy, shall have equally to work for this Federation. This way lies her only safety from any possible complications of either Pan-Islamism or Pan-Mongolianism. This is what every Indian Nationalist must clearly realise. Nationalism in India has no other future before it. In its own interest, Indian Nationalism must seek to keep up the British connection. Ideally, Federalism is a higher thing than Nationalism. Practically, federations do not grow to order, but gradually evolve out of the existing relations of different peoples. Why seek federation with Britain, and not with China or Japan ?—is, therefore, a foolish question. We cannot seek federation with China or Japan for the simple reason that there is, at present, no basis for it. There are no historical conditions or possibilities that force the new relation upon both India and China or India and Japan. In the next place, there can be no federation between an independent and sovereign State on the one side and a dependency of another State on the other. But the federal relation can naturally and easily be worked up between a Sovereign State and its Colonies and Dependencies. In fact, in our time this is the only way to preserve the integrity of extensive world-empires. And these are the reasons that compel us to seek Federation with Great Britain instead of with China, Japan, or any other country. This is the easiest and the most reasonable thing for us to do, with a view to realise the highest Nationalist Ideal. And I strongly deprecate the spirit of bitter antagonism to the British connection which seems to have obsessed some of our people, because it threatens to seriously hinder this natural evolution. It is this bitterness which lends silent support to the propaganda of political violence in the country. This anarchical propaganda finds excuse for bureaucratic repressions. These repressions, in their turn, increase and deepen popular discontent, and make active revolutionaries of those, especially among the youthful and the most impressionable section of the community, who had before been only indifferent spectators of this degrading conflict. This propaganda of crime and this policy of repression, which, the very secrecy of the criminal propaganda forces to be more or less indiscriminate in its application—these two acting and reacting upon each other, are continually increasing this spirit of bitterness in the community. And no Indian Nationalist, who has any appreciation either of the true Nationalist Ideal or of the fearful possibilities of the present world-situation, can afford to allow this bitterness to grow in the country. For unless we are able to induce a more sober and reasonable attitude in our people, any outside enemy of England, either Mongol or Moslem, may take advantage of this growing unrest and simultaneously sever Britain's connection with India and kill India's hope of national autonomy. To combat the unreasonable excesses of the present unrest in India is, therefore, the common duty of the Indian Government and the Indian Nationalist.

Lord Hardinge's Difficulty.

Unfortunately, however, there has so far been very little real co-operation between the Government and the leaders of the people in a matter of such vital moment to both. There is as yet very little basis of it. The very first condition of this co-operation is a frank and unreserved acceptance by the Government of the Ideal of an Imperial Federation in which India shall be a free and equal partner with Great Britain, Ireland, and the British Colonies. We know that the actual working out of this ideal will take considerable time. Both parties will have to be educated in the idea, and trained by practice for the due and efficient discharge of the ultimate federal functions. We do not demand an immediate formation of a Federal Constitution. It would be foolish to desire it. But we may well demand an assurance from the responsible Ministers of King George that they frankly accept this as the ultimate goal of the Imperial Policy of Great Britain. Lord Hardinge suggested it in his Despatch. But Lord Crewe repudiated it in Parliament. This was a very unwise thing to do. Of course, the fate of nations is not determined by royal pledges and promises, or by the despatches and pronouncements of particular statesmen or administrators. Public policies, though enunciated by politicians and administrators, are really formed by actual pressure of historic or economic situations. I set considerable value upon Lord Hardinge's Despatch because I see at the back of it a clear consciousness of the world-situation as it is slowly but unmistakably evolving before us. The value of that Despatch lies in the fact that it takes silent note of the rejuvenescence of China, the birth of Pan-Islam, the needs of a closer and formal union between Great Britain and the British Colonies, and the quickening of a new life in India itself and the consequent presence among us of the "Unrest" which represents really the "growing-pains" of our teeming multitudes. The statesmanly policy shadowed in Lord Hardinge's Despatch has grown out of a sober consideration of all these various forces. His lordship honestly believes that his policy will be for the good of India. But if these forces disappear altogether from the present Indian and world-situation, his policy will also lose inevitably its reality. Lord Hardinge's Despatch may then go the way of the earlier documents of the British Government concerning the ideals or the methods of their Indian Administration; though it will not impugn his lordship's sincerity, or disprove his good-will towards India. Public policies are not the result of personal feelings, but are controlled by inexorable historic needs. There is, however, very little chance of these needs disappearing from modern world-politics altogether. And because of the reasonable certainty of these various forces persisting for many years to come, that I think, a frank and unreserved acceptance of the Federal Ideal for India also, on the same lines in which it is being gradually accepted for the Overseas Dominions of Great Britain, will have a very healthy effect upon the Indian mind, and clear the ground for that mutual confidence and co-operation between the Government and the people without which the present situation can never be saved. It seems to me that Lord Hardinge is not unwilling to declare this ideal and thus rally the sober and saner Nationalist sentiments in the country around his Indian policy. But his difficulty is with his official superiors on the one side, and with his own countrymen in India on the other. Lord Morley is still the force behind the India Office in London ; and he is a child of the middle nineteenth century. His lordship's social and political philosophy moves still in the grooves of the old and attenuated British Liberalism of Gladstone and Bright. His lordship has no acquaintance with our culture and character, except what he has made through books written by men who themselves understood us less. He has, therefore, no appreciation of the Indian Problem. Lord Crewe's last word is that the future of India is on the knees of the gods and we must leave it there, and rest content with doing the day's work during the day. It is not possible for such lazy and improvident statesmanship to offer any lasting solution of so complex and far-reaching a problem as that which faces the Government of India to-day. With the possible exception of Lord Haldane, I doubt if there is any prominent Minister in England now, who understands or appreciates the significance of Lord

Hardinge's Indian policy. There is much less understanding of it in India, among those upon whom every Viceroy has, of necessity, to depend for the due execution of his ideas. They do not seem to understand what Lord Hardinge's policy means both to their own country and to India. In fact such statesmanly grasp of complex political issues are not found in the permanent officials in any country. They spend their lives working out the details of the Administration which they serve; and have neither the time nor the training to recognise large principles or understand broad and far-reaching policies. In other countries, permanent officials are carefully kept in their places, and are not permitted to meddle with public policy or play at state-craft. The Indian Civil Service is, perhaps, the only body under the sun, which claims this right and enjoys this privilege to a very appreciable extent. There are, undoubtedly, men of very superior intellectual calibre among Indian civilians, who have got the making not only of the successful administrator but even of the capable statesman in them. But their number is, naturally, very small; while the traditions of the service to which they belong, and the loyalty to their class which, almost from the birth of this service, has been demanded of every Indian Civilian as a great public virtue, make it very difficult for even these few men to get out of the old grooves of thinking, and take any broad and original view of the growing and changing complexities of the situation in India. The social atmosphere in which they live is also unfavourable to the growth of high statesmanly qualities in them. And it is they to whom the Indian Viceroy, coming to rule a country of which he had little or no previous experience, has necessarily to look for help and guidance. The Viceroy comes for five years and goes away just when, perhaps, he begins to feel his ground a little ; while these permanent officials remain to impart their knowledge and their prejudices both, to the new ruler. Even Viceroys are men, and have the common weakness of all conscientious men not to go against larger experience and expert counsel. Lord Hardinge's first difficulty is that neither the British Ministry nor the Indian Civil Service, as a body, have a clear grasp of the Indian situation.

THE CONGRESS IDEAL : CONFUSION OF THOUGHT.

On the other hand, his lordship has, I am afraid, so far received but little help from those who are accepted as leaders of Indian opinion, in this matter. The Indian National Congress, which has still the ear of the British bourgeoisie, as the spokesman of educated India, has done so far practically nothing to clarify public opinion in these matters. Frankly speaking, the Congress has not been renowned for very clear thinking. With very rare exceptions, the pronouncements of the Congress have been marked more by perfervid repetitions of the catch-phrases of English politicians than by any original analysis of Indian life and thought or any direct knowledge of Indian conditions. The arguments of the Congress have been inspired by the political philosophy of European Democracy and have been based almost exclusively upon the Blue-Books of the Indian Government. The Congress, during the last twenty-seven years of its life, has not collected, I am afraid, one scrap of original information, regarding either the economic condition of the people or how their life and evolution are affected by the current methods of British Administration of the country. The Congress platform has only been resonant all these years either with official quotations or patriotic declamations. The inevitable result has, therefore, been only increased antagonism to the policy and measures of the Government, without any clear thinking of the actualities of our situation or any definite policy or programme of our own. It is, therefore, that there has, so far, been but little real appreciation of Lord Hardinge's Indian policy in Congress circles. The only thing that the Congress leaders seem to have recognised in this policy is its sympathy and leniency. They are thankful to Lord Hardinge for the Repeal of the Partition, and the slight relaxation of the rigours of the Minto *régime*. In a vague way, some of them have recognised the value of the policy of "Provincial Autonomy" enunciated in his lordship's Despatch. But few Congress leaders have given so far, any convincing proof of their appreciation of the far-seeing statesmanship of that memorable public document. On the contrary, the very commendation of the Congress-leaders of Lord Hardinge's Despatch, as a proof of the acceptance of the ideal of Self-Government by the Government, as the regulating principle of British Administration in India, has lent support to the opponents of his lordship's policy, both in India and England. The Anglo-Indian Press, especially, in Bengal, smarting under a sense of wrong which the removal of the Capital from Calcutta inflicted on them, condemned the Despatch as offering a false and dangerous ideal to the Indian politician. The British Press, and even responsible Ministers of State in England, found it easy to openly repudiate the interpretation that India put on Lord Hardinge's Despatch, because of the utter impossibility of the realisation of the declared ideal of the Congress, without practically sacrificing every British interest in India. This so-called Colonial-ideal, which forms the very first article of the Congress-creed, is a false ideal for India. Either we understand its falsehood, and use it only as a cover for something more substantial and fundamental, which we have not the courage to proclaim ; or we do not know and understand what the Colonial relation implies and actually is, and have set it up simply to save the face of the Congress, which could not, for obvious considerations, accept the more inspiring cry of Swaraj. In either case, this so-called Congress-ideal stands self-condemned. The Colonial relation is based upon racial unity. The self-governing Colonies are attached to Great Britain by pure sentimentalities in some cases, and by considerations of pure self-interest in others. So long Great Britain offered protection to the Colonies by her naval and military resources. So long the Colonies needed also very little actual protection from the Mother-Country. But still, the moral support was there, and that was all that the Colonies required in the past. But recent developments in world-politics have been creating new and real needs of self-protection for the British Colonies. Australia stands in mortal fear of Japan and China ; while the growing naval strength of the Continental Powers has created nervousness in all the British Colonies, that are exposed to the sea, and have no navy of their own to protect their extensive sea boards, which, in the event of a Continental War, will be at the mercy of Great Britain's enemies. And with this new consciousness of danger, there is also a corresponding anxiety in all the Colonies to build Dreadnaughts and contribute to the Naval strength of the Empire. These developments will demand, by-and-by, the building up of a formal Constitution for the British Empire, the different members of which hang together very loosely now, by mere sentimentalities. And if the present loose relation cannot possibly subsist for long between Great Britain and her Colonies, how can it be set up as a permanent ideal of her relation with a Dependency like that of India ? We have nothing in common with Great Britain, neither race, nor religion, nor language, nor literature, nor tradition, nor history. The things that inspire British patriotism, and evoke the devotion of the British Colonials to the British Empire, have no appeal for us. The British Colonies are, to all intents and purposes, so many sovereign States, that have, in their own self-interest, hitherto imposed certain limitations, more or less formal, upon themselves in return for the real prestige and the protection which the British connection gives them. Neither this prestige nor this protection will be a condition of the political existence of a self-governing India ; and, consequently, Colonial self-government cannot mean the same thing in India, as it means in Australia, or Canada, or even in South Africa. Anglo-Indian publicists and British statesmen have every force of logic and statesmanship on their side, when they condemn this Congress-ideal of Colonial self-government as unreal, and dangerous to their interest in India. To interpret Lord Hardinge's ideal as shadowed in his Despatch of August 1911, as the same as this Congress-ideal of self-government, is to convict his lordship either of rank folly or deliberate dishonesty. And Lord Crewe repudiated only this foolish interpretation of that Despatch. But neither Lord Crewe, nor any other intelligent politician, with any perception of the Indian situation on the one hand, and the slowly evolving world-situation on the other, can so loftily dispose of the interpretation that Indian Nationalists have put upon Lord Hardinge's Despatch. The ultimate political ideal for India can never be this so-called Colonial-ideal. It should not be, for the reasons indicated above, that of isolated, sovereign, independence. The continuance of the British connection is a necessity, both ideally and practically, for the fullest fulfilment of the ideal of Indian Nationalism. It is as great and imperious a necessity for our self-fulfilment under existing conditions, as national autonomy itself. And in a true and real federation of the different members of the Association, now known as the British Empire, there is the only possible ground of reconciliation between these two imperious needs of Indian Nationalism. A federal constitution, with well-defined rights and obligations of the Federated States, must first of all be formed, before any real and substantial measure of self-government can be secured by India "within the Empire." The British Empire is visibly evolving towards this federal type. The final passage of the Irish Home Rule Bill will be the first step of a new reconstruction of the United Kingdom, upon a federal basis. Home Rule in Wales and Scotland, each with a local Parliament of its own and an Executive subject to the authority of that Parliament, will soon follow the establishment of Home Rule in Ireland. And this will lead to a reconstitution of the British Parliament upon a federal basis, preceded, of course, by the establishment of a local Parliament and a local Government for the English counties also. All these developments will come about within the life-time of a generation. And when the time comes for the reconstitution of the British Parliament upon a federal basis, to meet the needs of the new developments in the United Kingdom, the British Colonies also will put in their demand for their proper place in the Imperial Parliament. Even the blind may see all this. And then will come the real crisis in England's relations with India. Will India be left out of this Federation? *Can* she be left out? Will it be possible, will it be safe, to leave her in her present "dependent" position, to be lorded over not only by the Britishers, but also by *parvenu* Colonials? There are many things which India may suffer, for "auld lang syne"—from Englishmen; it is inconceivable that she will suffer the same things from the Australian or the Boer. India *must* be given an equal place with the others, in the coming Federation of the British Empire. This *must* will admit of no excuse or apology. Lord Hardinge clearly foresees it. And his scheme of Provincial Autonomy is the first step towards the training of India for this coming Federalism. His lordship knows that Provincial Autonomy can never be reconciled with Imperial Autocracy. The growth of Provincial Autonomy will inevitably develop National Autonomy; which will be bound to seek and find organised expression in a truly Federal Government for All-India. This is the inner meaning of the transfer of the Capital from Calcutta to Delhi. This is the significance of the constitution of a new Province subject to the direct control of the Imperial Government, like that of the District of Columbia in which Washington is situated, in the United States of America. His lordship is not a reckless rhetorician. All his life has been spent in the silent atmosphere of modern diplomacy. His lordship has been trained to weigh every word that he uses before uttering it. He could not have, possibly, referred to Washington, and Sydney and Toronto, in his Despatch, while discussing the question of the transfer of the Capital from Calcutta, without a full sense of their significance. His lordship knows that he has to deal here with an educated community who knows the value of these words. His lordship would not use words that would simply create a false enthusiasm in the public mind. His reference to Washington, Toronto, and Sydney is deliberate and carefully-considered. His pronouncement concerning Provincial Autonomy is equally deliberate and carefully thought out. And all these indicate that his lordship wants to lay down a policy for the Government of India which will gradually evolve something like a United States of India in the country, and this, in turn, will form the basis of a real Federation between India and Great Britain and Ireland and the British Colonies. This is how we read Lord Hardinge's Despatch. This is the only rational interpretation of the policy which it indicates. Its supreme value lies in the fact that it offers a true synthesis of the Indian political situation, and provides a basis of permanent reconciliation between Indian Nationalism and British Imperialism. Our people should clearly understand and frankly recognise it. British statesmen in England

and British Administrators here should seize the inwardness of this far-seeing statesmanship and loyally support it. Anglo-Indian publicists should ponder over it, and accept it in their own interest. If all parties are once agreed upon this policy, mutual co-operation for fighting the criminal excesses of the present unrest will not be difficult. This is the only basis of any such co-operation. There is none other.

Calcutta, May 1913.

CHAPTER V.

THE PRESENT INDIAN PROBLEM.

THE PROBLEM STATED.

In politics and statecraft, there is, I think, only one vital problem before the Government and the people of India at this moment. How to work up a reasonable reconciliation between the legitimate requirements of Indian Nationalism on the one side and of the British Empire on the other, is that problem. All other political problems that face us dwindle into utter inconsequence before it. The value of every political or administrative programme or policy in India must now be judged by its capacity to help this reconciliation. And the worth of every political or administrative reform must be determined by the same test.

AN UNAPPRECIATED PROBLEM.

Unfortunately, however, it is so far practically an unappreciated problem. There are not many people—neither among Indian Nationalists nor among British Imperialists—who seem to have got as yet a thorough grasp of it. The Nationalists, as a body, are inclined to take a very narrow view of Nationalism; while the so-called Imperialists have no conception of the real meaning and significance of the Empire-Idea as a lofty and uplifting social synthesis. The Nationalist, distracted by the passions and prejudices of the passing conflict between the ideal and the actual in his present political life, cannot seize the universal aspect of his own Nationalism or recognise the trends of modern world-politics which will really determine the course of historic evolution in his own country as well as in other countries, in the near future. At one time he had an exaggerated notion of England's power and strength. That hypnotic spell is practically broken. But the counter passes have apparently been much too strong for him; and he has got into the habit of taking an equally exaggerated view now of his own powers and possibilities. He has still to recover his sense of proportion. He fancies that he can stand by himself against almost any world-combination. His secret ambition is to be like one of those great nations of Europe, the extent of whose greatness is measured by the degree of menace which their physical and mental strength offers to all neighbouring nations. He has lost his vision of the future when the war-drum shall throb no longer, and the battle-flags of the nations shall be furled—

> "In the Parliament of man, the Federation of the world."

The Real Meaning of Indian Nationalism.

He has forgotten his ancient MANTRAM—Jagaddhitāya Krishnāya—"In the name of Shree Krishna, for the good of all the world"—by which he had been taught of old to consecrate all his thoughts and works. This Jagaddhitāya Krishnāya—in the name of Krishna, for the good of the universe—has been the Regulative Idea in Hindu history. This has been the purpose of God in India. It is for the realisation of this Idea that India has, in almost every respect, been a miniature of the whole world. It is for this reason that, in the course of its gradual historic evolution, India has become the meeting-place of almost all the great world-cultures of our time. From almost the very beginnings of our social evolution, the trend of Indian history seems to have been to evolve a unique federal ideal among us. The Hindu religion has been, for countless centuries past, a federation of many religions. The Hindu society has been, similarly, a federation of many practically-autonomous communities or castes. The Hindu ideal of the State, when there were Hindu States in India, was a truly federal ideal. With the advent of other religions and cultures into India this ancient federal idea has received further developments among us. America has concretised the federal ideal only in one single department of life, namely, that relating to the State. India has evolved this federal type in almost every department of life. We have been clearly trained for countless centuries in this federal idea. Our appointed part and function in the coming history of the world is to lead humanity into this Universal Federation, universal in every sense of the term. This is the real meaning of the Nationalist Movement in India. The leaders of the Movement have, no doubt, fully seized this ideal. Bankim Chandra had fully realized it; and, therefore, he presented the Permanent Form of the Mother as Mahā-Lakshmee seated on the lap of Mahāvishnoo: The Nation standing eternally related to Humanity. Every Nationalist leader since has preached this Nationalism, not as a mere political ideal, but as a high religion. It is the Cult of the Mother. And this Mother is a term of universal connotation with us. Kālee, Durgā, Lakshmee, Sarasvatee, all these are synonyms of the Mother, and they are all at once both particular and universal. This is what Max Muller really meant by Henotheism. The Mother in Bandê-Mātaram, is not only our Mother but the Mother of all. She has many appearances but one essence. This is the fundamental idea of the true Nationalist Creed. Nationalism has, therefore, an essential humanitarian reference. It is not an end unto itself, but must realise its special and particularistic ends in and through the universal ends of other social or socio-political units, and the collective ends of Universal Humanity. Nationalist conflicts and competitions are, therefore, only passing phases of the evolution of Humanity, and not its permanent elements. Their end is to help a closer union, and not to create wider discords. Even the present conflict in India must ultimately lead to such a union. These are, however, very feebly realised as yet by the general body of Indian Nationalists. And it is, therefore, that there is little or no appreciation of the vital problem that faces us just now.

The True Meaning of Imperialism.

Neither is there any correct appreciation of this problem among British Imperialists. If some Indian Nationalists have taken a wrong and distorted view of Nationalism, the British Imperialists also, with possibly a few solitary exceptions, have taken a similarly wrong and distorted view of the Empire-Idea. The superior ethical value of the Empire-Idea consists, as I have repeatedly tried to point out, only in its capacity to offer a much higher and wider formula of human association than the Nation-Idea. And a synthesis implies the rational reconciliation of antecedent conflicts. A true empire is that which can, in its corporate life and constitution, offer a rational reconciliation of the particularistic conflicts and competitions of the different national units comprised within it. To realise this right Imperialist Ideal, the British Empire must find adequate means for the reconciliation of the particularistic interests and ambitions of the different national units that compose it now. This reconciliation must be worked in and through the larger life and constitution of the Empire. An Empire that will not or that cannot do this can never endure. British Imperialism must, therefore, in its own interest, seek to work out a timely and permanent reconciliation between Indian and Egyptian and Irish and Welsh and Scotch and Australian and South-African and Canadian Nationalism with one another and with itself. Such a reconciliation can be worked only upon a truly federal basis. An Imperial Federation alone will enable British Imperialism to fully realise itself. To seek self-fulfilment in any other way would be to court ruin and failure. This true Imperialism is very different from that Jingoism which has tried to pass itself off as such all these years. And the reason of it is that there are not many British Imperialists who have any clear perception of the true Imperialist Ideal. Their Imperialism means really the usurpation of the authority and function of the whole Imperial Organism by certain favoured parts and limbs of it. Their conceit of Imperialism is a false and unhealthy thing; it is based upon conceit of superior brute force or of superior cunning, or of a combination of both. It has no true and lofty philosophy at its back. Like the Nationalist with a narrow vision of Nationalism, the

Jingo Imperialist also has absolutely no sense either of actuality or proportion. It is inevitable, therefore, that he should have no appreciation of the true character of the problem that faces him in India.

Conflict of Nationalism and Imperialism.

The Indian Nationalist, whether he belongs to the so-called Moderate or the so-called Extremist section, is moved simply by a more or less strong passion for National Self-Rule. He desires to be in his own country what other great nations of the world are in their own country. He has not been encouraged or tempted to think, in working out the problem of Nationalism in India, of the world-wide Empire of which, whether he likes it or not, his country is just now an integral part. This Empire has so long been practically a sign and symbol, not of his freedom, but of his servitude. He has hitherto been treated by the other members of the Imperial concern in a way that has not helped to draw him closer to the Empire, but has rather prevented him from feeling any intimacy with it. He has not been a participator in the glories of this Empire, and has not been trained to feel that he has any vital stake in it. He has, therefore, absolutely no call to approach his problems from what may be called the true Imperial stand-point. The very idea of seeking any reconciliation between his Nationalist aspirations and the requirements of the unity and strength of the Empire, does not enter into his thoughts. He is anxious only for the fulfilment of his own Nationalist ambitions, but does not care a pin for the fate of the Empire to which, for good or for evil, he now belongs.

If the Indian Nationalists are utterly unconcerned about the fate of the British Empire, the British Imperialists, as a class, are equally unconcerned about the future of Indian Nationalism except in so far as it may affect their suzerain interests or hurt their conceit of culture or pride of race. By the British Empire they understand only a dominant White Confederacy mainly of British or Anglo-Saxon origin, holding political sovereignty over multitudinous non-white peoples. If this position of absolute superiority of the Anglo-Saxon in the work and prerogatives of the Empire goes, the Empire itself might go then, it would not be worth having on those conditions. This is how the narrow Imperialist feels. He is the last person, therefore, to seriously think of any reconciliation between his Imperialism and the Nationalist movement whether in India or Egypt. All that he wants is to crush and kill this impertinent ambition of the Indian or the Egyptian to be an equal co-partner with the white members of the Empire. There is, thus, an irreconcilable antagonism between narrow Nationalism and Jingo Imperialism. One does not admit the possibility, and the other the necessity, of any reconciliation between themselves. Consequently, there is no appreciation on either side of the real value and significance of the Indian problem, as I have stated it here. And this is, to my mind, the greatest difficulty in the way of a statesmanly settlement of the present trouble in India and the Empire.

Lord Hardinge's Statesmanship.

Lord Hardinge seems to be one of those few people who have a clear grasp of this problem. He is perhaps the only official in this country who has a seasin of the case, as the lawyers would say. And it is impossible to deny that his Lordship has been pursuing a policy of real reconciliation between the legitimate requirements of both Indian Nationalism and the British Empire. It is because of this policy of reconciliation that his Lordship has been able to very considerably relieve the tension of the Indian situation as Lord Minto had left it. This situation would have improved a good deal more if only Lord Hardinge had the unstinted sympathy and whole-hearted support of the Indian Bureaucracy and the Anglo-Indian press. There is, of course, no open opposition to his Lordship's policy from the subordinate officials in the country; but there is no intelligent appreciation of it among them. It is hardly their fault either. Statesmanly grasp of complex and far-reaching political issues can hardly be expected from a body of permanent officials in any country, trained only to the routine work of the administration. Least of all, is it reasonable to expect it in a highly organised Administration. The more perfect and efficient is an administrative machinery, the lesser is the need there of any statesmanship in the permanent officials in the country. For, the lack of any superior statesmanship in the subordinate officials there does not in any way interfere with the efficient working of the administration.

But the situation in India is very peculiar. There is hardly any parallel to it either in ancient or modern history. The Government of India is, undoubtedly, a huge and complex machine, and the individual officers are mere parts and limbs of that machine. The Governor-General in Council and the Heads of the various Provincial

Administrations with their respective Executive Councils, are, each in his own sphere, engineers and foremen of this complex machinery. It is they who lay down the policy of the State, initiate changes and reforms, and direct and control the Administrative Machinery. The subordinate officials have, at least in theory, simply to carry out the orders passed on to them from headquarters. Theoretically, these officials are only parts and organs of the Administrative Organism. But practically, they are a good deal more. The District Magistrate in India, for instance, is not merely a limb and organ of the Administrative Organism, but is, in a peculiar sense, the Organism itself. He is not only the local representative of the authority of the Government, but is, above all things, the fleshly and visible embodiment and incarnation of the spirit and character of the State. He is not merely the executor of the policy of the Government, but is also the interpreter not only of the meaning, but also of the inner spirit of that policy. People in India, therefore, judge of the character of the Government not by the words of the Head of the State but by the acts and attitudes of the officials. Consequently, the policy of the Head of the Government, enunciated in his public pronouncements, can have absolutely no influence upon the people unless it is clearly understood, thoroughly appreciated, and loyally translated into their everyday conversation and conduct, by every official in the country. This, I am afraid, is not being done by Lord Hardinge's subordinates in the country, in the way and to the extent, it should be done, to meet the requirements of the present situation and to help a clear understanding of his Lordship's statesmanly policy by our people.

The New Policy in Delhi. The Old Spirit in the Districts.

Ever since Lord Hardinge took up the reins of Government from Lord Minto, there has been a grateful change of heart at head-quarters ; but the old Adam is still very much in evidence in the District Administrations, more or less everywhere. And this is largely responsible, I am afraid, for the smouldering of the old unrest still in the country. The notion entertained even by Lord Hardinge, that because revolutionary anarchism has been found impossible to kill entirely in Europe, it will inevitably remain always with us even in India, seems, to my mind, wholly unwarranted. This anarchism in Europe is an indigenous product, the growth of many centuries of historic and social evolution, and has an organic affinity with the inner psychology of European humanity. Philosophically, it is the necessary logic of Christian culture, with its excessive individualistic emphasis, and its dogmas of social rights and equality. Politically, it is the direct fruit of centuries of oppression of the masses by the classes and their kings. The gulf that separates men in society, has been far more wide in Europe, since the break up of the old Feudal System, than it has ever been in India. Not to speak of Islam, whose spirit of democracy is so unique in human history, even Hindu division of caste, except in the South, has never been so destructive of human fellowship as the secular class distinctions of Europe, with its excessive emphasis on the accidents of material possessions. And all these are mainly responsible for the birth, growth, and perpetuation of the anarchical propaganda in Europe. None of these causes and conditions are, however, present among us. The so-called anarchism in this country is an exotic. It is of distinct European origin. It has been borrowed by a section of our Europeanised youths, from the revolutionary literature of France, Italy, and Russia. One has only to glance over the Indian literature of this propaganda, to see how much of its inspiration has been derived from foreign sources, and how largely its deductions are based upon indiscriminate study of European works. And this being the real origin and history of this so-called anarchism in this country, there is absolutely no warranty for the conclusion that because revolutionary anarchism has not been entirely stamped out in Europe, it has come to stay here, with us, in India also. With us the malady is not constitutional, as it is in Europe, but only functional. And if it has not been cured completely as yet, the responsibility rests more with bad doctoring than with anything else.

The King-Emperor came all the way to India to help heal the sore created by the tactlessness of the Curzon Administration and deepened by the panic-begotten policy of Lord Minto. And His Majesty's visit has done a lot towards healing that sore. Lord Hardinge's statesmanly policy, as enunciated in his Lordship's memorable Despatch of August 1911, has had the same end in view. It has considerably relieved the irritation in the public mind. But it can hardly be denied that the Indian Bureaucracy as a whole, and the Anglo-Indian publicists as a class, have not as yet entered into the spirit of the King-Emperor and the Viceroy. They still seem to fancy that "military law and no d——d nonsense" would have settled the unrest much quicker and more effectively than all this weak-kneed parleying with sedition and rebellion. It is inevitable, therefore, that while the Viceroy is pulling one way, the officials and the foreign merchants and traders and newspaper scribes are all pulling Britain's Imperial policy in India in another and a contrary way. And this want of living response on the part of the District Administrations to the inspiration of the Supreme Government is very largely, if not entirely, responsible for the continuance of this unrest. No one would say or suggest that the District officials should be less watchful now than they had been before. I, for one, would not even care to ask for an open repeal or reversal of the unwise measures of the last Administration. A law that exists only on the Statute-Book of the realm, does not necessarily hurt a people. The evil comes only through its application and administration. And what the situation absolutely demands in India to-day is a change of heart and spirit in all the branches of the Administration, from the highest to the lowest. There is evident proof of this change in the head of the Government, and to some extent also at provincial headquarters; but none practically in the lower places. The District Administrations are being conducted in most places just as under Lord Minto. The District officials have not as yet clearly realised it that watching is one thing and nagging is quite a different thing. Lord Minto did not understand the truism that nagging is not administration. The officials habituated to the methods of the Minto *régime*, have yet to learn it. And it is the general opinion among intelligent students of current history in this country, that this nagging by the officials on the one hand and by Anglo-Indian scribes on the other, is very largely responsible for whatever unrest there is still in the country. Existing methods of police surveillance of sensitive patriotic youths, creates, I think, oftentimes more political criminals in the community than the wildest raphsodies of contraband revolutionary circulars of the Yugantar class could ever expect to do. Political "suspects" may be watched as vigilently as possible : every Government have to keep an eye upon people whose opinions and activities are-likely to create trouble for them. They are watched everywhere. But it is a great mistake to subject the "political suspect" to the same kind of watching, which is usually kept over ordinary Police-Register-criminals. I do not know if Lord Hardinge is aware of it, but in Bombay, at any rate, people convicted under Sec. 124-A, the Sedition Section of the Indian Penal Code, have to give their thumb-mark and other particulars like the P. R. prisoners. And it shows the spirit in which "undesirable" politicians are treated by the subordinate administrations. It is not necessary to cultivate this spirit of persecution for the preservation of peace and order in the country. And yet it rules the treatment of political "suspects" in almost every district. Any one who had ever been tempted to betray the least little sympathy with the Nationalist propaganda is treated with ill-concealed suspicion by the local executive. His movements are watched openly, almost insultingly. Relations and friends he may visit are pestered with harassing police enquiries. Humbler Nationalists find it difficult to earn an honest living. With the police perpetually at their heels, they are turned out of every place that they may secure, and are not allowed sometimes to make their own living even by starting any trade or business of their own. I am sure that neither Lord Hardinge nor Lord Carmichael nor any other superior officials know of these things. I do not think that these things are always done under orders from, or even with the knowledge of the District Magistrate. I do not blame even the police for these petty persecutions. The police had received certain instructions during the Minto *régime* to meet a peculiarly trying and novel situation. That situation has visibly changed, no doubt ; but the lower officials cannot be expected to understand that this change is entirely due to the inauguration of a new policy of reconciliation by Lord Hardinge. They generally attribute the comparative quiet of to-day to the severity of the repressions of yesterday. They are, therefore, quite naturally unwilling to relax the old rigors immediately. This is the correct psychology of the general official attitude, and particularly of the attitude of the police towards political "suspects."

The Need of the Present Indian Situation.

And a change of spirit of the lower District Administrations is, to my mind, the most imperative need of the present situation in this country. Nothing less, and nothing else, will kill the propaganda of political crimes among us. We are as much eager as any official to stamp out this criminal propaganda. It is not merely a menace to the peace, but is equally a very serious obstacle in the way of the progress, of the country. Every thoughtful and responsible Nationalist is anxious to settle this revolutionary unrest. But what are we to do, if all our attempts to induce a sober and reasonable attitude and temper in our young people, are frustrated by the acts and attitudes of the lower official body on the one side, and the reckless writings of the irresponsible Anglo-Indian scribes on the other. And as long as a more reasonable and conciliatory spirit has not been infused into the rank-and-file of the British Bureaucracy in India, and the Government has not assumed an attitude of stern aloofness from the Anglo-Indian publicists, and treat them openly and scrupulously as they treat the Indian press, resenting their impertinence in always arrogating to themselves a special relationship with the State on the strength of their chromatic or sartorial kinship with the King-Emperor, so long, I am afraid, Lord Hardinge's statesmanly policy in India will not bear fruit, not at any rate in its fullest measure.

The Trend of Lord Hardinge's Policy.

Lord Hardinge clearly recognises both the possibility and the need of a complete reconciliation between the legitimate demands of Indian Nationalism and the true interests of the British Empire. I use the adjectives "legitimate" and "true" deliberately and with a full consciousness of their implications. All human conflicts, whether between individuals or between communities, are due always to unreasonable pretensions on the one side and unjust usurpations on the other. Both unreason and injustice are based on falsehood. The present conflict in India is caused by a false view of Nationalism on our side, and an equally false view of Imperial interests on their side. Legitimate Nationalism can have no quarrel with true Internationalism or Imperialism. True Imperialism also cannot be destructive of legitimate Nationalism. The real and rational value of the Empire Idea, as I have repeatedly declared in these pages, consists in the fact that it offers a much wider and higher formula of human fellowship than the Nation-Idea. Imperialism must, therefore, offer a higher synthesis of all national conflicts and competitions than what can be found in mere Nationalism. The legitimate demand of Nationalism is that it must have the fullest and freest scope to realise its own special life and ideals, consistently with the larger life of Universal Humanity, without any let or hindrance from any other national units or national groups. An Empire is a unit composed of many Nationalities. An Empire is a large Social Organism, composed of many small Social Organisms, which are its limbs and organs. The true interest of any organism cannot be in conflict with the legitimate freedom and self-realisation of its organs, but rather it is furthered and protected by the protection and furtherance of the autonomy and self-fulfilment of these different organs. The true interest of any Empire cannot, therefore, be served through the suppression of the freedom of its component Nationalities but only and always through the promotion and perfection of that freedom. Isolated independence cannot be a legitimate demand of any National unit that has been placed by force of its own historic evolution in vital relations with other National units. Usurpation of the right and scope of free development of any National unit comprised within an Empire along its own line, towards its own specific and organic cultural ends, is not required in the true interests of that Empire. And it is in view of this true and advanced social philosophy, that I hold that there is, in truth, no irreconcilable conflict between Indian Nationalism and what is called British Imperialism. Whether it be from the view-point of this social philosophy, or from considerations of far-seeing but practical statesmanship, from whatever motives it may be, Lord Hardinge seems to have recognised that the present conflict between Indian Nationalism and British Imperialism is not absolutely irreconcilable.

And his Lordship clearly realises this also, namely, that to work out any sort of permanent reconciliation between these, there must be a good deal of give and take on both sides. His Lordship, therefore, fully understands it that the present position of the British Government in India will have to be materially amended, before there can be any sort of permanent reconciliation between itself and the aspirations of Indian Nationalism. The Government of India must gradually cease to be autocratic, and become more and more truly representative of the highest thought and culture of India, controlled and worked by the composite Indian people, through their accredited spokesmen and officers, just as the Colonial Governments are—before it will be able to completely reconcile itself to the legitimate requirements of the Nationalist Ideal. In other words, there must be complete National Autonomy in India, before it can be rightly incorporated into the British Empire as an organic part and limb of it. Lord Hardinge, as I have repeatedly said in these pages and elsewhere, recognises all this, and is fully prepared for this line of development of Indian politics. This is the only meaning that can be reasonably put upon his Lordship's Despatch of August 1911. His Excellency can evidently think, without fear or sorrow, of a time when India will be autonomous, like the self-governing Dominions of Great Britain—an autonomous State, or, more correctly speaking, a congeries of autonomous provincialities federated to one another and represented in their collective life and authority by a Central Federal Government with its seat in the historic District of Delhi. His Lordship clearly sees that this way lies the coming course of political evolution in India. He further sees that this way lies also the only safety of the British Empire and the preservation of its strength and integrity. He understands that the only way to perpetuate the British connection with India lies along this peaceful historic evolution. All this is distinctly implied in the policy that he has enunciated in this Despatch. This policy has clearly the fullest support of the King-Emperor, otherwise His Majesty would not have put his seal upon it by coming out to India to personally initiate it by announcing the repeal of the Bengal Partition. It has also the support of the British Cabinet, without whose sanction all this could not have taken place. The plinth and foundations of a reasonable reconciliation between Indian Nationalism and British Imperialism have thus been already definitely laid. What is wanted now is that all parties should forget and forgive the past and loyally work together to help the building up of the noble edifice of an Imperial Federation, the first really of its kind in history, which will stand for all time to come as a model for all the races and nations of the world to imitate with a view to ultimately usher in an era of universal peace and progress, freedom and happiness, which will release the vision of the prophets and the dream of the poets of every race and land. Thus through the development and perfection of our national life, in and through the larger life of a world-wide imperial federation of Hindu, Christian, Zoroastrian, Buddhist, and Moslem cultures of the world, as represented by some of the best representatives of these, we shall at last realise, in and through our social and political life, our ancient ideal, enunciated in the sacred formula—Jagaddhitāya Krishnāya—for the good of the universe to Shree Krishna the Lord of All.

The Education of the Bureaucracy.

I am so enthusiastic over Lord Hardinge's Indian policy and have been urging every Nationalist to lend it his loyal support, because I clearly see what it means for the future of Indian Nationalism. I am confident that every British official and Anglo-Indian publicist in the country would lend it his whole-hearted support, if only he could as clearly see what this policy really means for the future of British Imperialism also. Unfortunately however, they do not seem to have so far realised the true inwardness of this policy. And what is needed just now is to devise some means for the education of the subordinate officials, and, if possible, of the Anglo-Indian publicists also, in the ground principles of that high and synthetic philosophy of Imperialism which evidently lies at the back of Lord Hardinge's Indian policy. If only they could be made to see the utter impossibility of perpetuating the present constitution of the Indian Government, in the face of the growing opposition of the leaders of articulate public opinion in the country on the one side, and the fearful possibilities of either Pan-Islamic or Pan-Mongolian complications on the other; and understand that the very attempt to do so would increase the growing bitterness of the present relations between the rulers and the ruled in the country, and add immensely to the difficulties of a very difficult situation; and that the only possibility of perpetuating the British connection in India lies in working out a reconciliation between the legitimate needs of Indian Nationalism and the true interests of the British Empire; and that Lord Hardinge's policy indicates the only practical line along which this reconciliation may be worked up by slow degrees—if the British officials in the country could only be educated in these facts and ideas, I am confident they would at once throw the weight of their influence on the side of this statesmanly policy and carry it out to a successful issue. I do not think that the Viceroy has done anything so far to fully explain his policy to the subordinate officials in the country. I am not aware that any Viceroy ever did anything of the kind before. But there can be no harm in doing it even for the first time now. Since some time past British politicians, from Lord Morley downwards, have been talking of "personal government" as best suited to the genius of Oriental peoples. We know what the surface meaning of this prescription is, and the ignorance and short-sightedness that have combined to enunciate this policy. But if the ideal of so-called personal government is at all to be pursued in this country, there must, first of all, be much closer personal contact and intercommunication between the

Head of the Government and every individual official who represents him in every district. Whatever may be said either for or against the policy of personal government, a close personal contact between the Viceroy and our District Magistrates would, I think, go a very great way to improve the present situation in the country.

THE EDUCATION OF THE ANGLO-INDIAN PUBLICIST.

But like the British official in India, the Anglo-Indian publicist also requires to be thoroughly posted in the facts and arguments upon which Lord Hardinge's Indian policy is based. Whether they profess allegiance to the Liberal or the Unionist programme in regard to British politics, Anglo-Indian journalists belong, so far as India is concerned, practically, to one common school. They are, with one or two very rare exceptions, all committed to a policy of upholding, under every circumstance and in all matters, the superior position and special privileges of the foreign official and mercantile community in India, and consequently they are almost uniformly "anti-native." And it is impossible to deny that a good deal of the irreconcilable attitude of many of our people, specially of the younger generations, is very largely due to the writings of the Anglo-Indian press. I wonder if any responsible British statesman sent out to act as the King-Emperor's representative in India, has ever tried to realise how seriously the Government is hurt, in the eyes of its Indian subjects, by the intolerable arrogance of the irresponsible Anglo-Indian scribe. These people have created far more sedition in the country than either the Congress or the Svadeshi-

and-Boycott agitation ever did. One can understand their position as spokesmen of a particular community, who, as such, have, as a matter of course, to always protect every special advantage or prerogative of their clientele. One may even overlook their interested opposition and abuse. These are not the things that really matter or that actually hurt the Government. What does so is the pretension of these scribes as having a special right, owing to their country or colour, to identify themselves with the Government and speak in its name. When every Anglo-Indian publicist or politician, speaks or writes of the British Government in India as "our rule" and proposes all sorts of preferential measures in the interest of "their" Empire, the situation becomes ridiculous to those who have a keen sense of humour in them, but intolerable to the many whose sensitive patriotism is very much hurt by these presumptions. And, frankly speaking, the Government of India has done so far precious little indeed, to take this mischievous conceit out of these insensible people. Like the British officials in India, these Anglo-Indian publicists also must, therefore, be thoroughly educated in the ideas and ideals of the new Indian policy, as enunciated in Lord Hardinge's Despatch, if it is to fully realise its purpose. And here again, I think, a few confidential and personal interviews between the Viceroy and individual Anglo-Indian editors would be exceedingly helpful. Of course it goes without saying, that to avoid misunderstandings, such interviews will have to be granted to or sought with Indian publicists also, irrespective of all considerations as to whether they are called "Moderates" or "Extremists." In fact, I think, the Indian Viceroy is likely to get more light from the latter than even from the former.

THE EDUCATION OF THE INDIAN NATIONALISTS.

The Indian Nationalist also equally requires to be educated, first in the true philosophy of his own Nationalism, and, next, in the actualities of the Indian situation on the one side and those of the general world-situation on the other. For it would serve no useful purpose to shut our eyes to the fact that the general body of Indian Nationalists have as yet no appreciation of the need of reconciling their Nationalist aspirations to the continuance of the British connection with India. To the Indian Nationalists, whether they are called Moderates or are condemned as Extremists, the most vital problem now is, really, not how to reconcile their ideals and ambitions with the perpetuation of the British connection, but simply how to cleverly nullify, or violently get rid of, the British control. It needs a much keener political insight than what we have acquired as yet, and a much wider vision than what has so far been vouchsafed unto us, to realise the supreme necessity, in the interest of the future of Indian Nationalism itself, of keeping up the British connection, while carefully eliminating the taint of servitude from India's present political position in the Empire. The Congress-idea of "self-government within the Empire" is, to many people, a mere meaningless cant, that helps to save one's reputation for patriotism, without risking one's freedom through sedition. By its confusion of thought in the earlier stages, and its timid diplomacy subsequently, the Indian National Congress, more perhaps than any other body, has helped to confirm the feeling among many people that Indian autonomy is inherently irreconcilable with the British connection. The very idea of any such reconciliation is voted, therefore, out of court by many people in this country, as absolutely utopian.

There is, however, a still greater obstacle in the way of a clear and correct appreciation of this problem by our people. And that is the low and limited view that many Indian Nationalists take of their ideal and duty. It is due to alien influences. Most of us are Nationalists more in the European sense of the term than after our own true social philosophy. Jagaddhitāya Krishnāya—dedicated to Shree Krishna, for the good of the world—this has been, as I have said, the formula of consecration of all our works, sacramental and social both. This is how the rich among us always consecrate every public work they construct, be it a temple or a tank; and it shows the universal reference of all our social duty. Our modern Nationalist Ideal has not yet reached this lofty spiritual level. The idealism of the Indian Nationalist rarely rises, in fact, above the lower European plane of it, where it concerns itself almost uniformly with the carnal conflicts of political and economic competitions between one nation and another. Even this narrower idealism has raised our young men far above the meaner joys and pains of their individual life, and has trained, at least some of them, to completely identify themselves with the larger life of their country and their people; but it has not as yet enlarged their vision from national autonomy or independence to that of Universal Federation. Their idealism has not as yet been able to transcend the passing particularities of the mere national life, under the inspiration of the divine vision of the Universal revealing and realising Himself in and through the endless diversities of various national ideals and activities. Nationalism has so far done very needful and valuable spade work. It has somewhat cured us of our selfish ambitions, which is the bane of the life of all dependent peoples. It has taught some of our people to care more for their country than for their own self or family or friends. This is no small moral achievement. But the Indian Nationalist has yet to learn the supreme truth that the highest and truest fulfilment of Nationalism is not really inside, but beyond itself. Indeed, this unceasing call of the Beyond is the soul of all idealism. It is the incentive of the devotee, the inspiration of the poet, the intoxication of the martyr, and the dynamic element in all human evolution. The man or woman who is not impelled by this call of the Beyond, even in the midst of the pursuit of his or her immediate objects of life, does not live, but simply vegetates. This call of the Beyond is the sign and covenant of our Divine origin and destiny. The individual who hears not this call, is killed by the dead weight of his own individualism. A nation that sees and seeks nothing beyond its own isolated and narrow national interests, and pursues only these with deathless determination, is destined to be consumed to ashes by its own heat. We must realise all this. And when we do so, we shall realise both the need and the possibility of a reasonable reconciliation between Indian Nationalism and Indo-British Imperialism.

A MOST VITAL PROBLEM.

And it is in view of all this that I hold that, to reconcile the requirements of Indian Nationalism with the maintenance of the British connection, is the most vital problem before us just now. The future of India, the future of Great Britain and her Imperial family, and in no small measure the future even of modern humanity, depends upon the solution of this problem. Great Britain and India joined together in an honest and honourable federal relationship, will hold the peace of the world and the fate of the modern world-cultures in the hollow of their hands. Separated from each other it may be impossible for both, either to save themselves in the coming clash of nations, or help the salvation of others. Every reconciliation of rival claims means a good deal of give and take on either side. To work out a real reconciliation between them, both Indian Nationalism and British Imperialism must make up their minds to sacrifice what may seem just now as pleasant, to what is really good for all time to come. British Imperialism must renounce its natural desire to perpetuate the present relations with India as a Dependency of Great Britain. Indian Nationalism must also amend its equally natural ambition to attain the status of an isolated and independent sovereign State. And both parties should do it in their own interest. Indian Nationalism should seriously think over the fatal risks of recklessly pursuing the ideal of isolated independence in the face of the general world-situation. British Imperialism should clearly realise the absolute impossibility of keeping a continent like India in a state of perpetual tutelage and helplessness, specially in the face of the gathering of rival forces in modern world-politics. A free and honourable federation with Great Britain and her Colonies and Protectorates will not hinder but, on the contrary, materially help the realisation of the true ends of Indian Nationalism. The absolute autonomy of the Federated States is the only basis upon which such a federation can be built up. It will thus secure to us that freedom of self-development, which must be our one and only plea for desiring national independence—without calling upon us to run the risk of a fresh period of soul-killing servitude under Moslem or Mongol. These are what we should consider on our side, while seeking for a reasonable compromise with Great Britain. Great Britain too, on her side, should realise that while a dependent and helpless India must, on the one hand, be a source of fatal weakness to her Empire, an autonomous and strong India, with her own national Militia and Navy will, on the other hand, make that Empire absolutely invincible against every possible combination of her enemies. And, above all, such a Federation will also be a guarantee of the world's peace, such as nothing else is likely to be.

CHAPTER VI.

NATIONAL INDEPENDENCE, OR IMPERIAL FEDERATION?

NATIONALIST CONTRIBUTION TO INDIAN POLITICAL THOUGHT.

THE much-abused Indian Nationalist has done at least one great good: he has forced the consideration of ultimate ideals both upon the political leaders of his people and the representatives of the Government. The Government of India has hitherto been guided by what can be best described as a policy of pure drift. The British Empire in India was built up by force of outer circumstances over which the builders had admittedly little or no control. This wonderful structure is the work of historic accidents. It never had at its back any conscious plan or purpose. It has never or rarely been guided by any clear forethought or high ideals. A few idealists did, no doubt, come to be prominently associated with the Indian Government in the early years of the last century; but they could not supply any vital and permanent inspiration to the Indian Administration, or lend any potent regulative idea to the evolution of British policy in India. The early years of the nineteenth century in Europe were steeped in the idealism of the French Illumination. Children of this idealism, Mill,

Macaulay and others, brought no doubt their noble humanitarian philosophy and enthusiasm with them, to the work of the Indian Government; but all that they could practically do, was to furnish some moral justification to the unmoral acts of the British East India Company, and to support the irresponsible authority of the new rulers of the country, on the plea of humanity and civilisation. But though their humanitarian idealism failed to exert any deep and abiding influence upon the course of public policy, it helped, very considerably, to strengthen the inherent pharasaism of the British conscience, and thereby to really obstruct the realisation of the very ideal which they had meant to supply to the Government of India. In spite, therefore, of Mill, Macaulay and others, the Government has had, up to now, really no settled policy or vital idealism at its back. It is moved by no conscious aim, except of course the universal aim of all organisms, whether biological or social, namely, to preserve its own life and secure its own safety. The only settled policy of the British Government in India has thus been that of self-preservation. But even this aim has not been able to lend any intelligent unity to this policy. For it has received different interpretations from different Viceroys according to their individual views of this "self" in the Government of India.

Like the representatives of the Government, the leaders of popular political agitation also has hitherto had no consciousness of any ultimate ideal or abiding principle of their own endeavours. Popular political activities were confined absolutely to the consideration of particular political disabilities or specific administrative grievances, which had no conscious reference to the future that would be wrought by the redress of these very wrongs. The Indian National Congress, which brought into a focus the current political thoughts and ideas of the articulate Indian populations, formulated, thus, only a number of specific demands; for instance, *viz.*:—the reform and expansion of the Legislative Councils upon an elective basis; the increase in the minimum age of candidates for the Indian Civil Service Examinations; the separation of the executive and judicial functions of the Indian Magistracy; the repeal of the Arms Act and the admission of Indians into the higher offices in the army; the admission of Indians into the Volunteer Corps; the reduction of military expenditure and the Home Charges; and so forth. But the Congress-leaders do not seem to have been at all troubled with any thought regarding the future which these reforms would lead to, or how, in that future, the British authority in India would stand in relation to a people, who practically made their own laws and manned their own army, and could command, at any moment, an enormous body of Volunteers of their own countrymen. All these reforms demanded by the Indian National Congress, practically tended towards a vision of the future when India could, only if she so desired, get rid of the British altogether; or if she did not desire it, when England would have only to mount guard on her frontiers and protect her enormous seaboard with her navy, while Indian politicians could rule the country as it suited their wishes or interests. Such a future, however comfortable to us, could never be acceptable to the British. And the innocent humour of the whole situation was that Great Britain was seriously asked to do all these things out of regard for abstract justice and humanity; and by placing all its weapons of self-defence in our hands, to generously commit political hara-kiri for our sake. The more intelligent British administrators and politicians saw, however, from the very beginning, where the success of our agitations would lead to. They knew, what our leaders seem to have ignored, that unless Great Britain definitely made up her mind about the future of her Empire in India, the removal of the isolated grievances complained of by the Congress, would only add to the complications of an already very complex situation, and enormously increase the difficulties of her rule. There was as yet no imperative call upon her to make up her mind about these matters, that lay still "on the knees of the gods." This is the psychology of the earlier opposition of the Anglo-Indian Bureaucracy to the Indian National Congress. Neither they themselves, nor the people who were clamouring for wresting the authority of the administration from their hands, had any vision of the future. Neither party had any plan of peace and reconciliation with the other. Neither party had any programme or policy that could command the acceptance of the other party by its irresistible logic, or enthuse it with its lofty and soul-stirring idealism. If both the parties could come to some clear and honest understanding about their respective ultimate ends, the bitter conflicts of the past quarter of a century and more, might have possibly been largely avoided, or at least these might have been far more reasonable than they have actually been.

The Nationalist Ideal.

The appearance of Nationalism, as an irresistible force in Indian history and politics, commenced visibly to change all this. The first note of this Nationalism was, necessarily, one of protest and antithesis. The confusion of current political thoughts and ideals called loudly for it. Neither the people nor the Government had any clear vision of the future. The leaders of our popular political agitations and the representatives of the Government were both engaged in tinkering the administrative machinery. This new Nationalism, with its firm grasp of actualities, its relentless logic, and its soul-stirring idealism, attacked simultaneously both the official and the non-official political thoughts of the country. It commenced to demolish popular shibboleths on both sides. The amorphous politics of the Indian National Congress had been simply sowing widespread discontent and disaffection among the people, without offering any real constructive policy or inspiring ideal. It timidly avoided all thought of the future. The same improvidence and timidity, the same confusion and inanity, marked the official policy and attitude also. The Indian National Congress had never dared to challenge the moral basis of the British rule in India; which had, therefore, no call to examine and justify itself. There could be no moral or rational justification of any existing order and method of Government, except in the light of some ultimate ideals or objectives which these sought to reach or realise. The immediate result, therefore, of this Nationalist challenge was to shift the emphasis of current political thoughts in India, both of the Government and the governed, from questions of individual grievances and isolated reforms, to the fundamental question of the ultimate ideal. Nationalism not only demanded a declaration of ultimate ideal from the Indian National Congress and the Government, but presented its own ideal also at the same time. Autonomy, it declared, was the only true and legitimate ideal of Indian Nationalism. Though mistaken by the multitudes for absolute independence, this word autonomy conveys a much deeper and more rational meaning than independence. In the first place, autonomy is a positive, while independence is a negative, concept. In the next place, autonomy has a much wider range than independence, which could only be used, in the literature of any nationalist movement, as a predominantly political term, while autonomy embraces all the various departments of the life of a nation. Literally, autonomy means living according to "one's own law," from its roots, *autos* self, and *nomos* law. But our law does not come from the outside. It is not something that is superimposed upon us, but is really involved in the very make of our constitution and being. The Greek *nomos* conveys very closely the idea of our own *dharma*. *Nomos* is that which holds together and controls the relations of a thing with its own inner components as well as with other things. That is also our *dharma*, from the root *dhri* to hold together or support. Autonomy, meaning the right or act of living according to one's own law, bases itself, therefore, upon one's own inner nature and constitution, upon one's own individuality or personality, upon one's own *being*. National autonomy, the declared ideal of Indian Nationalism, meant much more, therefore, than the attainment either of Colonial self-rule under the ægis of Great Britain, or of absolute political independence. We might gain these and yet lose our national autonomy. We might not gain either Colonial Self-Government, or absolute independence, and yet attain true and substantial national autonomy. Nationalism, therefore, did neither demand the importation of Parliamentary Government like that of England or her Colonies into India, nor the absolute severance of Great Britain's political connection with her. Its only demand was to live and grow as an individual social organism according to its own special law, engraved upon its own nature and constitution, and revealed through its past historic evolution. It was the demand of the *self* in India, which is her spirit, her soul, her being—to fulfil and realise itself. And the challenge that it offered to the present Government in the country, was in regard to this fundamental demand only. The Government was called upon to justify itself not by its railways and irrigation canals, nor even by its schools and colleges or its organisation of medical or famine relief, nor by its police that has offered peace and protection to the people, or its courts that have brought justice to their very door, but by what it has done, and can do, to help the Indian peoples to live completely according to their own law, and grow, without outside let or hindrance, after their own fashion, towards the ideal-end involved in their own special nature and individuality. It raised its protest against economic exploitation, not because it was simply draining the economic resources of the country to the economic loss of her own children ; but primarily for the false and fatal ideals of capitalism and industrialism which were being insidiously introduced among them. Its protest against current methods of administration, and especially against the present officialised system of public instruction, was similarly more fundamental than that of the Indian National Congress, which simply wanted to change the *personnel* of the Administration in its different branches, while allowing the *spirit* and the *ideals* to practically remain as they are. From one point of view, the conflict between Nationalism and the present Government was thus more fundamental, from another point of view it was less so, than what the conflict between the National Congress and the Government ever was or could be. But from both these points of view, it offered a very bold challenge to British authority in the country, as well as to those Indian politicians who were carrying on a clamorous agitation against the Government, to justify their ways and principles, in the light of ultimate ideals.

The Congress Ideal.

Sir Henry Cotton was, I think, the first among the Presidents of the Indian National Congress, to consider the political future of India and make some definite forecast of it. The "United States of India, under the ægis of Great Britain" was the forecast that Sir Henry presented to us in 1904. Careful students of current history know, and Sir Henry himself admitted it, that this declaration was more or less influenced by the new Nationalist thought that had already commenced to quicken in the country. A new spirit of criticism was abroad. It had commenced to apply itself to a thorough examination of the ideas and methods of current political agitation in the country. Under the influence of this new criticism, Mr. (now Justice) Ashutosh Chaudhuri, as President of the Bengal Provincial Conference, at Burdwan, had proclaimed that "A subject nation has no politics." And he had, therefore, asked the people to give up the degrading methods of "political mendicancy," and apply themselves to the more substantial and needful work of social reconstruction and economic advance. Mr. Chaudhuri's was the first authoritative declaration of the Nationalist ideal of self-help and self-reliance, from which all our subsequent patriotic endeavours derived their main inspiration. Mr. Chaudhuri's pronouncement fell as a bomb in the Congress-camp. It caused consternation among Congress-leaders, and commandeered the allegiance of the more thoughtful section of our educated community, who had already commenced to feel sick of the inanities of Congress-politics. The new criticism, voiced by Mr. Chaudhuri, did not, however, stop with simply exposing the weaknesses of the Congress-propaganda ; it simultaneously drove public attention to questions of ultimate ideals ; and the Nationalist organs in the press commenced to discuss the future with great persistence and considerable power. And all these things combined to force the consideration of the ultimate political ideal of India upon the President of the Indian National Congress, and Sir Henry Cotton, presiding over the Bombay Congress of 1904, proclaimed the above ideal.

Sir Henry Cotton's declaration, however, failed of its purpose. He had observed the quickening of a new thought and criticism among the articulate sections of the Indian people, which threatened to divide the Congress itself into two opposing parties—one the party of self-help and the other the followers of the old methods of prayers and petitions ; and he clearly sought to unite these two in their devotion to a common ideal, namely, that of this "United States of India under the ægis of Great Britain." But instead of bridging, his declaration rather widened this gulf. The new Nationalist criticism was applied to this new ideal as it had been applied to the older methods ; and exposed its unreality as ruthlessly as it had exposed that of the old "mendicancy." How would the British suzerainty be maintained over a "United States of India" which would be so only in name, unless it was a free and self-governing State ? Sir Henry had not considered, and had no reply to this fundamental question. He tried to offer a reconciliation between the two schools of political thought in the country. But the time was not yet ripe for it. A true and complete reconciliation in the realm of our thought, must be of the nature of a rational synthesis. But there can really be no synthesis before the full and complete development of its antecedent antithesis. There can be no rational and permanent synthesis between two inchoate and nebulous thoughts. The old political thought was invertebrate and incoherent ; the new thought was as yet only in its infancy, more or less nebulous. The conflict between them was not yet fully pronounced. Their mutual claims were not clearly formulated. The time had not yet come for them to recognise their respective limitations, without which there can be no incentive to any real reconsideration and reconciliation. This is why Sir Henry's pronouncement failed of its purpose. This pronouncement was itself inchoate and amorphous. It did not boldly tackle the problem of the future relation between Great Britain and India.

The next declaration of the ultimate political ideal of modern India was made, in 1906, by Mr. Dadabhai Naoroji. It was somewhat clearer than Sir Henry's pronouncement. "Self-Government as in the Colonies or Great Britain," said Mr. Dadabhai, was the ultimate political ideal of the Indian National Congress. Mr. Dadabhai gave a new and indigenous name to this ideal. He called it "Swaraj." Here was, after all, something which people could understand. By using the word "Swaraj" Mr. Dadabhai practically allied himself to the new Nationalist School of Indian politics. By interpreting this "Swaraj" as Colonial Self-Government, he spoke in the terms of the older political thought in the country, and by adding the explicatory phrase, "or Great Britain," he cleverly reconciled the two terms, Colonial Self-Government and Swaraj. Critically considered, Mr. Dadabhai's declaration was, in fact, the highest and fullest embodiment of the Nationalist protest and antithesis. By using the phrase, "Self-Government as in the Colonies or Great Britain," Mr. Dadabhai simply kept to the older Congress terminology, but really gave the whole case for the old Congress-ideal away. While keeping continuity with the Congress-traditions in name, he completely changed the essence and substance of the old Congress-ideal altogether. By this wise stroke of policy, Mr. Dadabhai opened a safe way for the Congress to practically adopt the new thought in the country, without any open rupture either with the

Government on the one side, or with its own past on the other.

But the antitheses of the early phases of our Nationalist thoughts, still dominate the thought of the Indian National Congress. While Nationalist thought in the country has commenced to slowly move from its old negations and antitheses, to a new assertion and synthesis, the National Congress has slowly advanced from its old state of thesis, with its inchoate and incoherent inanities and fanciful imitations, to where the earlier Nationalist antithesis had brought the country ten years ago. The tendency of all antithesis is towards separation and conflict. And this tendency, however timidly expressed, is manifest to-day in the thoughts and ideals of the Indian National Congress. It is still dealing with inconsequential particularities on the one side—crying for the old reforms and ventilating the old isolated grievances—and looking forward to a future when, trained and tutored by her present masters, India will be a free nation among the free nations of the world, a sovereign State among other sovereign States.

The Dream of Sir Ibrahim Rahimtulla.

Not the Indian National Congress alone, but almost every school of political thought in the country, seems to have been captured by the spirit of protest and antithesis of our earlier Nationalist thought. And even the All-India Moslem League, representing a community that had hitherto been violently opposed to the ideals and methods of the Indian National Congress, has publicly proclaimed this isolated and sovereign independence, as the ultimate political ideal in India. Sir Ibrahim Rahimtulla, the President of the last (1913) session of the Moslem League, made thus, this significant confession of political faith, in course of his presidential address :—

"I am one of those dreamers, who firmly believe that, given a sufficiently long spell of British rule in India, we are bound to become united as a nation in the real sense of the term. When that time arrives (as it is sure to do), we shall have qualified to rule the country ourselves and self-government will be absolutely assured to us ....No country such as India is, can for ever remain under foreign rule, however beneficent that rule may be; and though British rule is undoubtedly based on beneficence and righteousness, it cannot last for ever...... India is our Motherland, our proud heritage, and must, in the end, be handed over to us by our guardians. I regard the connection of England with India in the nature of guardianship over minor children."

Sir Ibrahim Rahimtulla's dream has not even the distinction of being a new revelation either. It was the dream of Macaulay too. It has been the dream of the Indian National Congress also. And like most dreams it lacks substantial reality. The guardianship-idea is introduced evidently to save the pronouncement from directly coming under the sedition section of the present Indian Penal Code. Either Sir Ibrahim Rahimtulla's politics has no relation to our common human nature, or it is not sincere. It is absolutely contradictory to every thing that we know of ordinary human nature, to sincerely believe that a guardian who manages and enjoys the estate of a minor for two or three centuries can give up his rights and prerogatives, of his own free will, at the end of that long period. It was an old Anglo-Indian plea. But even Anglo-Indian politicians have commenced to see the hollowness of it, and no longer repeat it in the way they used to do at one time. The Nationalist challenge has completely dissipated these fancies and falsehoods for ever.

Sir Ibrahim Rahimtulla dreams of the day when India will be "handed over to us" by our guardians. But he has not, evidently, cared to dream of the process by which this will be done, nor of the relation, if any, that will be established between India and her present guardians, after their stewardship is over. One can understand what the political position of India will be, when she is "united as a nation, in the real sense of the term" as Sir Ibrahim puts it. When that condition is fulfilled, and India is relieved of her guardians, she can reasonably hope to be a great power among the great powers of the world. She has ample resources, both human and economic, to occupy her rightful place as a great world-power. But what about her present guardians ? Will they too be able to maintain their world-position if the Indian connection is absolutely severed ? The thing is simply unthinkable. And this simple fact which even a tyro in current history and world-politics can clearly understand, proves the utter unreality of Sir Ibrahim's pleasant dream. To maintain her world-position, Great Britain must follow one of two possible courses open before her : she must either continue her Indian connection, even if she may not be able to keep up her political suzerainty in its present or indeed in any form in India ; or, failing this, she must gradually federate with other sovereign States, and form a powerful Pan-Anglo-

Saxon, or join a Pan-European Federation. There is no third course. Which of these two possible courses the actualities of the coming historic evolution of modern world-politics will force upon Great Britain, no one can definitely foretell just now. But both India and England have still a choice of these two courses open before them. The realisation of Sir Ibrahim Rahimtulla's dream of isolated sovereign independence for India, is, however, the only contingency that will force Great Britain inevitably to an Anglo-Saxon or European Federation, which, if it is actually formed, will spell a fierce and world-convulsing conflict between the White and the non-White populations of the world, divided into two opposing camps. It will neither work good for India nor for humanity at large. To India of our time, Providence has given the choice of determining the course of the future historic evolution of the human race—to India and Great Britain jointly, to speak more definitely. But neither our "moderate" politicians nor our Moslem fellow-countrymen seem to have any appreciation of this offer. They are, therefore, dreaming of a future for India when she will stand by herself, as an independent and sovereign, that is, an isolated, State, among the independent and isolated States of the world. Neither party seem to have any clear idea of the fearful trends of world-politics, or any vision of the high mission and destiny of their own Motherland in the coming Federation of the World.

The Vision of Mr. Archer.

This lack of insight and vision is painfully evident in the thoughts and ideals even of "advanced" leaders of

British public opinion also. While the Jingo politician can think of no future for the British connection with India, except a practical continuance of the present autocratic and irresponsible overlordship; the advanced Liberal politician also can conceive of no future except that of absolute and isolated independence for India, as a constitutional monarchy, with a hereditary King of the House of Hanover at its head. This is practically the vision of Mr. William Archer, the well-known author and dramatic critic, whose dream has recently been published in the *Daily News and Leader* (London). Mr. Archer paints this future in the form of the last function of the "Last Viceroy" who will deliver the seals of his office and authority into the hands of the "Princes and Citizens of India" on the 31st December, A.D. 2000. In course of his last official pronouncement in India, this "Last Viceroy" is imagined as saying:—

"I could name to you some of the greatest British soldiers and administrators who saw and declared that British rule could not be an end unto itself, but only a means to an end, and, that it must consciously and deliberately, and sincerely address itself to the realisation of that end—a self-governing, self-protecting, United India. But not many Englishmen were at that time—I speak of a century ago—able to take so large and clear a view. The prevailing tendency was to assume that the glory and prestige of England demanded the eternity of the British Raj, and to regard as disloyal the most reasonable and law-abiding aspiration towards self-government. What is to us a truism was to that generation an inadmissible paradox, namely, that England's mission was not to perpetuate her rule, but to render it as brief as was consistent with the safety and well-being of India. Few could then realise that the most glorious day in the annals of England would be that which has now arrived—the day on which her great work accomplished, she could lay down her stewardship and say to a self-controlled, self-reliant India, 'Hail and Farewell'."

Mr. William Archer's vision of the Future of India, is as unreal as that of Sir Ibrahim Rahimtulla. Ten years ago, I should have unhesitatingly characterised the former as exceedingly mischievous, having for its object the perpetuation of the fatal inertia and stupor of the Indian peoples. But the old spell is broken. The ancient māyā has been almost completely dispelled. The new Nationalist upheaval in the country has thoroughly disillusioned us. But though I may not view these fancies in the same light to-day, I cannot deny that they are equally, if not even more, mischievous now, from another and a no less serious point of view, than perhaps they could have been before. Ten years ago these fancies might hinder the quickening of our national self-consciousness : to-day they are almost sure to strengthen the revolutionary propaganda in the country. Sir Ibrahim Rahimtulla's dream is the ideal of the Indian revolutionary. Like him the revolutionary nationalist in India also believes that "no country such as India is can for ever remain under foreign rule." He too thinks, like Sir Ibrahim, that the present foreign domination "cannot last forever." Only, not being a responsible and respectable politician, the youthful revolutionary does not add to his belief the saving clause about the beneficence and righteousness of this foreign domination. In fact, these questions concerning the motives and morals of this domination, are contemptuously dismissed by the revolutionary nationalist as absolutely irrelevant. The only real difference between the Indian revolutionary and the President of the last (1913) session of the All-India Moslem League is that between recklessness and prudence, between rash and intrepid youth and cold and calculating age. Sir Ibrahim thinks his people to be minors, he believes that they are disunited and unorganised, and that a "sufficiently long spell of British rule" will unite them, and by the time this is done, they will attain their majority, and their guardians will faithfully make over to them their "proud heritage." The revolutionary thinks differently. And few men will deny that he has a firmer grasp of actualities than Sir Ibrahim. And he will subject Mr. Archer's vision also to the same candid and searching criticism, and equally dismiss, not the ultimate ideal, but the plea for patience with which it is joined in both these cases, as mere mischievous moonshine. The effect of these fanciful excursions into the future, in the present state of the country, can, therefore, lend only additional strength and inspiration to the revolutionary propaganda.

Absolute Autonomy: The Early Nationalist-Ideal.

The times are too critical and the problem before us too serious to justify these playful excursions into dream-land. We too did our humble part in quickening a lusty desire for political independence in our people. Absolute autonomy was the first cry of our new Nationalism. The preaching of absolute autonomy was a supreme psychological necessity of the situation that faced us ten years ago. The inanities of Congress politics, steeped as it was in fancies and falsehoods, could not have been killed by any other ideal or message. But still it was the dogma of an antithesis, the bitter cry of an indignant protest. Antitheses and protests are necessary moments in all evolutionary processes. It is only when the half-truths of an antithesis or a protest are accepted for good, as the final and the whole truth, that evolutionary reforms are made impossible by revolutionary impatience. It has happened in certain quarters among us also. The patient who had been prescribed a salutary dose of vinum gallici to keep up his low vitality, has continued the habit even after its need and justification have gone, and has consequently been developing fatal symptoms of delirium tremens. It is criminal quackery to prescribe fresh doses of the same stimulant for him now. The nurse who secretly supplies him with it, helps only to kill him. And yet this is exactly what many of our so-called "moderate" politicians are doing. While cleverly keeping themselves at arm's length from the law of sedition, they are helping the youthful intellectuals to keep up an attitude of mind that will make the new synthesis and reconciliation more difficult than ever.

A SINISTER IDEAL.

This synthesis and reconciliation is the most urgent need of the present situation in Indian politics. The Government, in the person of the present Viceroy, is in an exceedingly conciliatory mood just now. The sober and thoughtful section of the Indian community also are tired of the unequal fight in which some people are engaged with the present Administration. There is a dawning consciousness in high political circles in Great Britain of the impossibility of perpetuating the British connection with India without very considerable modification of the present spirit and form of the Indian Government. There is an equally growing consciousness among the more thoughtful section of our own articulate classes, of the impossibility of attaining absolute political independence for India, without running the very serious risks of a fresh spell of foreign servitude, whether Moslem or Mongol. All these have been clearly opening the way for a rational synthesis and permanent reconciliation between Indian aspirations and the enlightened self-interest of Great Britain. To preach at this moment, any ideal of absolute and isolated political independence, which must necessarily sever the British connection altogether, even if it has to be attained by peaceful and constitutional methods, or as the result of an act of supreme self-sacrifice on the part of a Christian nation—is really to hinder this much-needed synthesis and reconciliation. And those who are doing it, whether they are Indians or Britishers, stand convicted, to my mind, of either crass ignorance or egregious insensibility or of sinister designs against both Indian Nationalism and the British connection. In fact, I find it very difficult to understand the meaning and motive of these belated dreams of our Pan-Islamist friends. And I trust I should be doing no injustice to Sir Ibrahim Rahimtulla if I were to take him as a leader of this Pan-Islamist school in India. It is impossible to deny that the leadership of the Moslem League has practically passed into the hands of the party of Mr. Mahomed Ali, who makes absolutely no secret of his "extra-territorial patriotism." And it is as plain as plain can be, that apart from the small band of revolutionary nationalists in the country, the Indian Pan-Islamist is the only person among us who has a distinct interest in keeping up the present conflict between Indian Nationalism and the British connection. For both are in his way. The success of Nationalism, as well as the perpetuation, not of the British subjection, but of the British connection with India, in any shape or form, are the only two conditions that will defeat the ends of this political Pan-Islamism in India. The longer any complete and reasonable synthesis and reconciliation between Indian Nationalism and the British connection with India is delayed, the greater chance would this Pan-Islamism have of securing its separatist ends. And in view of this inevitable logic of the Pan-Islamist position, one cannot help being moved by some secret suspicion regarding this sudden accession of a new love for the political independence of India in our Pan-Islamist friends. The whole propaganda lends itself to a very sinister interpretation. In any case it is to be hoped that Indian Nationalism will not be duped by these dreams of Sir Ibrahim and his friends.

Imperial Federation.

It is high time, indeed, that the Indian Nationalist fully recognised how vitally the realisation of his fondest hopes and ideals is bound up with the perpetuation, not by any means of the present British subjection, but certainly of the British connection. And the only way to maintain this connection without this subjection, is through the evolution of an Imperial Federation, in which India—herself a union of a number of provincial autonomies federated with one another and forming one large federal whole—will be a free and respected partner, an equal among equals—combined with the other partners, including Great Britain herself, into one large organic political whole, co-operating with one another for the furtherance of their respective national interests and the progress of universal humanity. We must clearly realise that this Federal Imperialism is a much higher objective, not merely ethically, but even from the point of view of practical politics, than isolated sovereign independence. This federal idea alone offers a perfect basis of reconciliation of particularistic national interests. Federation does not imply national subjection, but rather on the contrary, it means a much larger freedom for national life than what could be ever attained by isolated independence. Knowing and understanding all these things, the Indian Nationalist should set his face sternly and resolutely against the syren song of those who have commenced to preach, at this late hour of the day, the beauties of isolated and sovereign independence for India.

CALCUTTA:
March, 1914.

CHAPTER VII.

"PROVINCIAL AUTONOMY" AND THE DESPATCH OF 1911.

THE full import of Lord Hardinge's Despatch of August 1911, does not seem to have been seized by the leaders of political life in this country. The Bengalee leaders acclaimed it, first because it annulled the Partition of their Province, and second because it accepted and openly proclaimed Provincial Autonomy as the ultimate objective of the new reforms introduced into the constitution of our Legislative Councils by Lords Morley and Minto. Even this appreciation was anything but unanimous. The younger Nationalists treated it with ill-concealed contempt, taking it to be just another of those public documents which make sweet promises to the ear, only to break them to the heart. Many "moderate" politicians saw both in the redistribution of territories with which the repeal of the Partition was associated, and in the transfer of the capital from Calcutta to Delhi, only a sinister attempt to break the power of Bengal, while outwardly conceding to its demand for the annulment of the Partition. The true meaning and significance of this document, and of the policy which it enunciated, have thus failed, it seems to me, to be grasped by almost every school of political thought in the country.

OFFICIAL DISCLAIMERS.

I am not sure if Lord Hardinge's colleagues themselves fully realised the import of the document to which they put their seal and signature. Within three months of its publication, Lord Crewe, who had fully approved of the measures proposed by this Despatch, disclaimed the one idea which lent to it its permanent worth and importance. The redistribution of territories which, accompanying the repeal of the Partition, actually dismembered the old Province of Bengal, by taking both Behar and Orissa from it; and the transfer of the seat of the Supreme Government from Calcutta to Delhi deprived Bengal of the superior position which she had held as the Metropolitan Province. There was no compensation for these in the repeal of the Curzonian Partition. Bengal, though saddled with a Governorship, was actually made smaller by the repeal of the Partition than what it was before, while the permanent transfer of the capital from Calcutta, deprived the Province of the safeguards which the direct control of the Viceroy over the local executive was believed to provide. This is how good many people viewed the changes introduced by the Despatch of August 1911. And unless there was something beyond what appeared on the surface, unless these changes were dictated by some far-reaching and comprehensive policy or ideal, this popular interpretation of this document could not be contested or refuted. Some people at least had read a deeper meaning and significance into this document. They had accepted and acclaimed it as the enunciation of a new policy which aimed at working out a real and effective settlement of the issue between Indian Nationalism on the one side and the British Empire on the other. But this policy, which fully accepted the ideal of National Autonomy for India, did not appeal to Anglo-Indian sentiments. It did not commend itself to the British Bureaucracy in India. It was attacked by Tory politicians in both the Houses of Parliament, and all this seems to have forced this disclaimer from the Secretary of State for India.

We are not intimately acquainted with the forces that work behind the scene in British Parliamentary life, and we cannot say if this disclaimer was really called for in the interest of the silent and peaceful pursuit of the policy which was, thus, publicly disclaimed. But we know that it had a very damping effect in India. Already there was an almost universal disinclination in the public mind to take Lord Hardinge's Despatch very seriously; and this disclaimer by Lord Crewe destroyed whatever enthusiasm the proclamation of the ideal of Provincial Autonomy had evoked. People did not recognise the real inwardness of this proclamation. They did not realise the fact that it was prompted not by generosity but by necessity. At the back of the entire policy of Lord Hardinge there is a thorough appreciation of the forces of the Indian unrest on the one side, and those of current Asiatic and world-politics on the other. Mere unrest in India might be crushed out. Any combination of world-forces, in the absence of any fearful ferment in the subject populations in India, might also be successfully overcome. But the real gravity of the Indian problem, from the view-point of British Imperialism, arises out of the possible combination of these two disturbing elements.

Lord Hardinge has clearly realised this possibility. And one finds this recognition in the policy enunciated in the Despatch of August 1911. Those who have any insight into current world-politics, did not, therefore, take Lord Crewe's disclaimer seriously. But their number is not large. This disclaimer has had, therefore, a very depressing effect upon the people at large, and it neutralised, to a very considerable extent, the effect which the publication of this important document had commenced to produce.

The Despatch Analysed.

The Despatch of August 1911 stands divided into two parts: one part proposes certain changes in the Administration; the other indicates, cautiously and by implication, a new policy which demand and justify these changes. The repeal of the Partition of Bengal, the redistribution of territories, the elevation of the Bengal Administration from a Lieutenant-Governorship into a Governorship, the transfer of the capital to Delhi, and the institution of a new Province including the Delhi District and its approaches, to be directly administered by the Governor-General in Council—all these are the changes proposed by this document. These, sanctioned by the Secretary of State for India, and approved by the King-Emperor, have been carried out. If the Despatch of August 1911 contained nothing else, it would have hardly met the requirements of the situation as Lord Minto had left it. A complete annulment of the Partition of Bengal, whether by a re-constitution of the old Province under the old Lieutenant Governorship, or by a change into a Governorship, without any redistribution of territories, except the reinstitution of Assam into a Chief Commissionership once more, would not have been consistent with the prestige of the Government. And no Government that does not receive its authority directly from the people, can be forgetful of or indifferent to its prestige. The Government could not surrender itself openly and unconditionally to this anti-Partition Agitation in Bengal. Such a course would not make for peace, but for greater trouble. The Bengal Partition might have been easily and honourably repealed, as soon as the Liberals came into office in 1906. Lord Morley lost his opportunity then. In 1911, after five years of the fiercest agitation and unrest that Bengal had ever seen since the transfer of the Government of India from the East India Company to the Crown, a simple repeal of the Partition and a return to the *status quo ante*, was absolutely unthinkable. The problem before Lord Hardinge was to discover a reasonable policy, wider in scope than what was required to pacify the anti-Partitionists in Bengal, a policy that, while repealing this evil measure, would, at the same time, ensure peaceful evolution in the future. His lordship had to enunciate a policy that would not only justify the repeal of the Bengal Partition, but would, at the same time, offer a real, effective, and permanent basis of reconciliation between the aspirations of Indian Nationalism on the one side, and the maintenance of the unity and integrity of the present British Empire on the other. This is, really, the central idea and policy of this important state-document. In this document Lord Hardinge has laid down, as clearly as his position and the circumstances of the country allowed it, the fundamental lines of the future historic evolution of India, as a part,—and, indeed, as a partner—of the British Empire. It is in this light that this Despatch should be read.

Provincial Autonomy has been mentioned in the Despatch of August 1911, not as a definite pledge, but as a distant ideal. Here Lord Hardinge's Government sowed, so to say, the seed of the future constitution of India. The ideal suggested by this document is practically the same as that of the United States of India, proclaimed many years ago, from the presidential chair of the Indian National Congress, by Sir Henry Cotton. Lord Hardinge clearly saw that the time was coming when India would be composed of a number of autonomous provinces, somewhat similar to the different States of the American Union, with a Federal Government directing and controlling them all, in all matters of inter-state or foreign policy and administration. Lord Hardinge not only dreamed of this future constitution of India, but he is so absolutely convinced of its gradual growth and evolution that he has started already to build up the scaffolding of this superb structure. The transfer of the capital to Delhi, and the institution of the new seat of the Supreme Government into a separate Province directly administered by the Viceroy and Governor-General in Council, prove this. Indeed, his lordship speaks in this Despatch of Sydney, Toronto, and Washington—all seats of Federal Governments; and of the District of Columbia where Washington stands and which is under the immediate administration of the American President. And all this shows the idea that has been working at the back of his mind, in the writing of this Despatch. All these show that he has been thinking here of the future United States of India. It is not a pledge but an idea, not a promise but a policy. A pledge carries with it the obligation of redeeming it, and a promise demands its fulfilment. But a policy involves no such moral obligations. Whether it will or will not be carried out, does not depend so much, if at all, upon the will of its enunciator, as upon the actualities of history. A policy is the indication of a certain line of administrative or legislative activities, calculated to lead to some definite and desirable result. A policy implies an aim, and a series of acts with a view to reach that aim. The aim here is the preservation of the unity and integrity of the present British Empire. Provincial Autonomy, leading, gradually, to the institution of a Federal Union for all India, which will be in a position to federate with the other parts of the British Empire, and thus help to preserve the unity and integrity of that Empire, in and through a scheme of real Imperial Federation—these are regarded by Lord Hardinge as the best, if not the only, means of securing this end. A careful consideration of present conditions, both inside and outside the British Empire, forces this idea upon those who are anxious to maintain, in perpetuity, the British connection with India. The policy indicated in Lord Hardinge's Despatch is clearly prompted by this consideration. And as long as the conditions remain what they are and develop along lines indicated at the present moment, so long this policy will be pursued by Lord Hardinge and his successors, in spite of any disclaimer that may be publicly entered on the subject by either Lord Crewe or Sir W. Meyer, or even by the Viceroy himself.

The Growth of Political Constitutions.

Provincial Autonomy is not a thing that can be *given* to the people by their Government. Such gift would not, really, be worth having. The people themselves must work up to it. In fact, no Government, not even what claims to be democratic, ever moves except under pressure of irresistible circumstances. The British constitution or that of France or the United States of America, has been the gradual growth of centuries, and every change in it has been forced upon the Government for the time being by the economic or political conditions of the time. Governments do not go after abstract idealities, but are always controlled and moved by concrete utilities. The impulse to move rarely comes from within the ruling classes, but always from without. Even when any ruler or ruling class initiate any fundamental change or improvement in the constitution of their state-machinery, the driving force for it comes from the irresistible conditions about them; and the motive is always self-preservation. The King and the aristocracy in England, for instance, have accepted and have occasionally, even initiated democratic reforms, curtailing their own powers and prerogatives, not out cf any burning desire for the expansion of popular freedom, but only from the conviction that unless they sacrificed a part, they would risk the whole of their prerogatives and powers. This is the story of popular political progress all the world over. We should bear this universal experience of history in mind, when approaching the problem of political advancement in modern India. Lord Hardinge's Despatch is not based upon any idle and abstract speculation of what will be an ideal form of Government for India. It is the demand of an imperious necessity. The ideal of Autonomy has commenced to possess people's mind. It has, indeed, already obsessed many youthful intellectuals. The youth of to-day will be the old man of to-morrow. And though the wild ardour of youth may somewhat cool down with age, the ideal that has already commenced to obsess their youthful imagination, will not be destroyed but simply lie dormant in them, only to reincarnate itself in their children with greater strength and tenacity. And the unrest will, thus, grow in intensity and volume from generation to generation, until it blazes forth in a world-consuming conflagration. This is the danger that looms ahead. This danger must, so far as may be, be avoided or provided against, in the interest as much of India as of the British Empire. This is clearly the view which Lord Hardinge has taken of the situation before him. And it is this view that has evidently led to the initiation of the policy indicated in this Despatch.

The Immediate Need in India.

And we should not forget or ignore that it is a mere initiation, a faint indication, of the line which the evolution of British policy in India will take, in the event of its being called upon to face the forces that have commenced to quicken in and outside this country. If these forces do not grow and come to a focus, or if time and experience reveal some other more effective means of successfully dealing with them, without any abdication of the existing absolute authority of the Executive Government at the head of the machinery of the state in this country, this policy will be naturally abandoned; and we shall hear nothing more about it, except perhaps, from the political demagogue occasionally holding forth before harmless audiences, on "the ancient and unredeemed pledges of an all-powerful Government." If, however, on the contrary, the forces that have compelled this pronouncement from the Head of the Government, are neither hypnotised by gilded concessions, nor dissipated in delirious and suicidal revolutionary outbursts, this policy will be bound to slowly materialise itself, until we have not only provincial, but real national autonomy in India, inside a broad and comprehensive scheme of Imperial Federation. Our duty now is to avoid these two dangers. But our "moderate" leaders have no appreciation of these facts. They are forgetting these gilded concessions. They do not seem to understand the very plain fact that neither provincial nor national autonomy can be established in India by an order of the Executive Government, or even by an Act of the Legislature. The case of Irish Home Rule has absolutely no application to India. Ireland has been used to the Parliamentary system of Government for many centuries past. She has her established Parliamentary divisions, and has been enjoying the Parliamentary franchise as fully as Great Britain. All that is needed now, to set up Home Rule in Ireland, is to transfer the supreme executive authority for the administration of Irish affairs from London to Dublin; and to make that authority subject to the control of an Irish Parliament. The Irish Members now sitting at Westminster will, under the Home Rule Act, go and sit in Dublin. The structure will be what it is, only the seat of executive and legislative authority and the personnel of the Government will be changed. And it is because of the existence of a complete machinery of Parliamentary Government in Ireland, that it is possible to establish Irish autonomy by an Act of the Legislature. But in India we have no such machinery. We are not used to these parliamentary methods. It is exceedingly doubtful whether we should at all seek to import them from Europe. Parliamentary or representative Government is just now upon its trial in almost every European Democracy. Almost everywhere representative Government has developed class-rule and oligarchies, against which the forces of modern democracy have already commenced to organise themselves. Political forces all over the European and American States are just now arming themselves for a fierce fight, and nobody knows what the end of this conflict will be. Self-government is as yet as much of an unrealised ideal in Europe and America as it is in India or China. It would be an act of arrant folly on the part of the awakening nationalities of Asia, to blindly go in for the failures of Europe, in search of their own political enfranchisement and self-realisation. We must profit by these failures, and try to develop our own systems of real national self-government in our own way, according to the special genius of our race and the traditions of our country. In India, it is of the utmost importance, at this juncture, that instead of encouraging the Government to introduce the European system of Parliamentary Administration among us, we should rather pray to be left alone, and given sufficient and reasonable scope and freedom to slowly beat our own music out ourselves. All that we want is that the Government should openly and unreservedly accept and proclaim national autonomy as the ultimate ideal and objective of our present historic evolution. Lord Hardinge has done this. And we should rest content with it, and nct try to force him to any definite course of immediate action in the matter. Lord Hardinge could not do more. I would not ask him to do more, even if he could.

FINANCIAL AND PROVINCIAL AUTONOMY.

In fact, to demand financial autonomy for the Provincial Administrations, under existing conditions in India, is really to hinder, and not help, the evolution of real Provincial Autonomy. The Provincial Autonomy mentioned in Lord Hardinge's Despatch, has reference to the ultimate political ideal in India. It is to be an element of the future United States of India, the vision of which stands at the back of Lord Hardinge's policy. This Provincial Autonomy means, therefore, a Provincial Legislature thoroughly representative of the people of the Province and completely controlled by them, *and* a Provincial Executive subject to this Legislature. Provincial Autonomy means the complete control of the people over all purely Provincial affairs. We have no Provincial autonomy now. Though our Provincial Councils have a non-official majority, this majority is composed partly of elected and partly of nominated members; and the latter though non-officials, are not in any way subject to popular control. And even these Councils have no control over the Executive Government of the different Provinces. They cannot control executive action in any way. They have no control over the pay and pension of executive officers, are not called upon to pass what are called civil service estimates, and by moving and passing amendments to these, they cannot even commend or condemn executive action or policy. To demand financial autonomy before this real political autonomy has been established in the Provinces, is really to ask, not for the expansion of popular freedom, but rather, on the contrary, only for strengthening the hands of the Executive Government in the Provinces.

That the Provincial Governments do enjoy a certain measure of fiscal freedom under the existing Provincial Contract system, cannot be denied. What some of our popular leaders want is more money for the Provincial Administrations, to spend upon the growing needs of their respective provinces. The Provincial Governments do need more money, and if they had it, it would undoubtedly be to the profit of the people. The real complaint is that the Government of India take more money out of the Provincial Revenues than what is actually wanted for strictly imperial purposes, and dole out this excess money back to the Provinces, for expenditure upon specific subjects, from year to year. This places the Provincial Governments at the mercy of the Imperial Government, and with the Imperial grants, which they receive from year to year, comes also needless and irritating interference with the Provincial Administrations, even in matters where they should have perfect freedom of action. This is the brunt of the whole offence of the Government of India. Individual instances have occurred of late in Bengal, where the interference of the Government of India has clashed with educated opinion in the Province. And this is the real reason of this demand for greater financial freedom for the Provincial Administrations. This is why the present system of "doles" which brings with it also a certain amount of irritating control by the Government of India, is condemned. But we should not forget that it was a mere accident that in some recent cases the Government of Bengal sided with educated opinion in the Province. Occasions may arise when the Provincial Executive may come into open conflict with the ideas and interests of our articulate populations; and in that case, the very people who are clamouring for provincial freedom now, will pray for Imperial intervention. A broad view of the present situation, in the light of future ideals and objectives, would, I think, rather favour the continuance of the existing financial arrangements between the Provincial and Imperial Governments, until such time, when real Provincial Autonomy, that is, a truly representative Provincial Legislature and a Provincial Executive subject to that Legislature,—is evolved and organised. Till then, the Imperial Government must be allowed to exercise its right of supervision and control over the Provincial Governments. This has its advantages and disadvantages both. But on the whole, the very aloofness of the Government of India from close contact with Provincial politics, which may sometimes lead to wrong judgments of provincial needs, will leave some chance of impartial arbitration by them, in all disputes between the Provincial Executive and the leaders of educated public opinion in the Province. From the point of view of the ideal of ultimate Provincial Autonomy, as part of a real scheme of Indian Federation, which will lead to the admission of the future United States of India, into an honourable co-partnership with Great Britain and the British Colonies,—any inconvenience due to the existing arrangement is far more preferable to this so-called financial autonomy for the Provincial Administrations, the inevitable effect of which will be to strengthen the hands of an already strong Executive who own no direct responsibility to the people. To talk of Provincial Autonomy now, except as a distant and ultimate idea, and ask for this financial freedom for an irresponsible Executive, in the name of this Provincial Autonomy betrays really considerable confusion of thought.

Indian Actualities and British Experience.

And all this confusion is due entirely to our present unreal education. We have been brought up in English ideas and ideals, whether in literature or sociology or religion or politics. We have not been trained to test these ideas by the actualities of our past experience or present conditions. We have been taught by every English historian and political or economic writer, for instance, that the freedom of a people is based upon their control of the public purse. The power of the purse constitutes the very life and soul of popular freedom in England. This is the secret of the power of the House of Commons. The British people fought for generations to secure this power of the purse. It is therefore argued, that we too must do the same if we are to advance popular rights in India. But we forget that the British people fought for this power of the purse, because their trouble was with an absolute monarchy, and this was the only means by which the monarchical constitution might be retained while divesting it of its absolute autocratic character. The King is the executive head of the State in Great Britain. His is the right of appointing and dismissing the officers of State. He alone has the right of declaring war against and concluding peace with other nations; and he is also the head of the national army. The discharge of all these functions requires money. And if the representatives of the people controlled the public finances, the King would naturally have to depend upon their advice and direction for the exercise of what are conceded to be, theoretically at least, his absolute rights and prerogatives. It is, therefore, that this power of the purse means so much in British politics. The control of the purse is a clever and cunning device by which the kingly power and office are reconciled with the supreme political authority of the people in a constitutional monarchy. This "power of the purse" is a very vital thing in all cases where the supreme authority in the State is divided between two parties, as, for instance, between the King and the Parliament in Great Britain. But it has not the same value in republican States, where the power of the purse, like every other function and authority of the State, is held by the representatives of the people, and where it is treated just in the same way as any other authority or function of the Government. The supreme value of this "power of the purse" in British history and politics, arose out of the peculiar struggles between the King and the people, through which the British constitution has evolved. Our struggles in India are not with an absolute monarchy; but with a foreign bureaucracy, subject to the authority of a constitutional monarch and his parliament—a bureaucracy that exercises, so far as the people of this country are concerned, absolute and irresponsible authority over all the affairs of the Government. In England they had to work out a compromise between popular rights and the royal prerogatives. The compromise that we in India are called upon to make, just now, is not between popular rights and bureaucratic authority, but between national autonomy and the imperial connection. Not constitutional monarchy, but federal self-government is the ultimate political ideal in modern India. We have no absolute monarch, as the head of the Indian Government. The King-Emperor, in whose name the Government of India is carried, is already a constitutional sovereign. Our problem is different from what the British people had to solve under the Plantagenets and the Stewarts. The solution of our problem cannot, therefore, follow British lines. We cannot accept British experience for our guidance. The terms of British political life and evolution have no reality to us. They are not only inapplicable, but positively misleading, to the work that lies before us. And it is time that we freed ourselves from the trammels of the catch-phrases of British history and politics.

"Nagging" and Statesmanship.

Ever since the appearance of an imitative and imported revolutionary school in our nationalist thoughts and activities, we have been anxious to work out a reasonable reconciliation and compromise between national autonomy and the British connection; and every year, the trends of contemporary world-politics have revealed, with increasing strength, the wisdom of this reconciliation, in the interests as much of Indian Nationalism as of the unity and integrity of the present British Empire. The first step towards any reasonable reconciliation of this character is a free and open acceptance of the ideal of National Autonomy for India, by the responsible representatives of the British Government and the British people. This is an absolute condition-precedent of any real compromise between Nationalism and Imperialism. The acceptance of autonomy as the ultimate political ideal in India, by the British Government, would be bound to lead to the acceptance of the British connection, as a profitable arrangement, by every Indian Nationalist who understands what Nationalism really means, and has a clear grasp of the evolving actualities of contemporary imperial and world-politics. We had repeatedly asked for this declaration, as an absolute condition-precedent of the settlement of the Indian unrest. Neither Lord Minto nor Lord Morley, however, recognised this need. They did not understand the psychology of this new trouble in India : few British officials or publicists, politicians or statesmen, understand it even to-day. They could not measure the strength of the new idealism that had possessed the Indian intellectuals. And they failed to do the one thing that might have at once eased even the tension of the Anti-Partition agitation. Had Lord Minto the courage and farsight of Lord Hardinge, and had he done in 1907 or 1908 or even 1909, what Lord Hardinge did in 1911, he might have completely taken the wind out of the sails of the youthful Indian revolutionaries. Lord Hardinge has, however, done this. And in the doing of it his lordship has combined clever diplomacy with very real and far-seeing statesmanship. The King's visit was a deep diplomatic move. The Despatch of August 1911, and the annulment of the Curzonian Partition of Bengal, and the redistribution of territories, and the transfer of the capital to Delhi, are acts of far-seeing and courageous statesmanship. And all these have practically saved the Indian situation. The direct result of the publication of the Despatch of August 1911 was to enlist the sympathies of the more thoughtful and sober section of the Indian Nationalists on the side of peaceful reconciliation and compromise. It removed the paralysing despair that the Minto-policy had created in the community. The old fear gave place to a new hope. The old demoralisation was gradually replaced by a new enthusiasm for an international or imperial ideal which did not destroy, but on the contrary, sought rather to help forward the narrower Nationalism of the earlier years, to a completer and fuller self-realisation. This is a thing of supreme moral worth. It is a great mistake to recklessly destroy this excellent effect which Lord Hardinge's Despatch and the far-seeing policy enunciated in it, has been undoubtedly producing upon the public mind. Indian statesmanship should rather help in every possible way to keep up and strengthen the ideas and sentiments which this important document has produced. The enemies of Indian Nationalism, the advocates of the Big Stick, all those whose economic or political interests and racial prejudices have been threatened and wounded by the spirit of compromise and conciliation of this great document, are already trying to repudiate it and neutralise its excellent effects.

They do not like this weakness, this parleying with revolution, this pandering to criminalities, as they describe Lord Hardinge's policy, and are only waiting to see a complete reversal of it. This fact at least should warn us against doing anything that is likely to neutralise the excellent effects of this Despatch. Others there are, both here and in England, both among officials and non-officials alike, who are only too anxious to explain away the significance of this Despatch. The right Nationalist policy in India should be to prevent these attempts and oppose these interpretations ; and we should do nothing to help these.

Lord Hardinge is reported to have remarked once that "nagging is not administration." Our own political leaders, especially the members of our Legislative Councils would do well, it seems, to realise the truth and significance of this wise observation. If it is unwise for the Government to "nag" the people ; it is equally unwise for the people's representatives and leaders to "nag" the Government. And these attempts, so common in our Legislative Councils, of our elected members to constantly throw the utterances or statements of the Viceroy or the Secretary of State for India, at their teeth, is very much like nagging. If nagging is not administration, neither is feminine petulence, politics. These attempts cause only needless irritation. They force the authorities to disclaim, under temporary irritation, what they had perhaps seriously meant in sober moments. In any case these ill-advised debates create needless misunderstanding at a time when a complete and frank understanding between the Government and the people is so essentially wanted in the interests of peaceful progress.

Thoughtful people had commenced to recognise in Lord Hardinge's policy, as laid down in this Despatch, a way to the ultimate reconciliation of Nationalist ideals with the continuance of the British connection, in and through some scheme of Imperial Federation, that would be honourable and profitable to both the countries. If, however, the conviction gains ground that this so-called Provincial Autonomy was a mere meaningless phrase, and the Despatch of August 1911 did not understand anything real or serious by it, it would lend fresh strength to the revolutionary propaganda in the country, and undo the excellent work which Lord Hardinge's policy and administration have been trying to do.

CALCUTTA,
April 1914.

CHAPTER VIII.

THE DELHI TRANSFER.

THE OPPOSITION TO THE DELHI TRANSFER.

I CAN quite understand why Anglo-Indian opinion in Calcutta should be so violently opposed to the transfer of the capital to Delhi. But I confess to my utter inability to understand or appreciate the attitude of a section of the Bengalee press towards this change. The Anglo-Indian community of Calcutta has lost a good deal, both politically and socially, through the removal of the seat of the Supreme Government from their midst. It has deprived them of the numerous opportunities which they had been hitherto enjoying, of controlling public policy through those subtle but powerful influences which their intimate social relations with the officers of the Government enabled them to exercise over those who are the real force behind the Viceregal throne in this country. The Indian community were never admitted to these intimacies. Their relations with the Viceroy or his court have always been of the most formal character. They have always been mere worshippers at the gate at all official functions and state-ceremonials. The Government of India have never entered into any intimate intellectual or moral relations with them. Politically, therefore, the transfer of the capital from Calcutta can mean really nothing to the Indian community of that city. Socially also, it is the Anglo-Indian community only who have been deprived of the more extensive and lavish hospitality of the Viceregal house, than what the smaller sumptuary allowances of a Provincial Governor are ever likely to offer. The Anglo-Indian community must naturally feel these deprivations more or less keenly. But these reasons do not exist for the Indian community. The apprehensions of the Calcutta land-owners that the transfer of the capital would depreciate the market-value of their properties, have not been verified by facts. Rents have not been at all affected by the departure of the Government of India from their old capital. A few of the bigger houses in the residential streets of Chowringhee may not fetch as high rents to-day as they used to do before; but with these very few exceptions, no one sees any tendency to lower rents in any part of the city. Nor has the trade of Calcutta suffered in any way owing to the transfer of the capital to Delhi. Trade follows the sea and large river-courses, and as long as we have the Bay of Bengal near us, and the Hugli at our door, to bring up heavy tonnage vessels to our quays, so long the trade of Calcutta will remain what it is and grow as in the past, unless it is diverted by the growth of new sea-port towns more advantageously situated. The Assam Bengal Railway, with its south-eastern terminus at Chittagong, may someday set up that ancient seaport town of Bengal as a formidable rival of Calcutta; and when Chittagong came to her own, and became once more the queen of the trade of East Bengal, the mere presence of the Supreme

Government in Calcutta would not save the maritime supremacy of the latter city. Karachi may gradually take a part of the sea-borne trade of the United Provinces that now passes through Calcutta. Coconada and Vizag may possibly compete someday with Calcutta in regard to the import and export trade of Orissa, Ganjam, and the Northern Sircars. All these are possibilities that may some day affect the trade of Calcutta. But these have absolutely nothing to do with the presence or the absence of the Government of India in or from Calcutta. The mere fact that Calcutta is the seat of the Supreme Government, cannot possibly prevent other cities, more favourably situated, to try to be the commercial capital of the country. The apprehensions of the Calcutta merchants and traders are, therefore, as baseless as those of the Calcutta land-owners. These have been so proved by the experience of the past two years. The opponents of the Delhi-transfer must know this by now. In fact no one urges these any longer, as arguments against the Delhi scheme.

THE QUESTION OF COST.

The only argument upon which this opposition is still sought to be carried on, both here and in England, is the financial argument! And the pity of it is that instead of exposing the hollowness of this cry of cost, even our leaders seem to be lending their support to this Anglo-Indian agitation against the Delhi-transfer. And it shows a very lamentable lack of political insight in the country. That Delhi will cost quite a mint of money, nobody denies.

Those who have the gift of historic imagination, and believe not merely in the spirit but equally also in the form of things, will, I think, be really sorry, if the Government were to allow any consideration of mere pounds, shillings and pence, to interfere with the scheme of building a capital for New India, worthy of its past traditions and symbolic of its future promise. Calcutta was not, and could never be, the capital of New India. It is the spirit of the trader that called it into being. It is the hand and brains of the salesman that have built it up. The Soul of India lies really crushed under the cranes and wharfs of this ugly city. Now that India is going to have a new capital, it must be made worthy of the Imperial Government, worthy of the people of India, worthy of their ancient culture and modern life, a capital that will express, in brick and marble, something, at least of the real Soul of this great country. The building of such a capital cannot be an inexpensive job. The Government of India has long ceased to be a mere merchant company. But the ancient malodorous memories of the factory still hang about almost all the modern cities of the Indian Empire. Bombay with her garish flippancy, suggestive of the thoughtless gaiety of modern Europe; Madras with her unsightly warehouses disfiguring her noble sea-view; Calcutta with her jetties and godowns, and in spite of her so-called palaces, unowned by any style of civilised architecture, are all reeking with the malodours of multifarious merchandise, so loudly reminiscent of the trading days of the East India Company. None of these throw upon their face the sacred reflection of the soul and civilisation of the composite Indian people. These were not built, but only grew. They grew not in response to the inner impulse of the soul and civilisation of the country struggling for outer expression, but under pressure of the needs of a body of alien commercial exploiters. They are the creations of the foreign traders, and grew from year to year to meet the material requirements of an expansive trading community and the needs of a Government largely controlled by them. All the old capitals of British India, —Calcutta, Bombay, Madras—were the creations of the days, when the Government was as yet uninspired by any vision of an Empire that is to outshine, if possible, even that of the mediæval Moguls.. Now that that vision has come, they cannot live amidst wharfs and quays, noisy with shrieking locomotives, and dusty with the perpetual processions of heavy laden wagons. There was neither conscious plan nor intelligent purpose in the growth of the old capitals, except the one purpose of satisfying their immediate animal wants. The *whole* was not consciously conceived before the *parts* were allowed to expand and take shape. Every building and every street grew unconsciously, as it were, to meet some urgent material need; and its future relations and evolutions were left entirely to the accidents of fresh needs that might arise in course of time. No large outlay had, therefore, to be made, all at once, nor every possible item of expenditure had to be forecast, at their very birth. But the new capital at Delhi has to be created. It is a rare privilege, a God-given opportunity, to a people or a Government to be called upon to plan and execute a capital city worthy of itself, reminiscent of its glorious past, and suggestive of its still more glorious future. America had this privilege;

and Washington is, to my mind, the finest capital city of the modern world. Though planned, evidently, after Paris, Washington is yet infinitely more beautiful than Paris. And the reason of it is that while Paris grew, Washington was made. Paris had to submit to the requirements of the expanding trade and commerce of her inhabitants. Paris is not merely the political capital of France, but its commercial capital also, to a very large extent. But Washington has not as yet, and will never be, subjected to these ugly necessities. Washington is only the Capital of the American Union. All its trade is limited to the requirements of the small official colony, and a few people who, originally associated with the Federal Government, have subsequently settled in the outskirts of the capital. And this freedom from the grosser requirements of expanding trade and commerce of cities like New York or Chicago or St. Louis, or even Boston, has enabled Washington to make and keep herself so supremely beautiful. Washington is a living picture of the soul of the composite American people. It is open, like the American mind. Youngish, like the American spirit. A thing of beauty, such as the young heart of America is perpetually seeking to attain. Apparently so small though Washington is—a couple of hours' walk is, I think, quite enough for "doing" the whole city and even a good part of its outskirts—it suggests, however, an expansiveness, a spacial indefinity or infinity, which one does not feel in London or Paris, New York or Chicago. And in this very suggestion of limitless space, Washington strikes the visitors at once, as beautifully symbolic of the spirit of freedom of her people.

IDEALISTIC IMPERIALISM AND SHOP-KEEPING FINANCE.

The plan and style, the poetry and symbolism of new Delhi is everything, the question of cost is nothing, and ought not to count in the execution of a really worthy capital of the new Indian Empire. The new city will take some time to build. The cost of it will consequently spread over a good many years. One might even seriously put forward the suggestion that the major portion of this cost should be met, not out of current revenues, but rather out of some borrowed capital. The metropolis of New India will be built, not merely for the benefit of the present, but for that of future, generations. In fact, it is they who will profit by it far more than the actual builders themselves. And it is neither unreasonable nor unjust to place a part at least of the cost of the undertaking upon their shoulders. This will be done by building the city with the help of borrowed capital, which will involve only a part of the cost being met out of current revenues. But howsoever it may have to be found, the question of cost should never be permitted to interfere with or cripple so great an undertaking. Had Anglo-Indian politics not been almost absolutely divested of all historic imagination, there would, in fact, have been no opposition to the Delhi scheme on the score of its cost. Had our own political thinking been adequately inspired by any lofty and prophetic patriotic imagination, our own publicists too would have paid little heed to this niggardly cry of their Anglo-Indian contemporaries.

The fact of the matter is, that few people have as yet been able to visualise all the possibilities of the Delhi transfer. Calcutta was not, and could never be, our own capital. The foreign associations of it are much too strong to encourage any real identification of the Indian or even the Bengalee people with Calcutta. It had no past before the East India Company. All its sites are reminiscent of the ugly times of Clive and Hastings. Old Calcutta has no inspiration for the people. New Calcutta too has hardly any soul-stirring national associations about it. It is English from beginning to end. So far as we are concerned, it has no traditions of the past, and can inspire no hope for the future. But Delhi is different. Delhi is older than both Pathan and Mogul. It is, like the Himalayas, an eternal witness of Indian history. It is both Hindu and Moslem in its traditions and memories. It is symbolic of the composite Indian Nation. The decision of the Government of India to remove their seat from Calcutta to Delhi is significant. It means that they do not desire any more to stand aloof from the central currents of Indian life and evolution. It is a silent tribute to the spirit of Indian Nationalism, with which they desire henceforth to more and more intimately identify themselves. It is the first practical step towards working out a *rapprochement* between Indian Nationalism and British Imperialism. As such, the value of this transfer must infinitely outweigh the heaviest expenditure that the building of the new National Capital may involve. In fact, the real motive of the opposition of the Anglo-Indian trader and the British jingo to the Delhi scheme is to be found in this very political significance of it. Any reconciliation or *rapprochement* between the spirit of Indian Nationalism on the one side, and British Imperialism on the other, must naturally be distasteful to the Anglo-Indian trader, who has hitherto been so eager to run the Government of India as his own special concern. He has always called it "our rule." He has oftentimes even forced the hands of the Indian Government to the prejudice of the real interests of the people. He has systematically tried to keep the Government apart from the governed. The new policy of Lord Hardinge, as enunciated in the Despatch of August 1911, of which the Delhi transfer is a most important part, has boldly struck at the very root of Anglo-Indian domination in India. The nationalisation of the Government of India is the objective of this policy. Lord Hardinge has clearly realised it as the only means of perpetuating the British connection with India. Delhi is to be the capital of this new national Government in India. It is to be the seat of the Federal Government of the future United States of India. And when we approach it from the stand-point of the broad and far-seeing statesmanship that has enunciated this new policy, the question of the financial outlay required for the new capital seems too insignificant to deserve any serious notice, except perhaps to prevent any niggardliness in the matter of expenses, from interfering with the beauty and splendour of the seat of the future Government of India.

A Peep into the Future.

Those who are raising these questions have either no perception of the real motive of the Delhi-transfer, or, if they do understand it at all, are in deadly opposition to it. It is not a mere whim of the present Viceroy. Nor did the idea originate in the *contretemps* that arose out of the shameful Kabuli riots in Calcutta, when Sir Edward Baker was our Lieutenant-Governor. The removal of the capital to Delhi is a vital part of the larger policy enunciated in the Despatch of 1911. That policy, as I have repeatedly said, has for its objective the ultimate building up of a United States of India, composed of a number of provincial autonomies. The Government of India will have, in the gradual evolution of this far-reaching policy, to be slowly transformed into a Federal Government, which, in its turn, will have to be thoroughly representative of the different autonomous provinces of the Empire. Provincial Autonomy can never grow under an Imperial Autocracy. Autonomy in the Provincial Administrations will gradually compel the transformation of the Central Government into a thoroughly constitutional and representative state-authority. This evolution will involve a division of the present dual functions of the head of the Government of India. He is now both Viceroy *and* Governor-General. But in the future, the office of the Governor-General will have to be separated from that of the Viceroy. The Governor-General will be the executive head of the Government of India. As such he will be subject to the control of the Imperial Council of India. But the Viceroy will be the King-Emperor's representative, discharging those functions only that belong to the Monarch in a strictly constitutional State. The Governor-General, as well as the Provinial Governors will be something like the Ministers of the Crown in Great Britain, responsible for their acts and policies, to the Viceroy on the one side and to their respective legislative councils on the other, and subject to their authority. With the separation of the present dual office of the head of the Supreme Government in India, we shall most likely always have some member of the Royal Family as our Viceroy. All these are presaged in the Despatch of August 1911 ; and it is in the light of all these that we should consider the question of the Delhi-transfer. And when this is done, it will be seen, that though the enemies of Indian Nationalism may have very good reasons to oppose the Delhi scheme, no Nationalist would be justified in joining this short-sighted and mischievous agitation.

Calcutta : May 1914.

CHAPTER IX.

INDIAN "COUNCIL-REFORMS" AND INDIAN CULTURE.

Council Reforms and Public Sentiment.

It is notorious that Lord Morley's Council "Reforms" aroused very little enthusiasm even among our English-educated countrymen who had for so many years been crying out so loudly and persistently for them. It may have been partly due to the tense political situation in the country at the time these Reforms were first announced and introduced. But though that situation has very considerably changed for the better since Lord Hardinge took up the reins of Government, it cannot be said that the old attitude of indifference of our educated community, at least on the Bengal side, towards these "reformed" Councils has changed in any appreciable degree. On the contrary, there seems to have grown among the more thoughtful classes at any rate, a distinct want of confidence in these imported methods of political progress.

The New Thought and the Old Ideal.

Thirty years ago, we were completely under the spell of the European Illumination. We knew little then of our own ideals and institutions, and had not the capacity, therefore, to judge and weigh the ideals and institutions of Europe that had commenced to overwhelm us. Since then a great wave of social reaction and religious revival has passed over the country. All reactionary movements have an element of unreason in them everywhere. Our own movements of social reaction and religious revival were not free from unreason. These excesses are inevitable in all antithetical and protestant movements. But they wear off in course of time, and the ultimate residuum which these movements leave behind them, takes the course of social evolution up to a position which is distinctly higher and saner than both the reactionary movements themselves and the antecedent movements against which they had started to work. The new thought in India is, therefore, neither inherently revolutionary, like the earlier movements of social or religious or political reforms, nor, in any sense, reactionary, like the subsequent movements of social preservation or religious revival, but is essentially a movement of reconciliation and synthesis. And this new thought is very largely responsible for the present apathy of our educated classes towards these Council-Reforms.

WEIGHED IN THE BALANCE.

Plainly speaking, the more thoughtful section of our people have been losing their old faith in the modern ideals and institutions of Europe. The almost absolute superiority of the European over the Indian ideals and institutions, which was at one time an important article of the creed of the Indian social or political reformer, is being persistently questioned to-day on all sides. We have gradually come to see that Europe has not as yet solved a single one of her numerous outstanding social or political problems by her so-called modern and rational methods. Her freedom is a fancy, her democracy a falsehood, her individualism anti-social, her patriotism anti-humanitarian. Her wealth creates direr poverty than what the world has ever known. Her inventions, while testifying to the superior intellectual powers and equipments of a favoured few, are killing the intellectual and moral life of the many. Her splendid organisations, while calling out the capacity for initiative and leadership in a few, are practically reducing the masses to mere automata. All these are being recognised by the more thoughtful classes even in Europe. They are, perhaps, being still more vividly realised by the more thoughtful classes in this country. And this new knowledge has considerably cooled down the old enthusiasm for following the lead of Europe of large and increasing numbers of our educated countrymen.

The Illusion of "Representative Government."

In fact, even in Europe itself the highest thought and culture of the twentieth century will be bound to gradually demand a more or less radical reconsideration of many ideas and ideals that had been accepted as the truest and the best by the speculations and aspirations of the eighteenth and the nineteenth centuries. And possibly among the very first to be so re-considered will be the shibboleth of Representative Government. In England and America at any rate, Mill's Representative

Government still dominates, it is true, the most advanced political thought of the people. But in England and America, again, the Government is absolutely in the hands of what is called the bourgeoisie in France. It is the educated middle-classes who, belonging neither directly to the aristocracy nor to the people of the country, almost absolutely control and guide the machinery of their Government. At one time this middle-class was practically nowhere in the political life of their nation This system of so-called Representative Government was their special device to wrest, for themselves, in the name of the people, the political power and authority that had lain in the hands of the landed aristocracy of the country. But the masses in England no more govern themselves even to-day than the masses in Russia or Tibet or Timbuktu. Representative Government means, thus, simply a replacement of one small body of rulers by another equally small body who, though ostensibly "returned" by the people or at least by a section of them, are neither of the people nor are really controlled by them.

Those who have any acquaintance with the way that Parliamentary Elections are conducted in Great Britain know what little freedom the voters have in the matter, and what judgment they exercise in the disposition of their votes. At one time votes were almost openly bought and sold. The special laws that regulate and control Parliamentary Elections now, have penalised these ancient practices. But no law can prevent the application of various kinds of "moral" pressure to force the voters to give their votes not to men of their own choice but to somebody else's friend or nominee. The class that owned the nation's land ruled the people at one time, in the name of the King and under cover of the authority of the Crown. The class that own the works and factories rule them now, in the name of Demos and under cover of the authority of the People. But, as before, so even now, the real people are practically nowhere. Thus, this so-called Representative Government upon which the political life and philosophy of the eighteenth and the nineteenth centuries so much prided themselves, is being gradually found out to be a mere clever device of the intellectual middle-classes, to exploit the masses in their own personal or class interest. And there is absolutely nothing in the political thought of the eighteenth or the nineteenth centuries that can hold out any hope for the redress of this new evil of bourgeoisie-rule.

Ninety years ago, great hopes were entertained in England, for instance, of the Reform Bill. That Bill became law. But though it enfranchised the intellectual middle classes, the proletariat were practically left where they had been before. Since then, Parliamentary franchise has extended very considerably; but what is the actual result? The law has given the vote to many people; but the law could not secure to them absolute freedom in the exercise of their franchise. Neither could the law endow them with intelligence to understand the complex political or economic issues that are placed before them by rival candidates, or with a sufficiently keen conscience to do the right even when they have understood it.

Democracy and Industrialism.

No law can, indeed, do it. Mere extension of the franchise will not touch even the outermost fringe of the real problem of modern statecraft. Self-government, in the true sense of the term, will be absolutely unattainable in industrial Europe or America without a complete reconstruction of the present economic structure of western society. Economic slavery and political freedom can never go together. The wage-earning classes all over Europe and America are more or less at the mercy of their employers. Men do not buy and sell the modern labourers as they did the Negro slaves in the plantations of the Southern States of America at one time. But these "free" labourers are really free in one respect only, namely, to starve and die, if they prefer it, to rendering obedience to the wishes of their employers. Otherwise, these modern labourers, grinding their life away with a view to find profits for their employer, are practically as much slaves as the old Negroes were. And so long as this new form of slavery is not entirely abolished, so long true self-government will be absolutely unattained and unattainable by even the most free peoples of Europe.

The Problem of High Living.

Nor is this only an economic problem, which a fair and equitable method of distributing the produce between employer and labourer might be able to solve. We have frightful poverty in India, but as yet not that debasing economic slavery which they have more or less in every western country. And the reason is that, among other things, we have not as yet gone in for that so-called higher standard of living, which Europe and America have accepted as an essential element of civilisation.

This standard of living is really responsible for this new form of economic servitude in Europe and America. Owing to his peculiar climate the European or American labourer wants many things, it is true, which are not required by the Indian working-man. But even after making ample allowances for these, it must be admitted that the European or American working-man can do with much less than what he wants now. And if he could do so, he might easily secure much greater freedom for himself than he is able to enjoy at present. His style of living makes, therefore, for the perpetuation of his present economic slavery as much as the greed of his employer. And it is in view of all this that I think that true self-government will never be attained by the people of Europe or America, unless there is an almost structural change as much in their economic as in their social life and institutions.

EUROPEAN IMITATION AND INDIAN WISDOM.

And the question before us in India is :—are we acting very wisely, in blindly following the lead of Europe in this matter and setting up stupid imitations of political institutions that have not as yet been able to render a very satisfactory account of themselves even in their original home and habit, where they have centuries of experience, experiments, and disciplines at their back ? The usual contention of the Anglo-Indian Bureaucracy that European institutions are not suited to the genius of the Indian people, though always urged in a very offensive way, and without any deep knowledge either of Europe or of India, has, after all, some substratum of truth in it. At one time we strongly resented these statements, because they implied that the Indian was intellectually and morally inferior to the European. We stoutly denied the truth and validity of these contentions, because they suggested our inherent incapacity for self-government. And our resentment was high in proportion as our ignorance of our own past history and traditions in regard to political life and thought was great. Thus it was that because we could not present anything from our own records that could stand comparison with the free political institutions of modern Europe, the statement that these institutions are not suited to our genius and civilisation, hurt our racial pride; and we challenged our opponents to put us to the test and see how we could prove ourselves as capable of working their democratic political institutions as any European people. This, indeed, has been the psychology of all our Congress-politics.

ANCIENT HINDU POLITY.

But the Nationalist agitations of the last few years have changed the entire venue of our present political problem. In the first place, we are gradually coming to understand that the Hindu system of polity was always constitutional, and never despotic. The essence of despotism is that the will of the king is law to his subjects. But the Hindu king was never a law unto himself. Ages before the birth of modern constitutional governments in Europe, the Hindu had worked out a complete separation between the legislative and the executive functions of his Government. His king was, therefore, only the chief magistrate of the country, who had to conduct his kingly office in strict obedience to laws which he himself did not make and which he could neither change nor amend as it suited his wishes or interests. In the constitutional monarchies of Europe, like that of Great Britain, for instance, the king enjoys what is called the right of veto, indicating that in these countries there is not as yet that absolute separation of the executive and legislative functions of the State which is a fundamental test of free political institutions. The Hindu had completely worked up this separation ages before, indicating his superior genius for true constitutional government. Theoretically, the constitution of the Hindu state and society was theocratic no doubt; but not practically. In theory, the Law which governed both the king and his people, was no doubt of divine origin. This Divine Law was the embodiment of the immemorial traditions and customs of the race. But though without any divine sanctions, these traditions and customs form the basis even of the state-constitutions of most of the modern democratic countries of Europe. In fact, the British Monarchy cannot exist for a moment, if absolutely divested of these ancient sanctions. But a fixed body of traditions and customs, even though claiming divine sanctions, cannot meet the changing conditions and growing needs of the historic evolution of any people. New conditions require new arrangements. New evils that arise in course of the advancing life of a people from simpler to more complex stages, demand new prescriptions. And these were provided in the old Hindu society, not by the enactment of new laws, as is done in modern Europe, but by progressive interpretations of the old "Divine Law" itself. And for this progressive interpretation of the Law, the Hindu polity provided a body of councillors of the king, to whom the king had to look up for sanction, whenever the situation in the country required the adoption of any new measures for the preservation or furtherance of the social well-being. In fact, all the paraphernalia of the most advanced form of constitutional government was furnished by ancient Hindu polity for the management of the state-affairs of the Hindu people. Recent researches into ancient Hindu civilisation are bringing these facts out. And in proportion as our knowledge of our own past history and culture is expanding, and we are coming to know how we too had a very superior political philosophy and had developed a very advanced state-constitution, the old eagerness to prove our capacity for self-government by submitting ourselves to be tested by the standards of Europe, through the actual introduction and working of modern European institutions in our country, is gradually waning. And with the birth of a new national self-consciousness we have gradually been gathering sufficient courage even to question the absolute superiority of European institutions over anything that we ourselves had in the past or what we may by and by evolve at present in consonance with our special genius and culture for meeting our present requirements. We are, therefore, no longer afraid of recognising and even openly admitting, any element of truth or reason that may exist in the indictments of our European critics and opponents.

A Straightforward Admission.

We are, thus, no longer afraid of admitting that the institutions of so-called self-government as they have been developed in Europe may not be entirely suited to the special genius and culture of our people. And we feel absolutely no shame in making the confession because it does in no way prove our incapacity for true self-government. On the contrary we have an idea that Europe herself is far less endowed with the moral and mental qualities that fit any nation for real self-government than ourselves. The whole philosophy of what is called Representative Government in Europe is essentially individualistic and inherently anti-social. It has been so far worked up on the assumption that there is an inherent antagonism between the interests of one individual and another as well as between those of the different classes of the community; and Representative Government is the best device that Europe has so far been able to think out for the safeguarding of these separate individualistic and sectional interests against the attacks or encroachments of their respective rivals and competitors. We see it proved every day in every Representative Assembly in Europe, which are only so many arenas for the different classes of the country to fight out the interminable battles of their class-interests. The sense of the organic unity of the nation is lost everywhere in the clang and clash of these class-wars; and it only comes occasionally to the surface when the nation goes to war with another nation. And even then this patriotic outburst is only a poor particularistic sentiment, unrelated to the ideal of Universal Humanity. And this being the true character of the Representative Institutions that Europe has been able so far to develop, what reason is there for us to hang down our heads in shame and humiliation if we are told that these are not suited to our genius and character, or if we ourselves openly confess it ?

India and the Modern Ideal.

In fact, it is a rudimentary principle of Indian Nationalism that European institutions should not be bodily imposed upon us by the authority of the British Government in the country. For it holds that all such superimpositions, however kindly meant, are more likely to hinder than help the real progress of our people towards the highest modern ideal. This modern ideal is no more the special possession of Europe than it is of India. It is the result of various forces that are more or less operative as much in India as in Europe or America. It is the common heritage of all the civilised peoples of our time. The West is no nearer to the realisation of it than the East. And ultimately this ideal will be bound to realise itself in diverse forms, through diverse methods, in the different countries of the world. Europe has been seeking to realise this ideal in her own way, following her own special genius, along the course of her special historic evolution. India, with a different genius and character, a different course of past historic evolution, will, if left to herself, develop her own lines of progress towards the same common ideal. These are very commonplace sociological speculations. Unfortunately, however, Europe has not yet been trained to study the course of social evolution in the light of any general philosophy of human nature. Had Europe done so we would have much greater appreciation of other world-cultures and the social and political institutions of other peoples than what we see at present. Even our own English-educated classes have but very feeble appreciation of these facts. If they had it there would have been a more cautious and critical attitude towards many of the "reforms" that are being introduced by the Government.

It is for want of this cautious and critical spirit that our English-educated classes so enthusiastically welcomed Lord Ripon's scheme of Local Self-Government as an inestimable boon. Lord Ripon, no doubt, meant well. But his Lordship had no appreciation of the peculiarities of our national genius and history. His Lordship practically ignored the fact that not only had we a very superior form of self-government in our ancient village-communities, but that we had, even thirty years ago, in many parts of the country, an actual measure of communal freedom in regard to all such matters as did not fall within the purview of the laws and regulations of the British Government in the country. Our Panchayets, though deprived of their old quasi-political powers, were yet, even in Lord Ripon's time, a powerful instrument and vehicle of the corporate life of our villages and still ruled the life of the people to a very large extent. In many places these were the general judicial authority in the small village-communities which quietly helped the settlement of all petty disputes in a simple way without the costly intervention of modern lawyers and law courts. Lord Ripon's scheme practically ignored all these facts and imposed a new and alien form of municipal government which, though enthusiastically received by the English-educated classes for whose special benefit it was evidently created, was neither understood nor appreciated by the masses. The masses, in fact, had neither part nor lot in this new "Vakil-Raj" or lawyer-rule that Lord Ripon's scheme practically sought to set up in the country.

INDIAN SELF-GOVERNMENT AND EUROPEAN INSTITUTIONS.

And the experience of the last thirty years of our so-called municipal self-government completely proves how difficult, if not utterly impossible, it is to cultivate the true spirit of self-government in our country through imported foreign institutions and alien methods. Though municipal commissioners are elected in most places by the rate-payers themselves, there is really no self-government in any of our municipalities. The primary object of the franchise, whether municipal or parliamentary, is to provide an effective check upon the tendency of those who are entrusted with the duty of carrying on the administration of the town or of the State, to run the business in their own private or class interest. This check has not as yet become effective even in democratic countries like America or England, which have had a long training in the working of these so-called popular institutions. And it goes without saying that in our elected municipalities the rate-payers have not only failed so far to realise this primary end of the municipal franchise, but they have—the educated and the uneducated alike—no appreciation even of this primary end. It is not at all surprising, therefore, that our so-called municipal self-government has been, so far, a dead failure. And even where, as in some of our presidency towns, it has been somewhat of a success, it has not been of much use as an institution for the political education of the masses, which it was reasonably expected to be. Generally speaking I think it may be very safely said that in most places this municipal franchise is being sedulously exploited by a few English-educated men in their own personal and private interests. The same remark holds good with regard to our District and Local Boards also. A careful scrutiny of the records of these Boards would show in many cases, I am afraid, how the funds of these bodies are frequently utilised to increase the comforts and conveniences of the prominent members or to improve their private property. And the failure of these new institutions is due to the fact that they did not grow naturally from within the people themselves, but were imposed upon them from without. This failure does not prove our incapacity for self-government, but only the unsuitability of these to our national genius and traditions. For it is well-known that in our old village life we had at one time a real measure of self-government even without any voting register or polling booth. The spirit of centralisation that has dominated the British Administration in India almost from its very commencement has killed these old national institutions. The new institutions of local self-government have not been able to revive, so far, the old corporate life of our villages. They never will. The Government is gradually coming to see it; and it is, therefore, trying to reconstruct our old village-panchayets. But our rulers do not seem to realise it, however, that if the old village life and institutions are to be revived at all, the work must be left entirely to the people themselves. Official intervention in any shape or form would court the same failure here again, as has overcome the so-called schemes of self-government in our Municipalities and District and Local Boards.

The New "Reforms" Built on Old Failures.

The new and enlarged Legislative Councils in the various Indian Provinces are mainly built upon the Municipalities and Local and District Boards. There was really no other foundations on which these could be built. This fact may justify the new builders, but cannot impart to their structure any greater reality or strength than what those older bodies have had. The real people of the country are practically nowhere in the Municipalities, Local or District Boards: they are equally nowhere, therefore, in the new and enlarged organs of self-government in their country. The Municipalities, Local and District Boards have hitherto been practically either official bodies or bourgeoisie organisations. They have been run, in many places, by the local officials after their own mind. Where the non-official element has been strong, these have been run by the English-educated middle-class not merely after their own mind, but frequently even in their own personal or class interests. It is no use shutting our eyes to these facts. And as these Municipalities, Local and District Boards constitute, under the present regulations, the largest electorates of the so-called "Reformed Councils," there is no reason to hope that these will not be run in the same way, namely, to protect and further the interests of the English-educated middle classes, more than to advance real popular freedom or safeguard the interests of the masses of the country. In the early stages of the struggle between the prerogatives of the Crown on the one side and the rights of the people on the other, the educated classes even in Europe made common cause with the uneducated masses and spoke and acted in their name. This way lay their only chance of success. We, too, have been doing this all these years. In all our past political agitations, we have also been speaking and acting for the masses. And we have generally been honest in this. Perhaps, there are many people among our English-educated classes who still sincerely believe that they represent the interests of their uneducated countrymen. But, as elsewhere, so here among us also, what is now an honest belief will gradually become a meaningless, if not a dishonest, cant. For, in proportion as the powers of government are gradually transferred from the present foreign bureaucracy to an Indian bourgeoisie, in that proportion will develop an antagonism between the interests of this new ruling class on the one hand and those of the general masses of the country on the other. It is the common experience of every democratic country in the West. And human nature being more or less the same all the world over, the same social, economic, and political conditions will be bound to produce, not exactly perhaps the same, but undoubtedly similar results everywhere.

The Evil of the "Reforms."

In fact these conditions will very likely produce much worse evils in India than they have done in England or America. In Europe, these so-called representative institutions have grown slowly, following the general course of the historic evolution of the European peoples. And where any social or political institutions grow in this natural way, they develop not only the needful checks and counter-checks for securing all the good that may be in them, while eliminating, as far as possible, the evils that are inevitably bound up with the good in every human institution; but, what is far more important, the social organism learns at the same time those subtle tricks of nature which every organism practices for purposes of self-preservation. When, however, any social or political institutions are imposed upon a people artificially, from without, these natural advantages are lost. And consequently the evil side of these grow here more vigorously than their good side. So there is much greater chance of an unhealthy middle-class rule growing here than there was in England, for instance. Because, in the first place, the struggle between the Crown and the People was both much keener and more prolonged in England than the similar struggle between the present Bureaucracy and the People of India is ever likely to be. In fact, the British Bureaucracy here, representing the British bourgeoisie, have already been willing to share the authority of the Government in India with chosen representatives of the English-educated Indian bourgeoisie. This is the declared policy of Lord Morley, the author of the "Reformed" Indian Councils. And the increasing participation of the

Indian bourgeoisie in the rights and emoluments of the present rule, will be bound to separate the interests of this class from the general economic and political interests of the uneducated masses. These Council "Reforms" make, therefore, not for the consolidation and strengthening of our new national life, but distinctly for the creation of new class-interests and communal antagonisms, calculated to weaken it.

The Test of These "Reforms."

The true test of all social or political institutions is not material but moral. The question, therefore, in regard to these "Reformed Councils" is, do they make for a larger manhood than what we have in the country? Do they make for the expansion of the interests of life? Or are they narrowing them? Do they make for the subordination of personal and private interests to the larger interests of the nation? Do they feed our enthusiasm for the public good, or do they simply help to give us a field for the satisfaction of our personal vanity? These are moot questions here. And judged by these questions, these new "reforms" stand self-condemned. The records of the latest Council Elections prove this very conclusively.

For, in almost every case it has been a mean and degrading personal contest. In Dacca, for instance, there was a fight between Babu Ananda Chandra Ray and Babu Ambica Charan Majumdar. Now, can anybody suggest any semblance of a decent reason, why these two gentlemen, each very estimable in his own way, both prominent Congress-men, who had never before been known to differ in their politics, fought this election against each other? Is it conceivable that either of these gentlemen could urge against the other anything except that he is either less able or less experienced or less honest than himself. In the absence of any conflict of political opinions or difference of political programmes between them, the contest was naturally a personal and mean one, in which both parties must have fought for purely personal and private ends and on purely personal grounds. It is not their fault, but their misfortune. In England, these two gentlemen would have likely belonged to opposite political parties, and might have fought each other upon the less degrading grounds of public policy and party programme. But there are only two political schools among those who would care to go in for seats on the "Reformed Councils" in India. One is the official school and the other, their rival, the Congress school. The officials are precluded by the Regulations from taking part in these elections. Consequently, all the fight is practically between one Congress-man and another. And the fact that Congress-men cannot select the best men for all the non-official seats from among their own leaders, but that these latter should be left to scramble for these in competition with one another, shows the nature of the political education and the type of public character that the agitations of the last quarter of a century have produced in the country.

As in Dacca, so even in Calcutta also, the same shameful story was repeated. Here also Congress-leaders fought with one another. There were about half a dozen Congress-men, including Babu Surendra Nath Banerjee, fighting for the Presidency-Division Municipal seats. There was just a chance of Babu Surendra Nath's not getting in. And what a humiliation to him, and what a scandal in our public life it would have been if this had happened! Why could not the Calcutta politicians bring the pressure of their own influence to bear upon the various candidates, and thus prevent the chance of such a scandal? In the Calcutta University, it is absolutely inconceivable upon what public grounds Dr. Deva Prasad Sarvadhicaree's seat was contested at all. Dr. Sarvadhicaree had done his work well both in the last Council and in the University. With the exception of Sir Gurudas Banerjee there is, perhaps, no other prominent member of the University who is in wider and closer touch with the educated classes in the city, if not in the Province, than Dr. Sarvadhicaree. And the fact that even such a man's seat was contested by people who have never been known to differ from his politics, exposes the character of these Council-Elections most clearly.

Super-Imposed "Reforms."

The fact of the matter really is that these evils will be bound to come in the wake of reforms that do not grow from within the life of a people but are super-imposed on them from without. The Indian Legislative Councils have, from the very beginning, been really such super-impositions. They did not grow out of any real and vital need of the people. When a people feel any vital need for any institutions, that need itself creates the organs that are best calculated to meet it, and these have then, necessarily, an organic relation to their general life and activities. They are rooted in the past of that people and are an expansion and evolution of some of their existing organs and institutions. The Indian Legislative Councils did not grow this wise. They were first instituted, not because the people wanted them or felt any need for them, but because the new British Administration found it both difficult and dangerous to govern an alien people, of whom they knew practically nothing, without the help and guidance of their "natural" leaders. When these Councils were subsequently reconstituted upon a partially elective basis by Lord Cross's Indian Councils Act, it was done, again, not to meet any vital need of the people, but to stop the clamour of the English-educated classes, who were kicking up a dangerous agitation against the present bureaucratic methods of government and were making the rulers of the country slightly nervous by the fervour of their denunciations and the growing strength of their political organisations. Lord Cross's "reforms" did achieve their object in a very large measure; for they did take the wind out of the sails of the Congress-agitation to a very perceptible extent and diverted the energies of the Congress-leaders from the old agitations against the Government to the new election-contests against one another. The Congress became, thus, as a direct result of Lord Cross's reforms, a "harmless" thing henceforth. When, however, the new Swadeshi agitation came into being, following in the wake of the Partition of Bengal, and the Government once more stood face to face with a tremendous popular upheaval, the like of which had never before been seen in the history of British India, a fresh need was felt by the authorities for a further reconstitution of the Indian Legislative Councils. This is the real genesis of Lord Morley's "Reforms." The people did not want them. They were asked for by a few representatives of the British-created bourgeoisie who scarcely live or move with or among the people and have hardly anything in common with them except their colour or their caste. And the Government gladly granted their prayers, with the professed object of "rallying" the so-called "Moderates" about them. It will thus be seen that from the very beginning our Legislative Councils have been only so many super-impositions on us. They have not grown out of the natural expansion of our own civic or political life, as they did in Europe. It is only inevitable, therefore, that these "reforms" should bring in their train new political and moral evils for which our social organism has not, as yet, invented or developed any remedy.

Under normal conditions, all institutions are the natural and legitimate embodiment of the complex life and ideals of a people. Political institutions are the natural expression and embodiment of a people's political life. The idea comes always with its expression. Immediately the life-force is quickened within, it is provided, by its own inner needs, with the outer organs and instruments of the organism's own self-realisation. With us, however, these political institutions have been set up before the birth of real political life. Or more accurately speaking, whatever political thought and life may have already commenced to quicken in the country, did not create these alien institutions and stands practically outside them. The institutions are larger and more complex than the real political life and thought of the people. The organisation is heavier than what the organism actually needs or can bear. This is the root of the evil. But however much we may feel their evil, we cannot do away, or even perhaps absolutely do without, these Councils now. They are parts of the Administration of the country. And they will have to be suffered even where they may not be actively supported.

The Only Remedy: Organisation of the Nationalist Party.

But since we cannot stop or alter these Councils, we must devise adequate means for minimising their evils and increasing whatever possibilities of good there may be in them. And the only way to do it is to strengthen and organise the Nationalist Party, which, with its legitimate ideal of self-help and self-reliance for the people and its policy of *laissez faire* so far as the Government is concerned, will at least be able to set up a powerful rival Party to that of the Congress in our present political life. Such a Party will largely remove the mean and demoralising personal emphasis from the Council Elections, and impart even to the debates in the Councils themselves a note of reality which they can scarcely have under existing conditions. The Indian Councils are built upon the model of the British Parliament, to some very slight extent. And the party-system is the very soul of the parliamentary institutions of Europe. Left to ourselves, we might have developed new institutions of popular self-government, in our own way. We may yet do so, by and by. But in the meantime, we cannot allow the existing Legislative Councils to grow in their own way, importing unknown evils into our country, and manufacturing a body of middle-class legislators, who, as the same class have done elsewhere, will exploit the Administration in their own interest. It is, therefore, the distinct duty, I think, of the Nationalists in the country, to actively take the field against these new and dangerous forces, and contribute their thoughts and labours to the work of the Administration. They cannot, without committing political suicide, stick to their old policy of aloofness from the Government any longer.

As on the one hand, we must throw ourselves into current political activities, taking our rightful place and part in the new Councils, so on the other hand, we must organise our forces and apply ourselves to the more real and useful work of training the rising generations of the country in the true Nationalist ideals, inculcating the duty of self-abnegation and self-restraint, in the interest of the common life of the nation. The immediate work before us is more moral and intellectual than political. It is more economic than administrative. And for this work, the decadent life of our villages must first of all be revived and reorganised. The new generation should, therefore, be encouraged in every possible way to keep to their own villages and lead and organise the economic and social life of their people. If we are able to do this, then political progress will come naturally of itself. But if we neglect to do this betimes, or fail in the attempt, no amount of political struggles or agitations will help to secure for our nation its rightful place in the coming Federation of the World.

CALCUTTA: *February*, 1913.

CHAPTER X.

LORD MORLEY'S "REFORMS."

THE INDIAN COUNCILS AND THE INDIAN PROBLEM.

THERE can be no more unhealthy condition in the political and administrative life of a people than that its Executive Government should always stand in an attitude of self-defence. Yet unfortunately, all our borrowed methods of political agitations and activities have actually brought this about among us. The constitution of the Government of India is essentially autocratic. It is not controlled, except indirectly, by the wishes and opinions of the governed. The methods of political agitation suited to a democratic country, where the Executive Government depend for their life and authority upon the suffrages of the people, cannot, therefore, apply to political agitation here. In England those who are in the Opposition to-day are called upon to change places with the Government to-morrow. Their one objective is, therefore, to lower their political rivals in the estimation of the people and create a large volume of sentiment against them in the country and thus drive them from office and step into their places. And the consciousness that some day, whether in the immediate or the distant future, they will have to face the same problems themselves, before which their rivals may be floundering to-day, exercises a secret sobering influence upon their inner ideas and attitudes. However acrimonious or uncompromising their criticism of the Government may be, the Opposition in the British House of Commons always acts with the Government in all matters of really vital concern. "Government by consent" —has long been the fact, whatever may have been the appearances of British party-warfare. In India none of our popular leaders have, under the present constitution, any chance of changing places with the Executive officers of the Government, without ceasing to belong to the popular party. They know that they will never be called upon to practically tackle the complex problems of the administration. They cannot possibly be inspired, therefore, with any real sense of responsibility. It is inevitable, under these circumstances, that their criticism of the executive government should be frequently uninformed and almost uniformly unsympathetic. Their presence in the council chamber and their comments on the various measures put up before them for discussion, are, therefore, a source of more or less annoyance and irritation to those who have to carry on the actual administration of the country. They cannot control but can only criticise, they cannot help but can only hinder— the real work of government. They cannot even offer any sound and helpful advice to the executive government. The Government do not take these councillors fully into their confidence. They are not placed in full possession of the informations in regard to any subject, upon which particular executive policies and actions are based. And in the absence of the actual data upon which the executive government proceeds in regard to any matter, these councillors cannot possibly offer any helpful advice to the responsible rulers of the country. They serve only as feelers of the trends of the ideas and sentiments of the more clamorous section of the subject populations. They are not in touch even with the deeper currents of their own national life. The slow and silent masses are as much strangers to our popular political leaders as they are to the members of the alien Bureaucracy which rule their civic and economic destiny. It is not at all strange, therefore, that Lord Morley's Reforms have absolutely failed to achieve even the petty ends for which they were introduced.

In fact, both Lord Minto and Lord Morley took a most superficial view of the situation that faced them. They were misled by those from whom they derived all their information regarding the nature of the unrest they were called upon to tackle. The psychology of this unrest was never properly studied or understood either by the Anglo-Indian publicist or by the British officials in India. They mistook it for a more aggravated form of the same political discontent that had hitherto been voiced by the Indian National Congress. The Congress agitation was practically killed by Lord Cross's Indian Councils Act. The new unrest, they thought, would also be similarly laid by a further expansion of these Legislative Councils which would "rally the Moderates" around the executive government. They did not see that it was the failure of the previous "reforms" introduced by Lord Cross, to satisfy the real political aspirations of the articulate classes in the country, which was mainly responsible for this new ferment, and it was not likely to be set at rest by a fresh and enlarged dole of the same "reforms." What was really wanted was not a reform and expansion of the Legislative Councils, but a reconstitution of the Executive Administration. The new patriotism craved really for neither reform nor reconstitution, but rather only for a little more freedom of self-expression and self-reliant civic activities. This was the inner meaning of the Boycott Movement and the organisation of the so-called National Volunteers. If the Government had tolerated the one, and allied itself with the other, all the later developments of the swadeshi agitation might have been materially modified, if not altogether avoided. An intelligent despotism would have placed itself cleverly at the head of a popular upheaval like this, and thus not only make it harmless, but perhaps turn it to its own use. Instead of this, the Minto-Government commenced to repress the only party which counted, and to conciliate that which had practically no hold upon the actual forces that had created this unrest. The "Moderates" have been "rallied," but the "revolutionaries" are almost as active as ever. These revolutionaries actually helped the Moderates to the enlarged privileges which the "Reforms" bestowed on them. And these very Moderates now, by keeping up a constant stream of unfriendly and unwise criticism of executive action and policy, are, in their turn, materially, though unconsciously, contributing to the strength of the revolutionary party. For, the failure of every Resolution brought before the Councils by the popular leaders, and the rejection of every amendment proposed by them in any Bill under the consideration of the legislatures, inevitably strengthen the conviction of the impossibility of working out any reasonable reconciliation between popular rights and the British connection with this country. Lord Morley's "Reforms" have, thus, only increased the difficulties of an already difficult situation.

The Right Nationalist Policy under present conditions.

But these "reforms"—however trumpery—are now settled facts. The history of the last seven or eight years cannot be re-written to-day. We must take things as they are, and devise the most effective means of counteracting the evils that these "reforms" are breeding. There was a time when the Nationalists avoided all associations with the Government. But there is no room for absolutism of any kind in politics and state-craft. Policies are dictated by the actualities of the political or administrative conditions. They are not the creation of abstract thinking or ratiocination. And when, therefore, the actualities of any situation commence to change, policies also must amend themselves to suit these changed and changing conditions of the life and problems of the people. The aloofness that was fully justified in 1905 or 1906 or 1907 or even 1908 and 1909, is not justified in 1913 or 1914. The problem before us in 1904-5 was how to awaken a real self-consciousness in the inert masses of the country; how to quicken in them a sense of their own strength, and a vision of their true destiny. The strange hypnotic spell under which the people lived had to be broken; the māyā had to be dispelled. And absolute dis-attachment was the only way to do this. The Nationalist rule of aloofness from all sorts of official associations and activities, except where the contrary was made positively binding upon us by law—was reasonable and justified then. It is no longer so now.

NATIONALISM *vs.* REVOLUTIONARY PATRIOTISM.

Revolutionary partriotism is the greatest danger before Indian Nationalism to-day. It is more dangerous to the true Nationalist cause in India than even Bureaucratic absolutism. The real danger to Indian Nationalism will come now, not so much from the British suzerainty as from the possibilities of Mongolian irruption on the one side, and Pan-Islamic intrigues on the other. British Imperialism will be forced, in the face of these fearful possibilities, to come to terms with Indian Nationalism, in its own interest. But there is absolutely no basis or chance of any such compromise between India and China or Indian Nationalism and the so-called "Extra-territorial Patriotism" of the Young Moslem schools both inside and out of India. It was never more true than it is to-day, that India and Great Britain must stand or fall together. Indian Nationalists must clearly realise this truth. They must realise, in the first place, what the continuance of the present bitter conflict must mean to their own future; and second, what the absolute severance of the British connection will spell for them, not only in the immediate but even in the distant future, as long as the Chinese menace and the Pan-Islamic danger have not completely passed away. These are common sources of possible dangers to the British Empire in India also. India must build a strong National Navy before she can hope to provide effectively against the Chinese menace. She must have a powerful National Army to provide adequately against the Pan-Islamic danger. And how is she going to have these? That is a most fundamental question before those who are dreaming of absolute and isolated independence as the ultimate Nationalist Ideal in India. Navies do not grow overnight, and armies are not organised and trained in a day. And should, by any chance, the British connection be forcibly severed in these circumstances, before we have the reign of universal peace in the world, neither China nor Pan-Islam will impose a self-denying ordinance upon themselves to allow India to first set her house in order, and then to organise these essential means of self-defence. These are vital considerations before every Nationalist in India; and they force the necessity of a reasonable compromise with the British Empire, upon us all. The same necessity is equally forced upon British Imperialism also to come to an early and rational compromise with the Nationalist forces in India. No Government, however powerful, can ever hope to defend itself successfully against any powerful outside enemy, unless it has the whole-hearted support of its own populations. It is absolutely impossible for a Government like that of India, whose authority extends over a wide continent peopled by a teeming alien population. To be able to successfully meet either China or Pan-Islam upon its eastern or western frontiers, the Government of India must win the absolute and whole-hearted and active support of the Indian populations. And there is only one way by which this can be done. The Government of India must be completely nationalised for this purpose, without severing the British connection. A reasonable compromise between Indian Nationalism and British Imperialism is, therefore, as much of an imperious necessity for Great Britain as it is for us. Common dangers and common interests, therefore, demand that both parties should apply themselves to the work of gradually modifying their respective claims and objectives, with a view to a friendly settlement and reconciliation of the issues between them. The earlier Nationalist antithesis, moved by the ideal of sovereign and isolated independence for India, must be gradually worked up to a reasonable synthesis, such as will reconcile the fundamental demands of Indian Nationalism with the maintenance of the British connection.

Evolution of Real National Government.

Nationalism is not a negative concept. The removal of all outside restraint or authority is, undoubtedly, an absolute condition of it ; but it is only a *condition* and not the thing itself. In the realm of politics, nationalism demands that the right of the *people* must be fully recognised and established, in the control and direction of their own state-organisation and state-management. In plain language, it wants that the *people* should frame their own laws, appoint their own officers for the execution of these laws, assess their own taxes and control the disposal of these taxes themselves. This is the utmost limit of the political demands of true Nationalism. At present, these various functions of our State are not discharged by the people, but by a foreign Bureaucracy. Nationalism demands that these shall be transferred from this Bureaucracy to the people themselves. And the Indian Nationalist should bear it in mind that the present Bureaucracy may be deprived of their powers and prerogatives and yet the real functions of the State may not come back to the *people* themselves. In place of a White Bureaucracy we may have a Brown one; in place of a White and foreign ruling class we may have a Brown and native ruling class; and this would not advance us any nearer to the true and real Nationalist Ideal than we are at present. And yet the entire trends of all our recent reforms, whether in the matter of the larger employment of educated Indians in the higher civil services or in that of the expansion of our legislative councils upon a so-called representative and elective basis, have been towards creating an Indian class-rule in the country, after the manner of England, to supplant the rule of the British bureaucrats. Representative Government—in which early nineteenth century thought in Europe believed to have at last discovered a *panacea* for all political evils, and an ideally perfect scheme of Government which reconciled individual freedom with the collective right and authority of the State to which the individuals belong—has been weighed in the balance, in the course of the last hundred years, and is being found wanting now. Neither in Great Britain nor anywhere else in Europe, except perhaps in the small Republic of Switzerland, do the people really govern themselves. The so-called Representative Government, in which eighteenth century democracy in Europe seemed to have found its highest ideal of a perfect state-organisation, has developed small and powerful oligarchies. Political evolution in Europe has, therefore, commenced, not openly as yet, but secretly and subtly, to change its old course. And Federalism is the new Idea. In the life-time of the present generation, the United Kingdom of Great Britain and Ireland will evolve into a Federation of at least four and possibly five small States, each with a local Parliament and an Executive subject to the control of that Parliament, and all of these will be combined for the management of all inter-state and foreign affairs in a Federal or Imperial Council with an Imperial Executive of its own. Nor will this new course of evolution be likely to stop here. Even England, Scotland, or Wales, or Ireland—whether it be preserved as a unit or be split up into two parts—will be found too large and unwieldy for real popular self-government ; and it is quite possible that the different counties, each having its own traditions and peculiarities, its county-life and county-pride, will gradually demand, and have, local home-rule ; and the United Kingdom will gradually become something like a second Switzerland, where alone there is at present anything like real, popular self-rule. In short, it seems not at all unlikely that history will have gradually to work itself back, to realise this democratic ideal of perfect and absolute self-rule, to the old system of so-called Aryan self-government, through self-contained and self-administered small, and more or less homogeneous, village communities. The old village communities were isolated units, without any wide outlook or outside concern. The new village communities will be free from these limitations. They will not be isolated units, but members of a large federation ; and they will have a universal outlook and will be moved by large and lofty ends, thereby relating the freedom of their own life with the universal federation of the world. This is clearly the trend of universal history and evolution in our time. The revived village-communities or county-parliaments, will be infinitely better organised and more vitally and organically related to the central and imperial governments, and will consciously and openly participate in the common duties and advantages of the federal commonwealth to which they will belong, than what the old communities had, perhaps, ever been.

Building From Below.

In India we have not as yet completely forged the chains that just now bind and clog the movement of European politics towards this inevitable solution of the complex political problems of our time. Modern industrialism with the inevitable growth of cities and the consequent decadence of the much simpler, more compact and infinitely more healthy, life of the villages, has not, as yet, possessed both our body and soul. Our old village life, though already considerably disorganised and tending towards decay, has yet, if not the actualities, at least the traditions of our ancient village autonomies. And though certainly difficult, it will not be altogether impossible to revive these ancient autonomies, with such alterations and amendments, both of organs and functions, as our new socio-political environments may imperatively demand. This is our first and immediate duty. And here we must ask the Government to give us the freest possible scope of self-movement and self-organisation. The Government have, since some time past, recognised the need of organising our village administrations. But they have been doing it for mere administrative purposes. The village was hitherto much too far away from the head of the District Administration, and the new move has been directed to bring it in closer touch with it. The ideal is greater centralisation. The object is to increase the hold of the executive authority upon the minutest details of the life of the people. The village panchāyets and the village chowkidārs are meant to be the eyes and ears of the District Magistrate, his attenæ, so to say, by means of which he may be able to keep himself thoroughly in touch with whatever ideas or activities may move and guide the village populations, and through which, he may, if necessary, pounce upon any person or movement that, in his opinion, may not be absolutely consistent with his own absolute authority and prestige in the District. The way that our village administrations are being sought to be revived makes, therefore, really not for ultimate national autonomy, but on the contrary, only for stricter bureaucratic control. The policy is mischievous. The idea is wrong at its very root and inception, and by provoking perpetual conflicts, instead of offering means of real reconciliation and amicable compromise, between the authority of the Executive Government and the legitimate aspirations of the people, it will be bound only to needlessly add to the complexities of the problems before them. Provincial Autonomy must be built upon autonomous village and district administrations, even as National Autonomy must be built, in a continent like India, upon Provincial Autonomies. If real self-rule is at all to be attained by us, we shall have to build up the structure from below. Its plinth and foundations must be laid in our village communities. The village must be re-organised as the unit of our Provincial Autonomies. And the system must be absolutely federal. The District Administrations must be a federation of autonomous village communities, and the Provincial Government must be a federation of autonomous District Administrations. This is the line of evolution that Administrative reform or reconstitution must take. Mere "decentralisation" will not do. "Decentralisation," as popularly understood by the Indian Bureaucracy, is the transference of a part of the power and authority of the bigger Bureaucrats to the smaller ones. The Lieutenant-Governors or the Governors-in-Council to be relieved of a part of their powers and responsibilities, which should be transferred to the Divisional Commissioners. The Divisional Commissioners to be similarly relieved, in their own turn, of a part of their powers and responsibilities, which should be made over to the District Executive, and the latter to be similarly relieved of part of their work, which should be entrusted to the Sub-Divisional Officers. This decentralisation does not mean, therefore, the loosening of the hold of the Bureaucracy upon the people, but rather, on the contrary, only a tightening of the bonds that bind them. The growth and expansion of real popular freedom and the consequent development of a nation's highest manhood come not through more and closer government, but through lesser and looser government. The demand for "decentralisation" for the Indian Administration, means, really, not greater but lesser freedom of movement and initiative for the people. The leaders of political thought and life in the country should, therefore, instead of welcoming, stoutly oppose all these schemes of so-called decentralisation. Not even the bribe of Advisory District Councils should secure their support for these schemes.

CALCUTTA: *April*, 1914.

CHAPTER XI.

THE EXECUTIVE GOVERNMENT OF INDIA.

The Viceregal Cabinet and the Civil Service.

Recent events have created a somewhat widespread impression in the educated Indian community that things are being done in the name and under the authority of the Government of India which have not had the fullest approval of the head of that Government, and it has raised the very important question whether the time has not come for a thorough reform and reconstitution of the Executive Council of the Viceroy. This Council is very largely dominated by the Indian Civil Service. It is a Cabinet which is almost entirely composed of the representatives of the permanent officials of the country who have risen to their high position, by slow degrees, following the regular course of seniority and promotion, from the lowest rungs of the official ladder. Long and extensive official training and experience have their undoubted value. They familiarise a man with the details of administrative work, and are of immense help in the direction and control of the huge and complex machinery of the Government. If the chief function of the Governor-General's Council were simply to control and manage the routine work of the Administration, nothing could serve this purpose better than the appointment of experienced officials to this Council. But the direction and control of the machinery of Government is, or ought to be, the least important part of the duty of the Executive Council of the Viceroy. Its chief function is to initiate policy, to formulate the principles which must govern the State, and to adopt such changes in the machinery and working of the Government as the evolving conditions of the country must from time to time call for. And long official training instead of being a help is inevitably a very serious hindrance to this work. The hardened habits of thought and work of the crystallised official make him naturally averse to changes. He does not understand the new conditions about him. He cannot, except in very exceptional circumstances, bring a fresh mind to the consideration of the complex problems before him. He has all his life viewed these problems from a particular stand-point. He has always put a certain interpretation upon the growing changes in the country, and has got, therefore, a fixed opinion about them. He has been a party to the conflicts through which these changes have gradually evolved. His views of the problems of the country have been tinged by passion and vitiated by prejudices and prepossessions. And these are not the highest qualifications of statesmanship. These are not the kind of moral and intellectual equipment necessary for the right study of far-reaching national problems. They are not helpful to that broad sympathy and far-seeing imagination which are so essential to a correct understanding of new social or political forces. The greatest asset of the trained and experienced official instead of being a help is necessarily a serious hindrance, therefore, to the work of a body whose chief function is to initiate progressive policies and principles of Government to suit the changing economic condition and political or social outlook of the people subject to its rule. These facts have long been recognised in all the progressive countries in the West. Permanent officials have, thus, practically no place in the British Cabinet. While the machinery of Government is worked there, as here in India, by a body of permanent officials ; the policy of the State is really initiated and controlled by people who never had, in all their life, to do anything with all this routine work. The British Cabinet is composed of men who, until their acceptance of office, had oftentimes no knowledge of the detailed working of the different departments of Government, but whose qualifications to their high office are their general culture, their political insight, their close acquaintance with the running currents of public thought and life in their country and their hold on certain important and powerful sections of their community. And this is how the progressive character of the Government is maintained in the British Isles and all revolutionary conflicts are avoided.

The Reconstitution of the Viceroy's Council.

And the time has come in India also, to reform and reconstitute the Executive Council of the Viceroy, with a view to give to the Government of India a progressive character, and thus minimise, if not altogether remove, the troubles and dangers of revolutionary unrest in the country. All revolutions owe their origin to the demand for changes in social, economic, religious or political institutions in a country, necessitated by the changed social, economic, religious or political outlook, ideal and condition of the people, on the one side; and the persistent opposition to these changes on the part of those having vested interests in the existing social, economic or religious or political order, on the other. And the function of true statesmanship is to initiate such lines of social, economic, religious or political evolution as will minimise the acuteness of this conflict and reconcile with one another the truest and the highest aims and ideals of both the contending forces. This is how revolutions are avoided. This is the only way to reconcile progress with order, to ensure the advance of society without violently breaking away from its own past. But to follow this "middle path," the personnel of a Church or Government must be men who, more or less untrammelled by any traditions or prepossessions, have yet a wide knowledge of affairs, a close acquaintance with the principles of general historic evolution, and an intimate insight into human nature, and, in our day, they must be men who are trained to study large and complex social or political movements in the light of common human psychology. I mean no offence to that capable body of officials who have built up the British Empire in India and who are, according to their light, still running the machinery of our Government with marked efficiency, when I say that they can lay absolutely no claim to these essential qualifications of the true statesman. In the earlier days of the British Empire in India—in the period of conquest and expansion—when their surroundings perpetually throbbed with unknown dangers, certain qualities of true statesmanship did develop in the officials of the East India Company. The Government had then, for the very life of itself, to be perpetually wide-awake, and to study, understand and propitiate whatever articulate public sentiment there was in the country, and avoid, at all costs, treading upon the tender susceptibilities of the people. The officials had then to study their environments with care, and conciliate the people under their rule with trembling and assiduity. They had to discover, at every step, the line of least resistance before them. But with the suppression of the Mutiny, the transfer of the Government of India directly to the Crown of England, and the gradual establishment of the Peace of Britain in the land, the terrible responsibilities of the Indian officials of the earlier generations were slowly removed from the shoulders of their successors. This was not good for the officials themselves, nor for the people placed under their authority. The establishment of unbroken peace, the consolidation of the Empire, the shortening of distance—both of time and space—between England and India by the establishment of the Indo-European cable and the opening of the Suez Canal, and the consequent transference of the centre of gravity of the administrative authority from Calcutta and Simla to London, and the growth of a large and self-sufficient European community in Indian cities—all these have combined to weaken the sense of fearful responsibility that weighed upon the older generations of British officials in India, and have removed from the life of the Anglo-Indian officials the old need of cultivating the leaders of the Indian community. The present generation of British officials live in a society of their own, in almost absolute isolation from the people about them. Following the example of their masters, the Indian subordinate officials also, from whom the higher officials derive all their knowledge of the people committed to their charge, create an atmosphere of similar isolation about them. The British officials have grown into a new caste in India, a new order of white-Brahmins. The Indian officials too, ignoring their real caste and pedigree, frequently create a new caste among themselves, almost as touchy and exclusive as the new British caste. Nor is this all. Even the "man-with-a-stake-in-the-country," who goes periodically to pay his "respects" to the higher officials, has caught the contagion and studies to establish a quarantine about him, to escape from every possible contamination from the seething currents of real public life and sentiment in his community. These people are, indeed, openly instructed to avoid all associations with that section of the public which really creates and controls the actual public life of the people. And the subordinate Indian officials and the men-about-official residences are the only two classes of the community who have the ear of our local magnates, and from whom the British officials receive all their knowledge concerning the trends of public sentiments in the country. And both these channels are no longer living, running currents, but only blind pools. The only people who are in direct touch with the officials on the one side, and the general masses of the people on the other, are the informers and spies of the political branch of the Criminal Intelligence Department. And a Government that seeks to build up its public policies on the confidential informations furnished by its secret spies rides always for trouble and disaster. And as long as the Executive Council of the Viceroy is dominated by the Indian Bureaucracy, it will always run this risk and find it exceedingly difficult, if not absolutely impossible, to pilot the barge of State with any effective statesmanship. The country has changed. The Civil Service has deteriorated. Unknown forces have been coming to a head. The sun-dried bureaucrat has no patience with these new forces and conditions about him. He is an anachronism in our day. The time has, therefore, come when, in the interest both of India and the Empire, the Executive Council of the Indian Viceroy must be thoroughly reformed and reconstituted, and the bureaucratic element completely eliminated from it.

CALCUTTA: *July*, 1913.

CHAPTER XII.

FIGHT AGAINST ANARCHISM IN INDIA.

ANARCHISM IN EUROPE AND INDIA.

EVER since the discovery of the so-called bomb-conspiracy in Calcutta, in 1908, various means have been tried to stamp out this new form of criminal propaganda in this country, but practically with little or no success. Judging these matters by the experience of Europe, there is even a tendency in many quarters to accept these crimes as a necessary evil of the modern civilisation, which may be watchfully provided against, but can never be entirely cured. But I think that, as in many other things so in this also, it is not very wise to go by European experience. Human sensibilities being the same everywhere, there must, as a matter of course, be a fundamental unity in both the origin and the evolution of any special form of anti-social malady that may appear in different countries. So far one must admit an affinity between the criminal propaganda of the European and the Indian revolutionary. But at the same time, we cannot ignore the very vital difference that exists between the social conditions and the national characters of Europe and India. The European anarchist is, mostly, a city-man or a city-woman. Even where they were born in distant villages, they joined the revolutionary gangs in city or suburban associations and thus practically became city-people afterwards. City-life is more favourable to the formation of secret associations than village-life. In the city no one cares to cultivate any intimate acquaintance with his neighbours ; least of all do people consciously keep watch over one another's movements or activities. In this country, and in our villages particularly, everybody lives an open life. Everybody knows everything about his neighbour's position and affairs, his thoughts and activities. In this respect, our rural life is different from whatever rural life there still is in England or America. And this freedom of intercourse is not destroyed even by our rigid caste-system, except possibly in certain parts of Southern India. It is, in fact, deeply ingrained in our national character and is not without its influence even upon our social life and relations in the cities. And this peculiarity of our social life and national character offers a much less favourable ground for the growth of secret revolutionary propaganda than what one finds in the West. And when we consider these, we find it difficult to believe that because it has so far been found impossible to stamp out criminal anarchism in Europe, it will never be stamped out here also in India.

Anarchism and Idealism.

The history of the birth and growth of criminal anarchism as a factor in modern politics, would be a highly interesting and profitable study. It would throw considerable light upon many an obscure problem of human psychology, especially upon criminal psychology. I have neither the equipment nor the time to present this history here. All that need be pointed out for my present purpose is that in its origin this anarchism is always associated with some lofty idealism, either patriotic or humanitarian or both. It is the revolt of the helpless against an all-powerful opponent. This is why this anarchism has sometimes enlisted some of the noblest of men and women in its service. Even Mazzini at first joined the Carbonari. But his moral nature, as well as his intellectual convictions, soon rebelled against that secret propaganda. It happened in the case of many another man of unselfish spirit and spotless character. But it does not always draw only such people. The instinctive criminal, the moral wreck, the greedy voluptuary, the selfish intriguer, all find here a powerful instrument and association for their criminal designs. It has been very largely so in Europe, where the expansion of popular rights has practically removed all honest political or patriotic motive from the anarchist activities. People have already commenced to entertain similar suspicions even regarding some, at least, of these frequent "political dacoities" that are reported from various parts of the country here. Some of these may, possibly, be actually the work of political malcontents; but that they are not responsible for all and every dacoity in the country, seems also to be equally certain.

The Strength of the Anarchist Organisations in India.

To lay the responsibility of all, or even a good number of the dacoities, said to be committed by armed and masked "Bhadrologues," or *bourgeoisie*, at the door of the political malcontents in this country, would be to credit them with a numerical strength and a wide-spread and disciplined secret organisation which no one who knows anything of our country, would accept as possible. It would be the merest affectation to deny that there is still very deep and simmering discontent in the country. And this discontent leads many people even to secretly enjoy the discomfiture of the police at the hands of a set of clever men, who seem to fall down from the sky, and having taken their loot, to vanish again into empty space. The masses nowhere take any long view of anything. Our masses also do not stop to think where these criminalities will finally land us all. For the time, they see the daring, the resourcefulness, the discipline of these unknown gangs, and admire these; and their innate dislike of the ways and character of the police lends an element of spicyness to this admiration. This is why nobody, except those who may be directly affected or threatened by these outrages, cares to discover the whereabouts of the criminals or help the police in bringing them to law. The mere spirit of adventure, I think, draws a good many young men to temporary associations with these bands. If I remember aright, there are indications of these casual associations in the records of some of these dacoity-cases also. These are matters of no moment to the police or perhaps, even to the magistracy; but they are of great value to the student of psychology and politics. They are supremely valuable to the statesman who has to grapple with these complex and dangerous situations.

WANTED: A PSYCHOLOGICAL DIAGNOSIS.

To fight this criminal propaganda successfully, we must take heed of all these facts. We must clearly understand that these criminals—so far as they are really political malcontents—belong to a distinct class. They are men at least of some education, and possibly, some of them at any rate, with a good deal of noble impulse, however misguided it may be. As the successful and experienced physician examines not merely the diseased organs of his patient, but perhaps with still greater care he tries to find out the source whence the suffering organism draws its vitality, and helps the patient to regain health and strength, by working upon his healthy organs; even so the criminologist, in his attempt to treat any criminal, must not only examine his morbidities alone, but must seek and discover the healthier parts of his inner moral nature and use these parts as a fulcrum to raise the man's whole character and cure him of his criminal propensities. Our criminal administrations fail so uniformly to reclaim the criminals, and so frequently increase the criminality of the community by their very attempt to cure it, simply because they do not work along this line. They take note of the acts of the criminal and the surface motives of his crime, but do not make any accurate psychological examination and analysis of the real genesis of the crime or the previous history of the criminal. They have commenced to pay heed to these things in Europe; but none, practically, seem so far to have done so here in India. But when society is threatened with apparently organised forms of lawlessness and violence like what we stand face to face with in India to-day, it becomes the positive duty of those responsible for the peace and good government of the country, to take note of all possible psychological considerations, and base whatever remedy they may propose for the social evil, upon them. Unfortunately, however, Lord Minto and his advisers never approached this problem from a psychological standpoint. They only considered the brute in our youthful revolutionaries, but paid no heed either to the man or to the God that was in them, as they are in every other human being.

Retributive and Remedial Measures.

It was not the fault of Lord Minto and his advisers, so much as it was their misfortune. Neither transcendental logic nor transcendental ethics has as yet secured any vital hold on current European thoughts and ideas. The ordinary European, therefore, finds it impossible to believe that a thing may be both true *and* false at the same time, or that an action may be *both* good and bad simultaneously. This is, however, ingrained in our very thoughts and sentiments. This is why our sages never care to fight false opinions, but allow these to drop off, like autumn leaves, of themselves, in their own proper time; and our saints never hate or shun, or even care to inflict any external punishment either, on men of evil temper or criminal habits or instincts. They see the good behind the evil, the shine behind the shadow; and knowing that the race is ultimately, always and absolutely, with the good, they are never impatient with the passing evils of life. Our sages and our saints fight, therefore, untruth with truth, evil with good, spite with love, niggardliness with generosity, and anger with forbearance. They do not fight the brute with the brute, but they seek to conquer the brute in man with the God that is also in him. And I think nothing short of this lofty philosophy and this divinely spiritual attitude will be able to conquer this new evil in our community. The Penal Code reveals really the animal strength of the State; for it is applied through sheer physical force either potential or actual, embodied in the Police and the Army of the Government. Without the Police and the Army, the Penal Code would be a dead letter. Government by penal laws is always of this kind. It is physical government, and not moral government in the highest sense of the term. The world has not as yet risen to that high level of moral elevation when the laws of the State would cease to work upon physical intimidation, but would be almost automatically executed by superior moral inspiration. We must have the Penal Code with us for a long, long time yet: but the spirit of criminal administration must slowly change all the same; and most of all, its present retributive ideal must give place, immediately, to its higher, remedial end, if criminality is not to increase with that intellectual and material advancement of the race, which is the essence of modern civilisation.

The Failure of Repressive Laws.

In India, at any rate, the Government will only court absolute failure, if they seek to grapple with these new forms of lawlessness in the country by either the old Penal Code or new and enlarged criminal laws especially designed to meet them. Lord Minto forged new weapons almost at every legislative session, and while they found new causes of anxiety and trouble for the timid and the peaceful, and to some extent demoralised certain sections of the people, they did not lessen, but on the contrary, visibly increased the very trouble which was sought to be cured; and while introducing every new measure, Lord Minto's Government had to openly confess the failure of its predecessors to meet the requirements of the situation. A partial salvation of that situation came, not from a continuance of the policy of Lord Minto, but really from its practical reversal by Lord Hardinge. The complete remedy has yet to come. But for the miscreant who marred the State entry of the Viceroy into Delhi, the situation would have been far more hopeful to-day than what it evidently is. But this sudden recrudescence of political outrages notwithstanding, the situation is not altogether hopeless. It will never be absolutely hopeless in India, unless the Government go back to the methods of the last Administration. And I have too large a faith in the statesmanly perceptions of Lord Hardinge to believe, even in the face of the new Conspiracy Act, that there will be any real recrudescence of the Minto-policy, as long as his Lordship is at the head of the Indian Administration.

A Constructive Proposal.

The real remedy of this situation will come from a calm and dispassionate study of the psychology of this criminal propaganda and a courageous application of the conclusions thus reached, through the enunciation of a new policy of confidence in and co-operation with the people. I think, a psychological analysis of the story of the present unrest will reveal the fact that the suppression of the Swadeshi Samities is very largely responsible for this new form of political lawlessness. It will serve no useful purpose to discuss the wisdom or unwisdom of that measure. The troublous condition of the country in 1908-1909 forced the Government of Lord Minto to suppress these Associations. But we have come to much quieter times now. The repeal of the Bengal Partition has, to a very large extent, removed the exciting cause of the unrest now. There is a sincere desire on the part of all parties to let bygones be bygones, and return to the old normal state of things. There is no reason, therefore, to keep up the old ban against these Samities now. But the Government cannot, perhaps, openly remove it either. Nor would it, perhaps, be wise to allow the reorganisation of these Samities in the old way, outside all official control. The best thing to do, therefore, would be to pass a permissive law, like the Indian Company's Act, for instance, under which people may openly and legitimately combine for the pursuit of general public good, by self-help, self-organisation, and self-taxation. They will determine their own objects, settle their own memorandum and articles of association, and frame their own laws and regulations; but will have to work openly, under official supervision of their accounts and official inspection of their proceedings. And as a price of this privilege, they may be held responsible, collectively, for the good behaviour of their members, and also be called upon to help the Administration to protect the life and property of the people in their jurisdiction. Such a law, giving an opportunity to the people to revive and reorganise the old Samities under legal restrictions and with legal sanction, will do more than any Conspiracy Act, to fight revolutionary anarchism in the country, and save a situation that is becoming almost hopeless.

CALCUTTA: *March*, 1913.

CHAPTER XIII.

THE PROBLEM OF POLITICAL CRIMES IN INDIA.

The Economic Theory of Political Criminalism.

It is high time that this problem of political criminalism was faced boldly both by the Government and the people. And the first thing to do is to clear the air of numerous misconceptions that have evidently gathered around it. Its genesis must be traced, its character thoroughly analysed, its strength fully probed, and whatever remedy may be reasonably suggested by this careful examination, must be fearlessly applied. There are some people, and even Indian publicists and politicians are to be found among them, who think that this criminalism has an economic origin. The increasing keenness of the struggle for existence, and the consequent increase in the number of the educated or half-educated unemployed in the country are, in their opinion, mainly responsible for these criminal activities. But those who think this wise forget the peculiar character and temperament of the class from which the political criminals in this country are drawn. They are, as a body, young men, some of them almost boys, with whom the so-called struggle for existence has had as yet absolutely no sort of reality. They are not as yet among the unemployed because they are mostly mere students not called upon to seek and find any employment to support themselves or their families. A very perceptible percentage of them belong to well-to-do families who do not feel the pinch of poverty and are not acquainted with the bitterness of what is known as economic struggle in Europe or America. Lastly, this economic struggle, even where it exists in this country, has not the same significance either physically or morally as it has in the western countries. Money counts for infinitely much less among us than what it does in European communities. Our kindlier physical environments enable us to live on much less than what the European or American people want. Our family organisations offer an insurance against starvation and nakedness which is absent in Europe or America. Our very system of castes, whatever other disadvantages it may have, has at least this one great moral advantage, that it prevents the dollar from being so absolutely almighty as it is in caste-less but capitalistic and industrial European society. Not necessity but avarice or greed make people thieves and swindlers here. And the avaricious young man is an exception everywhere. The economic theory of the Indian unrest, whether in its constitutional and non-criminal or in its revolutionary and criminal aspect, is absolutely untenable in the face of these undeniable facts. And we must trace it to some other cause.

The Gravity of the Economic Problem.

That there is a very serious economic problem in this country, calling aloud for timely solution, need not be denied. There is dire poverty in the land. This chronic poverty, more than either drought or flood, is responsible for the recurrent famines that decimate the rural populations of the provinces subjected to these visitations. This poverty is telling very seriously upon the physical and moral vitality of the people. All these are facts, and the evils due to them must be grappled with. But poverty, however dire and chronic it may be, never breeds the spirit of violent social revolt among us. Petty crimes do undoubtedly increase during famines and scarcities, but we rarely or never hear of any organised and wide-spread lawlessness in the country even when people die in their thousands and hundreds of thousands through famine and pestilence. We are a long-suffering people, with a large fund of moral and spiritual staying-power at our back. We are born fatalists. Men die when their time is up, not a second earlier or later. They cannot, with all their strength or wisdom or wealth or earthly influence, increase the allotted span of their life by even a hair's breadth. And when no man can live beyond his appointed period, it matters but little whether one dies of starvation or of cholera or of any other slower disease. This is the view that the Indian mind, whether Hindu or Moslem, takes of these visitations. They are ordained by God. It is the will of Isvara or Ālla. And they submit to the inevitable with almost stoic resignation. But for this inherent fatalism in our character and philosophy of life the Government of India by England would have been almost impossible, especially in the presence of the acute economic situation in the country and these recurrent famines. In fact, economic advancement will not remove, but simply increase, the political unrest in the country, and add materially to the complexities of the political problem ; especially if this advance should follow, as it is almost sure to do just now, the lines of economic progress pursued in Europe and America. The slow advance of industrialism is already repudiating all our ancient social and ethical values and laying the mines for a tremendous social transformation that must more or less revolutionise our mental outlook and moral temperament. The one saving grace in Indian history and evolution has been the noble idealism or spirituality of the Indian peoples. Modern industrialism threatens to deprive them of this one source of strength and sustenance that they have hitherto had. It is a distinct menace to our real national life. The success of this industrial propaganda would more or less spell the complete Europeanisation of the Indian mind. And that would be a very serious menace as much to our national life and culture as to the British connection itself. Indeed, the menace offered by what may be called Political Swadeshi or the Boycott propaganda of the Anti-Partition Agitation would seem absolutely contemptible, when compared to the dangerous possibilities, even politically, of the new industrial movement in India, which so far is only aping the methods and seeking to imbibe the spirit of the competitive capitalism of Europe and America. Any alliance between the hunger-driven socialism of Europe which is the inevitable fruit of this capitalism, and the hereditary fatalism of India, would generate forces of destruction which no political power or combination of political powers could hope to cope with. Lord Minto, with characteristic shortsightedness, did not realise the dangers of that "honest swadeshi" which he so enthusiastically commended as a set off against the Boycott Movement in Bengal. Few, indeed, of our own industrial and economic reformers are conscious of these dangers. They are absolutely obsessed by European thoughts and ideals, and cannot discriminate the generalisations of the particularistic economic experiences of Europe from the universal truths of economic science. This is why they encourage the false and foolish idea that the present political unrest, and particularly the criminalism with which it seems to be associated in certain quarters, are due to poverty and unemployment. And the greatest mischief worked by the propagation of this false theory consists in the wrong estimates of the inner moral strength of this criminal propaganda which this mean, materialistic view naturally leads to.

The Idealism of these Criminals.

In fact, this problem of political criminalism among us, would not have been half so serious if it had owed its origin to mere poverty or unemployment in the economic sense of the term. The real strength of this criminal propaganda comes not from the meaner impulse of hunger or want, but from the inspiration of a fundamentally loftier ambition. The young men who are being drawn into this revolutionary propaganda are not materialists but idealists. I do not want anybody to condone their crimes for that reason. As Lord Hardinge has truly said, an assassin is an assassin and a dacoit a dacoit—an enemy of Society, whatever be the motive that prompts him. On the contrary, the heinousness of his crime is just in proportion to the grandeur of his idealism. Idealism implies culture, refined sensibilities, and an educated mind. And when culture and enlightenment lend themselves to any anti-social propaganda, their criminality is not lightened but only deepened by it. But, however much we may condemn, the acts of these political criminals, we cannot honestly deny their idealism. Least of all should this idealism be ignored in the consideration of means and appliances by which this criminal propaganda must be fought. This plain fact has not, unfortunately, been as yet fully realised or frankly recognised by those who have so far set themselves to solve this problem. And this is why almost every attempt to control or cure these revolutionary activities has completely failed so far.

Results of Repression.

Lord Minto tried various forms of repression to fight this political criminalism, ignoring the universal testimony of history that the impatient idealist, who so frequently turns a political criminal, cannot be controlled or conquered by physical threats or chastisement. The very attempt to do so canonises the criminal and adds strength to his cause. It happened before our eyes in Bengal during the present unrest. These repressive measures inevitably restrict the legitimate freedom of the many as a punishment for the criminality of a few. This is their greatest defect. The failure of the Police to trace the authors of a political crime is visited upon the people at large with various new acts and ordinances affecting their right of free speech, free organisation, and free movement. And these restrictive measures inevitably create fresh grounds of complaint against established authority, deepens existing discontent, and confirms the conviction which the revolutionary is so anxious to produce in the community that there is a necessary and permanent conflict between what is good for the people and what is to the interest of the Government. True statesmanship would try, at all costs, to uproot this conviction where it may have already taken some root, and prevent its growth where there is still room for such prevention. For it knows that it is here, in this conviction of an unreconciled and irreconcilable conflict of interests between the rulers and the ruled in any country, that all revolutions take their birth, and that it is from this that all political criminalism draws its vitality and strength. Lord Minto did not understand this truism. The Anglo-Indian officials and publicists, as a body, have so far completely failed to realise this commonplace psychology of all revolutionary patriotism which is the parent of every form of political criminalism with which we are acquainted in history.

The Old Discontent and the New Unrest.

There was considerable discontent among the articulate classes in the country before Lord Curzon's time, but really no serious unrest. And the reason was that before Lord Curzon came among us, people did not recognise any irreconcilable antagonism between the gradual fulfilment of their national aspirations and the continuance of the British authority in their country. They were dreaming pleasant dreams of a future when India would be as free as England but live still in peace and happiness under the ægis of Great Britain. Lord Curzon's acts, and specially his candid utterances, dashed all these hopes down to the ground. He told the people in the plainest possible terms, that as long as the Government of India continued to be British, so long the supreme political authority in this country must vest in the representatives of the British people and that the people of India must be content to perpetually occupy a subordinate place. The higher functions of the State, in the due exercise of which the highest manhood of a people find scope and opportunity to fully realise itself, must always be reserved for the foreigner in India and not for the children of the soil. Not the evolution of self-government, but the establishment of good government was Britain's recognised mission and responsibility in India. And even Lord Morley lent support to this Curzonian ideal by declaring from his place in the House of Commons that the Government of India must, so far as his imagination went, continue to be a *personal* Government. This cruel truth had never before been so cruelly proclaimed in India or England by any responsible British statesman. It broke into our dreams, dispelled our illusion, and quickened a sense of the unreality of all our previous political ideas and activities. It generated the conviction that there was an irreconcilable conflict between the interests of India and those of England. And it was just this conviction which converted the old discontent into the new unrest.

PSYCHOLOGY OF THE INDIAN UNREST.

This is the simple psychology of the recent developments in India. Lord Curzon only sowed the wind. He did not see face to face the work of his own hand. It is impossible to say how he would have faced the music of the Anti-Partition Agitation in Bengal. In spite of his almost infinite self-esteem, Lord Curzon undoubtedly carries a much larger head-piece on his shoulders than Lord Minto, and it is quite possible that he would have avoided any violent and open conflict with the people he was called upon to rule. Trained in the free atmosphere of St. Stephen's, Lord Curzon could both give and take cruel knocks in political controversies, and was distinctly less fearful of violent speech or open antagonism than either Lord Minto or Sir Bampfylde Fuller or Sir Andrew Fraser, the three men who are so largely responsible, on the official side, for creating the recent troubles in Bengal. And neither of these administrators could seize the fundamental problem that faced them. They did not see that the real trouble arose out of the growing conviction of the people that Indian interests and British interests are absolutely irreconcilable in the present and even future political life and history of British domination in this country. Whatever measures they adopted to fight this new unrest, therefore, instead of weakening, helped only to strengthen and deepen this conviction the more.

The Root of the Disease.

Psychologically, this problem of political criminalism among us owes its origin to this conviction of the irreconcilableness of the highest aspirations and interests of the Indian people with those of the British people and the British Empire. This conviction is very widespread, if not absolutely universal, among the articulate classes in the country. Out of this conviction has grown the ideal of absolute political independence which is the avowed objective of the Indian revolutionary. I doubt it very much if it is not also the far-off ideal of many Indian politicians and patriots who have neither connection nor sympathy, however secret, with any form of revolutionary nationalism in the country. Even Mr. Gokhale would not impose any "limit upon the political ideal" or ambition of his people; but he accepted the ideal of Colonial Self-Government because it seemed to him more practical. The vision and far-sight, illumined by the ideal of Universal Humanity towards which all national evolutions tend as their ultimate end and goal—that could reveal the true basis of a permanent and reasonable reconciliation between Indian aspirations and British interests, have not so far been vouchsafed to many Indian politicians. And they are, therefore, divided as a class practically into two sections—the opportunist and the revolutionary. The opportunist can profit by the excesses of the revolutionary, and extend his power and improve his status with the Government by standing by them in their fight with the former; but he can never hope to cure or control political criminalism in the country. In fact this very coalition between the Government and the opportunist politician, directly helps to advance the revolutionary propaganda. It encourages the authorities in the pursuit of relentless repression. This repression, in its turn, increases the bitterness of the people and helps the spread of revolutionary sentiments in the community, and directly increases the facilities of the revolutionary politician to secure fresh recruits for his criminal propaganda. It is in this way that a shortsighted Bureaucracy, prone to fight unrest by repression, a body of opportunist politicians without any sound political philosophy or any lofty and far-reaching vision, and a gang of impatient idealists moved by a passion for freedom, the concept of which has evidently been borrowed from the inspirations of foreign history and alien culture, —these three have combined to create a situation dominated by almost universal unreason on every side. And the remedy can only come with the returning reason and the widening vision of all the three classes who have brought about the present impasse.

The Responsibility of the Indian C. I. D.

And I hope that Lord Hardinge at least has been thoroughly confirmed by this time in the conviction, of which we have had many proofs in his Lordship's acts and utterances in this country, that political criminality can no more be put down by rigorous repressions in India than it has been in other parts of the civilised world. Crimes, whether prompted by political or by personal motives, must be as severely dealt with, when duly detected, as the laws provide. But it is suicidal folly to set up a sort of political inquisition in the country, and encourage or allow the police to go about hunting sedition and anarchism in the community. It is suicidal, because these inquisitorial methods help the revolutionary propaganda, by inflaming the passions of sensitive youth. They never indulge in these methods in England. Lord Hardinge is thoroughly acquainted with the character and qualifications of the Criminal Intelligence Department in England, and need not be reminded that no police officer in London would touch any person without very substantial *primâ facie* evidence in his possession of the guilt of that person, however great may be his suspicion against him. More than one police officer in London told me that Scotland Yard was morally convinced of the complicity of a certain Indian student in London with the crime for which poor Dhingra, Sir Curzon Wyllie's assassin, paid with his life. But they gave him absolutely no trouble, except quietly and even respectfully shadowing his movements. Almost every Indian student in England, and more particularly in London, was treated practically as a political suspect in those days, and his movements were constantly watched by the officers of the London C. I. D. Some of these young men were living with Dhingra, in the same house, when Sir Curzon Wyllie was murdered. But while the police made a thorough search of Dhingra's rooms and took charge of his belongings, his Indian co-lodgers were subjected to no examination or annoyance whatever. There was no desire to hunt out Dhingra's friends and associates and connect them with his crime. Such wisdom, such patience, such scrupulous regard for the sanctities of private relations and personal freedom are practically unknown in this country. They are, practically, unknown even in Europe, outside the United Kingdom. It is to these virtues of the British Police Force that we owe the wonderful internal peace that Britain enjoys, in the face of the increasing virulence of her political factions and class-conflicts. But few Anglo-Indian publicists or officials seem to understand this plain truth. Every political offence, therefore, drives them to cry out for larger powers, but not greater wisdom or honesty—wider latitudes, but not more scrupulous regard for people's rights or liberties—for the Indian police force, and greater freedom from the restraints of law and procedure for the Indian Magistracy.

POLITICAL CRIMES AND POPULAR INDIFFERENCE.

It is not easy to say how and why many of these crimes go absolutely undetected. Political crimes are difficult of detection in every country. How many cases of arson evidently committed by the militant British suffragettes, have so far been brought home to the actual offenders? The percentage of undetected political criminals in England is not smaller, I think, but considerably larger than in this country. Yet no British publicist or politician arraigns the British public or any section of it either for shielding these offenders. What justification, then, has the Anglo-Indian scribe to indict the Indian public for shielding the Indian revolutionary? The majority of the British people are not in sympathy with the suffragette propaganda. They do not hesitate to condemn the acts and utterances of "these hysteric women." Yet they do not care to hunt out the woman or her male accomplice who not only destroys people's property but even commits mischiefs that may result in loss of human life. They do not simply care to employ their own time and energy in doing things for which they pay the Government to keep the police and the magistracy. This is also the meaning of the so-called indifference of the Indian public in the work of the detection of the political offender.

But there is also another, and a deeper reason for it. People in this country almost inherently shrink from causing harm to anybody, be he a friend or a foe of the social life. They have, no doubt, the common passions of humanity, and are as relentless persecutors of their personal enemies as are found in any other country or community. But that is due to their animalism. It is not their ideal. Resist no wrong is that ideal. They may, as men of flesh and blood, fight for their person or their property and demand even an eye for an eye and a tooth for a tooth, in their private and personal relations; but it is none of their business, they feel, to inflict sufferings upon another man or woman for any wrong that he or she may have done to another party. So far as the retributive functions of society are concerned, the Indian is practically devoid of what the European calls his sense of public duty. To his inherited lack of this sense of public duty has been added now a strong disinclination to get mixed up with the proceedings of the police. It is, indeed, more than mere disinclination. There is a distinct horror of the police in the Indian community. Neither as complainant nor as accused nor even as witness do people receive any, except the most irritating if not occasionally also the most oppressive, treatment from the Indian Police. It is not really the dread of the terrorist, upon which the ignorant and unimaginative Anglo-Indian scribe so constantly harps, that deters people from helping the police in the detection of political crimes, but it is rather the dread of the police themselves that prevents the public from offering whatever help it may possibly be in their power to render in the detection of these criminals. Any increase, therefore, in the powers of the police or of the prerogatives of the magistracy will not only fail to lead to greater detection or more effective prevention of political crimes, but will, on the contrary, simply increase the present antagonism of the people towards the police and shake their confidence in the integrity of the law courts, which is now, as it has always been, the greatest bulwark of the British Government in India.

The Moral Support of the Revolutionary Propaganda.

The fact of the matter, really, is not that the people are afraid of the terrorists, but that they are absolutely indifferent to the Government. With the illiterate masses this indifference is part of their inherent inertia. With the articulate classes it is, really, their only protest against the autocratic and soul-less methods of the administration to which they are subject. There are very few active revolutionaries in the country; but there is a very large class of people who, lacking the recklessness of the political anarchist, yet feel almost unconsciously glad at their criminal activities. Even those who sincerely condemn these activities, do so out of the dread of fresh oppressions which may follow in consequence of these outrages, and not out of any intellectual or moral conviction of the folly or sinfulness of the anarchical propaganda. But large numbers actually enjoy the discomfiture of the police and the embarrassment of the Government. It would serve no useful purpose to ignore or deny these facts. On the contrary, it is only from a frank recognition of these that there is any hope of the evolution of that wisdom and far-sight both in the Government and the people, without which this problem of political criminalism can never be satisfactorily solved. To advance this solution, it must be clearly realised that the strength of the revolutionary propaganda in this country is mainly derived from the almost universal conviction, among every class of the community, that the free and unrestricted self-fulfilment of the Indian peoples is absolutely irreconcilable with the perpetuation of the British connection. For want of a sound political philosophy and lack of vision of that Universal Humanity towards which —through nationalism, socialism, and a score other "isms" of our time, all the races of the world are slowly but surely moving: this is the real psychological origin and support of revolutionary unrest among us. The politician without any political philosophy; the patriot without the spirit of devotion or the capacity for sacrifice; the leader of public opinion whose only rule of conduct is expediency; the publicist without statesmanship who condemns in public —in the press and the platform, but commends in private, in unguarded talk with close friends and associates—the energy, the courage, the pluck and resourcefulness of the young anarchists and who reaps the richest harvest, in personal preferment and expansion of class-privileges, from their revolutionary activities—these are the real moral support of this criminal propaganda. And no repression can really touch these. These are the real enemies of peaceful progress in the country. And yet it is to these very classes that the Government have so often to look to for counsel and co-operation, in their fight against this so-called anarchism in our midst.

It is, indeed, high time that the Government and the non-official Anglo-Indian community clearly and fully realised the fact that not only would not the true cure or prevention of this revolutionary nationalism in India be effected by rigorous repression, but that the real remedy of this evil would not also come from the conciliation of the classes whom the authorities have hitherto been seeking to cultivate. It must be clearly recognised that the intellectual leadership of the country has completely passed out of the hands of the successful lawyer or the respectable landholder—the man with a stake in the country. The member of the local or the Imperial Legislative Council never was, and much less is now, the thought-leader of the community. The very expansion and reform of these Councils, under Lord Morley's scheme, have helped a visible depreciation of even the old market-values of these memberships. Council-elections, it is notorious, are never fought among us, upon grounds of public policy, but absolutely on private and personal grounds. These elections have not, therefore, been of any appreciable help in bringing only men with brains and character to the front, but have rather increased the opportunities for intrigue of the men with money, eager to secure the prestige and patronage that close association with the members of the Government is supposed to lend to the "Hon'bles." Neither the actual nor the potential members of council, have any real influence over the deeper currents of public thought and sentiments in the country. They are as much out of touch with the forces that contribute to revolutionary unrest as the officials themselves. It is absolutely of no use whatever cultivating this section of the community for fighting the present political criminalism in the country.

We have had ample evidence already of the exceedingly feeble hold that the Indian official or demi-official classes have upon revolutionary thought among us. The case of Gireendra Mohan Das* should serve as an eye-opener to the Government in this direction. Had Babu Yamini Mohan Das, whose loyalty and devotion to the Government he serves are absolutely above suspicion, any moral hold upon his own son, Gireendra could never have been so easily captured by the anarchists, as is alleged by the police. And Gireendra's is not a solitary case either, though it is the only one that has come to light. It is only natural that this should be so. For we cannot expect the selfish caution and wordly prudence of age from sensitive and impressionable youth. Least of all can these virtues be expected of young men brought up in comparative ease and affluence. The class that, in the older generations, swelled the army of wild and libertine youth, who wasted their substance upon publicans and prostitutes, now seem to find good many recruits for the revolutionary propaganda. The psychology of lawlessness whether social or political is really the same. In both cases it is due to the irresistible impulse of youthful animalism and enthusiasm that seeks an outlet for its exuberant energy and restlessness through these anti-social channels. And it is just here, in this universal psychological fact and experience, that we must seek for and find the true key to the solution of this problem of political criminalism in the country.

* Gireendra is the son of a Deputy Magistrate. He has been convicted and sentenced as a political criminal.

The root-cause of this evil is, as I have already pointed out, firstly intellectual, and secondly psychophysical. The conviction that the conflict between Indian Nationalism and British Imperialism is unreconciled and absolutely irreconcilable, is the intellectual cause of every form of revolutionary patriotism in the country ; and this conviction receives daily support from the reckless utterances of the Anglo-Indian press and the differentiating treatment, partly sanctioned by law but largely prompted by race-partiality and colour-kinship, as between the Indian and the European, received from unimaginative British officials in the country. It is unreasonable to expect the Viceroy to control either this press or these officials. But it is only right that His Excellency should know the real source whence the revolutionary movement receives its principal sentimental impetus. Lord Minto either did not see or could not correctly appraise the moral significance of these facts. He did not realise that the very support which the Anglo-Indian press gave to his repressive measures created more revolutionaries in the country than perhaps those measures themselves. The Viceroy may not control the Anglo-Indian press, but His Excellency can to some extent at least neutralise the evil it breeds, partly by the occasional administration of open rebuke of its reckless and irritating methods and largely by publicly disclaiming all association or sympathy with its wild counsels, whenever the discussion of any vital public question gives him an opportunity of doing it. Lord Hardinge has already shown, in the repeal of the Partition of Bengal and the settlement of the Cawnpore Mosque-dispute, that he is no worshipper of the Anglo-Indian fetish called prestige. There are minor occasions that come every now and then, when his lordship may well act similarly and withdraw or rescind any measure or act or policy that may be found to come into conflict with any vital conviction of the people, and that may lend any support to the impression, already very widespread in the articulate Indian community, that the development of the real manhood of the people is viewed with alarm and is sought to be repressed by the Government, in the interests of the existing political or economic ascendency of the British nation. And finally it would help the present situation more than most people can imagine just now, if His Excellency could place on record a reasoned statement of British policy in India, pointing out the possible lines of development worked by the pressure of the actualities of the present situation in the British Empire on the one side and in world-politics on the other, frankly and unequivocably indicating the bases upon which there can and must be a complete reconciliation between the fullest self-expansion and self-fulfilment of the composite Indian nation and the maintenance and consolidation of the present British Empire, a reconciliation that is essential as much for the future of Indian Nationalism itself as it is for British Imperialism. All this will remove, I do not say completely, but without doubt very considerably, the present conviction that Indian and British interests are absolutely irreconcilable, and consequently the only hope for India lies in the ultimate severance of their present connection with Great Britain, howsoever it may have to be worked out.

LORD HARDINGE'S POSITION.

But Lord Hardinge alone will not be able to do all that is required to remove the intellectual conditions that create political criminalism in the country. His lordship's position is exceedingly delicate and difficult. He has to consult the wishes of the British Cabinet and follow the instructions of the Secretary of State for India who directly represents the supreme administrative authority in the British-Indian Empire. He has also to consider the susceptibilities of the Indian Civil Service on the one side and of the powerful Anglo-Indian community on the other. His pronouncements, however statesmanly and sound, must necessarily be very cautious. His acts must, in the very nature of things, be tentative. He has not a clean slate to write upon. He is hampered by the policies and acts of his predecessors. He must keep up, in any case, a show of continuity with the past traditions and character of British rule in India. He may, if he likes, try to conciliate public feelings in regard to particular questions, but he cannot altogether remove the conviction already deep-rooted and widespread in the country, that the interests of the Indian people are as yet not only unreconciled but are eternally irreconcilable with those of the British Government and the British people. Besides his lordship cannot claim any long and intimate acquaintance with the psychology of the Indian mind or the inner ideals and possibilities of the Indian nation. He has, consequently, to move more or less in the dark, with his own intelligence and imagination as his only light. He has to take one step at a time, and wait for the actual consequences that it may lead to, before he can make another pronouncement or take another step. Lord Hardinge in his Despatch of August 1911 made a cautious but pregnant pronouncement. He indicated therein a policy of reform and reconciliation infinitely more statesmanly and far-reaching than what either Lord Morley or Lord Minto ever did. He did it, it is clear, almost in the teeth of the opposition of the Indian Bureaucracy and the British Jingo. And he had, necessarily, to wait to see the results of this pronouncement before he could either make his meaning clearer, or materialise the ideas and ideals of that state-document in actual acts and institutions. Sound administrative policies are always experimental. Unfortunately, however, Lord Hardinge's experiment did not succeed as well as its intrinsic merits deserved, and as, possibly, his lordship himself expected. The unrest was not visibly affected by it. Without completely or even appreciably conciliating Indian sentiments, the repeal of the Bengal Partition and the removal of the Capital to Delhi aroused the violent hostility of the commercial community of Calcutta and the secret antagonism of that subordinate officialdom which was mainly responsible for the repressive measures of Lord Minto. The Anglo-Indian publicist and the Anglo-Indian Bureaucrat correctly read the trends of this new policy and saw in it an attempt to weaken their hold upon the course of the administration of the country. But the Indian publicists also failed, as a class, to see that the repeal of the Bengal Partition and the measures with which it was joined meant a good deal more than what appeared on the surface. While everybody thanked the Viceroy for his generosity, few recognised his wisdom.

Some saw in the repeal of the Partition what they called the triumph of constitutional agitation ; others set it to the activities of the so-called extremists ; but very few saw in the new development a recognition of the irresistible forces of world-politics and the complexities of the problems of internal readjustment of the British Empire. They did not see how intimately was Lord Hardinge's policy connected with the rejuvenescence of China on the one side and the resurgence of the Moslem world on the other, under the inspiration of a Pan-Islamic sentiment that is rapidly spreading, particularly among the Mahomedan populations of India and Egypt. They did not see how these new developments in contemporary history and politics called for an early and permanent reconciliation between Indian and British interests, for the very life of the British Empire itself. Neither in the press nor in the platform, neither in the Congress nor anywhere else, was any attempt made by any Indian publicist or politician to seize the real meaning and significance of Lord Hardinge's Despatch and explain these to the people. That document, therefore, practically failed of its purpose. What slight impression was created in the country by the publication of this Despatch was destroyed by the ill-considered disclaimer of Lord Crewe. And there was not sufficient political far-sight or even diplomatic cunning in the country, to point out and prove the absolute worthlessness of this disclaimer in the face of the gathering forces of Imperial evolution and world-politics which had been creating an imperious need for the reconciliation of all conflicting interests within the British Empire, so that it may successfully meet all possible dangers of the new situation. Irish Home Rule, Egyptian Self-Government, and Indian Autonomy, along federal lines, these are all parts of the one and the same imperial policy and have for their object the consolidation of the British Empire. And no verbal disclaimer could alter historic conditions or prevent the pursuit of a policy that is based upon the primary instincts of self-preservation. This fact was never brought home to the Indian people. This is why Lord Hardinge's policy failed to remove the intellectual cause of the unrest to the extent it might and should have done.

The Duty of our Thought-Leaders.

There is, however, yet time for the leaders of Indian thought to co-operate with the Viceroy in creating public confidence in the feasibility of a reasonable and permanent reconciliation between nationalist aspirations in India and the fundamental requirements of the integrity of the present British Empire. But this co-operation must be different from what the Indian Bureaucracy have hitherto been wanting of the people. They never took counsel with us in either diagnosing the disease or in the determination of the remedy that is to be applied. They formed their own conclusions, prescribed their own remedies, and all that the leaders of the people were asked to do was to carry out the wishes and orders of the Bureaucracy in this matter. True co-operation was impossible under these circumstances. The former knew that the official diagnosis was incorrect. They saw that the official remedy would only aggravate the disease. But to question the correctness of the one, or to refuse the application of the other, involved serious personal risks. Every Indian was more or less under the shadow of suspicion. To refuse to accept the dictates of the Bureaucracy meant the registration of their names in the black books of the Police. No frank co-operation was possible, therefore, under the Minto *régime*. The Minto methods have therefore failed. Neither Lord Morley nor his "man on the spot" had any correct appreciation of the real problem that faced them. They did not realise the fact that the unrest which they were called upon to settle was fundamentally different from the educated discontent that had sought expression through the agitations of the Indian National Congress. At the back of the Congress agitations, there was no deep and strong conviction that the political and economic interests of India were irreconcilable with those of Great Britain. On the contrary, the Congress propaganda tacitly but firmly based itself upon the contrary conviction. The Bureaucracy did not understand that the new conflict was more of thoughts and cultures than of mere material interests. They utterly failed to see that this new unrest was due more to the spirit and attempt of self-preservation than those of self-assertion, of the ancient culture and civilisation of India against the onslaughts of aggressive European culture and civilisation. Above all they utterly failed to appraise the spiritual inspiration and significance of this new ferment in the country. The real conflict is between idealism and materialism. But neither Lord Morley nor Lord Minto nor their advisers had the training and equipment for dealing with a conflict of this kind. A child of the French Illumination, brought up on the philosophy of Mill and Bentham and the nineteenth century individualistic rationalism in England, Lord Morley is, in spite of his superior culture and mentality, an anarchronism in twentieth century thought and life. Lord Minto was a commonplace politician, without either vision or experience. And it is not at all surprising that neither of them had a correct understanding of the situation they were called upon to deal with. Lord Morley by his utterances and Lord Minto by both word and deed, indirectly contributed to deepen the conviction that political freedom in India, even of the type that is enjoyed by the British Colonies, was absolutely incompatible with the perpetuation of the British connection. While Lord Morley's utterances and Lord Minto's measures deepened this conviction, their so-called "reforms" and "concessions" did not at all touch the outermost fringe of the problem which it created. On the contrary, the creation of separate communal electorates for the Mahomedans lent strength to the belief that nothing was really further from the minds of these politicians than to help the evolution of national unity and the consolidation of the different Indian communities, with a view to gradually train them for any real form of self-government or political autonomy. The policy of cultivating the Moslems as against the Hindus, and of helping the so-called "Moderates" as against the "Extremists" was exceedingly foolish; for it created a new sense of self-importance in the Mahomedans, the fruits of which the Government is reaping in the present Mahomedan unrest; and by separating the so-called "Extremists" from the so-called "Moderates," it deprived the united political life of the country and, more particularly, the new forces which recent developments called into being—of the sobering influence of the older and more prudent politicians. Had there not been a complete break-up between these two schools of political thought in the country, the so-called "Moderates" would have to quietly advance, up to a certain point, towards the thoughts and ideals of the so-called "Extremists," and the latter also would have to accommodate themselves, to a considerable extent, to the susceptibilities of the former. This would have absolutely prevented the growth of any propaganda of revolutionary violence in the country. But neither Lord Morley nor Lord Minto had the insight and the far-sight to see all this. Lord Hardinge has a clearer vision of the situation, and this is why it is no longer unthinkable on our part to co-operate with His Excellency in finding a solution for the problem of political criminalism in the country.

The Principle of Reconciliation.

And our first duty, as well as of the Government here, is first to discover and then to publicly proclaim and accept some principle of permanent reconciliation between the passion for political autonomy and self-fulfilment of the articulate Indian populations on the one side, and the preservation of the unity and integrity of the association now known as the British Empire, on the other. Complete national autonomy in India, inside that Imperial Federation which is slowly building itself up in the British Empire, is the only reasonable basis of this reconciliation. It is on this basis that the Irish problem is being sought to be solved. On the same basis, and out of the same primary needs of the Empire, the Indian problem must also be sought to be solved. Lord Hardinge has practically, so far as his official position permitted him to do so, accepted this ideal of national autonomy for India. He has laid the foundations of this complete national autonomy, which in a continent like India, containing diverse races and cultures, must evolve on broad federal lines—by proclaiming "Provincial Autonomy," as the objective of the policy that has been materialised in the repeal of the Curzonian Partition of Bengal, the redistribution of territory with which this Partition has been repealed, and the transfer of the Capital to Delhi, which as the seat of the future Federal Government of the country has been formed, like the District of Columbia in the United States, into a separate Administrative Unit by itself. All these are clear proofs of the acceptance by the Viceroy of the ideal of an autonomous federation in India, which will be gradually incorporated, as an equal among equals, into the larger Federation of the Empire, towards which the historic evolution of Great Britain and her Colonies is visibly moving. And the *real*, as distinguished from the *verbal*, value of this policy of Lord Hardinge—which has evidently had the sanction of the British Cabinet and His Majesty the King-Emperor himself, for he personally came out to India to inaugurate these changes—is derived from the latest developments in world-politics, more particularly in China and the Islamic world, that have actually forced it upon our rulers in the interest of their own future. And if only we could realise the significance of these new developments to our own future also, we too would see that the pursuit of this policy is as much to our own interest as an infant or rejuvenescent nation, as it is to that of our present rulers. Never before was it more true and real than it is to-day, that the fates of India and Great Britain are indissolubly bound up together. And it is here, in the proclamation and preaching of this ideal and principle, in such a way as will open the eyes of both the rulers and the ruled to the danger of either party pursuing any other ideal, and thus create the conviction that this ideal and principle constitute a real basis of reconciliation between their conflicting interests and furnish the only line of least resistance for their common historic evolution in the immediate future—that the leaders of thought among us may well and effectively co-operate with at least the present head of the Indian Government. And in proportion as they will be able to do this, in that proportion they will deprive whatever political criminalism may actually be in the country, of every vestige of secret sympathy and moral or intellec tual support that it may be receiving from the people.

The Condition of Co-operation.

But the leaders of thought in the country will not be able to do this much-needed work, unless and until there is a radical change in the spirit of the local administrations. The present system of police espionage must be changed, root and branch, that is the first condition of this co-operation. The men who are usually employed to watch and report upon political speeches and writings are rarely fitted for the work entrusted to them. They are mostly without any liberal education and are steeped in the idea that their duty is not simply to report what is actually said or done, but also to interpret these and decide whether they make for sedition or not. They are always on the look-out for overt or covert political crimes; and the ordinary human mind is so constituted that it generally succeeds in finding out the purposes or meanings they are on the look-out for in other people's words or acts. It is foolish to wish or expect that those who are responsible for peace and order in the country can afford to abolish their Intelligence Bureau. The authorities must keep themselves fully informed from day to day of whatever is going on in the districts under their charge. Let them do so by all means, but let the information they receive be correct and reliable. Let men of educated intelligence and sterling honesty be employed in this most delicate task. Let them be men of proper education, properly paid, and above all, let there be no toleration of any untruth or carelessness or needless exercise of authority or of any the least attempt to cause wanton annoyance to people they may be set to watch and report upon. And above all, let them be so trained to keep their own counsel and conceal the fact that they are watching any one, that no one will suspect them of being an officer of the Political Intelligence Department. To do this successfully, all evidence of the members of this Political Intelligence Department, must be declared as inadmissible in any criminal proceedings for political offences. In a word, to enable the thought-leaders of the people to co-operate with the authorities in fighting political criminalism, the rights of free speech, free writing, free organisation for civic purposes, that have practically been taken away by the Government of Lord Minto, must be restored to the people. Unless this is done, even those who may be sincerely anxious to put down this criminal propaganda will find little or no opportunity of taking any rational steps in the matter. It matters but little whether the Minto-laws are openly repealed or not; but there must be ample and convincing evidence before the public that the old spirit no longer rules the acts and attitudes of the Government in the matter of popular political activities.

FREEDOM AND SOCIAL ORDER.

Indeed, it must be clearly understood that without a restoration of our old rights of free speech both in the press and the platform, the intellectual cause and origin of this political criminalism in the country will never be effectively removed. For it is not enough that we should co-operate with Lord Hardinge in proclaiming and preaching the principle and policy that reconcile the ideal of Indian autonomy with the continuance of the British connection and the maintenance of the fundamental integrity of the present British Empire, but we must also convince our people that under existing conditions this is the one only possible line of national self-fulfilment for them. Intellectual convictions are produced always upon certain psychological conditions. And the very first of these conditions is that there should be no conflict upon fundamental grounds. In arguing an individual out of any error, you must first of all accept the postulates of his position, and agree with him upon what he considers to be absolutely true or vital. In seeking to convert the Indian revolutionary, we must, therefore, accept his fundamental position, however provisionally it may be; nay more, we must fully and sincerely sympathise with his ultimate ideal. That ideal is, we know, absolute independence. In the abstract, there is no unreason or criminality in that ideal. National evolution up to our own age has almost universally been moved by it as its supreme regulative idea. Federalism or internationalism, as a higher stage and ideal of historic evolution, is a very recent revelation. Absolute independence is, as yet, practically a universal ideal of national existence in this world. It is no wonder, therefore, that it should appeal so powerfully to the awakened patriotism of the Indian intellectuals. And there can inherently be nothing criminal in what is so intensely natural. Those who seek honestly to fight this propaganda of political criminalism in the country, must recognise that it derives its main strength and inspiration from this passion for political independence. They must do more, they must freely and openly sympathise with this natural ambition of the people. For it is upon this sympathy alone that any real moral or intellectual relations may be established between them and those whom they desire to convince and convert. These are psychological commonplaces. Unfortunately, however, even these commonplaces were not recognised by the panic-stricken advisers of Lord Minto, and are perhaps not yet fully recognised by the ordinary Indian official. The faintest breath of this universal human passion was penalised by the Minto-Administration, that made all free discussion, however well-meant or rational it might be, impossible in the country. And it is high time that, in the interest of peace and order itself, this right of free discussion was openly and unreservedly restored to the people, subject only to such limitations as every civilised penal code everywhere imposes upon it.

For unless this is done, it will be absolutely impossible for us to thoroughly convince the youthful intellectuals in the country of the suicidal folly of revolutionary ideals and activities. We cannot point out their error, unless we are permitted to publicly discuss with them, every possible phase of this problem of political criminalism in the country. We must start with an open and free acceptance of the ideal of independence and then point out how impossible it is for us to attain that ideal in the present state of the country ; and how the very attempt to do so, must inevitably lead to a fresh period of political servitude ; and how our only chance of attaining practical, though not formal, national freedom or autonomy lies not in violently breaking up but in amicably preserving the British connection in and through a scheme of real Imperial Federation. To convince people of the criminal folly of the revolutionary propaganda in India, one must talk freely of its criminality, deal with it as tenderly and tactfully as a physician deals with his patient, honour its patriotic devotion, respect its convictions, however wrong these may be, and thereby establish that moral relation with those who are being secretly influenced by it, upon which alone can one person lead and control another's thoughts and activities. But this is practically impossible now. And unless the old rights and privileges of free speech and free movements are restored to them again, it would be idle to expect any real help from the actual leaders of thought in the country in effecting any rational and permanent solution of this problem of political criminalism among us

THE PSYCHOPHYSICAL ASPECT OF THIS PROBLEM.

But this problem has not merely an intellectual cause and origin ; there is also a very serious and important psychophysical aspect of it. Indeed, without the psychophysical conditions that have led to the birth of this unrest, the intellectual cause would not have at all been awakened into activity. And by psychophysical here I mean those physical conditions, created by either the political or the economic or the social constitutions and codes of a people, that powerfully affect their mental and moral life and contribute very materially to the birth and growth of certain overpowering emotions and impulses in them. And it is these overpowering sentiments or impulses, which, being denied their legitimate play and fulfilment, create all conflicts between individuals and individuals or between individuals and their social authority. The old, old story of Alexander and the robber illustrates this universal psychophysical reference of all our antisocial acts and attitudes.

Every crime has, indeed, a more or less psychophysical origin or reference. Every crime implies a violation of some positive law and a practical revolt, therefore, against the authority which promulgates that law and under which the individual violating it lives. These laws are the expressions, so to say, of the collective conscience of the community to which the individual belongs ; and have for their object the furtherance of social well-being, as it is apprehended and understood by that community. They seek, not merely, to secure social well-being but also to protect and advance the peace and well-being of each individual member of society, with which this social well-being is organically related. And considering how much it is to the interests of the individual also, that these primary social laws should be observed, no one violates these laws except under some strong and overwhelming impulse. Theft without any keen and overpowering sense of want and privation, and murder without some strong provocation, are rare, and wherever we find these crimes without these originating circumstances, they are due to inherited criminal impulses, that work almost automatically through what may almost be called unconscious cerebration. They are the acts of what are called instinctive criminals, and betray a kind of incipient insanity. These criminal habits are, like the drink habit for instance, due practically to physical or more correctly speaking psychophysical causes, the result, very often, of defective development or malformation of those physical and physiological organs, whose activities are closely and organically related to our mental and emotional life.

The Psychophysics of the "Circumstantial" Criminal.

But it is not only these instinctive criminals whose crimes have a distinct psychophysical origin; even those that are called circumstantial criminals whose crimes are due to some sudden impulse, owe it to some psychophysical cause. These crimes are due universally to the refusal of the social, sacerdotal, or political authority under which the criminal lives to grant adequate scope and freedom for the satisfaction of some natural, that is physical or psychophysical, want that he may strongly feel. Food, shelter, and clothing are primary necessaries of the human life. They are all primary physical wants. When men become thieves and burglars to satisfy these primary needs, the origin and cause of their criminality are distinctly physical. They are universally due to the denial to the criminal of legitimate and accessible or available means of satisfying his primary needs for food, raiment and shelter. This need is a purely physical need. The impulse to satisfy it is a physical impulse. It is the attempt of our physical organism to preserve itself. In the case of those whom we love and who may be more or less dependent upon us for their primary necessaries of life, the pain that hunger and cold inflict upon them affects us vicariously, through the natural capacity of our affections to identify the sufferings of those whom we love with our own senses and sensibilities—and when the privations of those whom we love impel us to criminal acts, the origin of these acts is not directly physical or physiological, but distinctly psycho-physical. We are driven to these criminalities by the refusal of the social or political authority under which we live, to grant us adequate opportunities to provide for our family and find them sufficient food and clothing and shelter. The true prevention of offences against property can only be effected by the removal of the physical and psychophysical causes that lead to them. And these causes, in their turn, can only be removed by some such socio-economic reform or re-adjustments as will secure to every individual member of the society adequate means to satisfy the primary wants of himself, his family and his dependents. And the course of socio-economic legislation in every modern state is visibly directed towards this end.

For the modern consciousness has fully realised the intimate relation between poverty or physical and physiological want and the most numerous class of criminality, namely that which is classified as offences against property; and modern statesmanship has applied itself to cure this criminality by working up some sort of a re-adjustment or re-arrangement of the existing economic or industrial life and organisation of society with a view to remove, or at least minimise, the impecuniosity of the poorer classes of the community.

Like offences against property, offences against person also have a clear psychophysical cause and origin. In the former case, the impulse comes from hunger or greed, in the latter it comes from anger. Indeed, from of old, anger has been known as "secret murder." Sometimes murder is associated with burglary; but the object there is not to kill but only to rob; and if any murder takes places here, it is incidental to the burglary, is due to the attempt of the murdered man to prevent the burglary or to apprehend the burglars. And the motive all through here, from the act of housebreaking to that of murder, is primarily mere greed, and secondarily self-protection, first against apprehension, and second, it may be, against subsequent detection and punishment. Barring these evident exceptions, every form of offence against person, from common assault to black murder, owes its origin to anger. And anger is not a pure and abstract mental or moral fact, it is organically related to our physical and physiological structure, is intimately and inseparably bound up not only with our brain-cells and nervous system, as all emotions are, but even with our motor muscles. Anger always manufactures a certain amount of physical or nervous energy in us that must spend itself through some sort of muscular movement. The wild movements of the limbs of the angry man or woman are due to this attempt on the part of their body to let off the steam or energy suddenly manufactured by this passion. This energy or steam, unless duly let off through the activity of our motor muscles explodes, sometimes within our brains and brings on paralysis or syncope, and even leads to death ; or it may also hold itself in reserve, embodied, so to say, as a relentless spirit of revenge, and seek quieter outlet through the contemplation of the future punishment of the person who excites our anger. But in whatever shape our anger may express itself, its essential psycho-physical character cannot be denied. And as anger is the almost universal cause of all offences against the person, the psychophysical origin and reference of this class of criminality also must be admitted. And here also, ultimately we find that it is the denial to the angry or injured man of positive and adequate scope and opportunity to satisfy his passion for retribution or revenge, that drives him to these acts of criminal violence.

Take, for instance, that increasingly numerous class of crimes that have reference to the sex-relation and the marital laws. Adultery and illegitimacy are far more prevalent in strictly monogamous communities than they are in communities where neither bigamy nor polygamy is punished as a crime. And the prevalence of these crimes in Europe and America is entirely due to two causes, namely, first, the rigid restraint that monogamy imposes upon the sex-impulse, and second, the almost endless latitude of free social intercourse between the sexes that obtain in those countries and that has an inevitable tendency to quicken this impulse in ordinary men and women whose higher moral and spiritual powers still await due development. This curious arrangement by which the sexual desire is being almost constantly quickened and inflamed on the one hand, and unnaturally sought to be repressed on the other, can only lead to one result, and that result is evident in Europe and America. The very constitution of modern Western Society—its individualistic social economy, its ideal of economic freedom, its habits of life, its food and drink, its recreations and amusements, its art and literature—all combine to create a set of psychophysical conditions that inevitably and constantly quicken the sex-impulse; while the laws of the State seek to impose the strictest restraint upon this—the strongest of all human passions. The institution of divorce originated with the recognition of this difficulty and was meant to relieve the very serious tension which the combination of monogamy with the peculiar social life and institutions of Europe threatened always to create. With the gradual passing away of the old chaperons, the advance in the average marriageable age of women, the improved means of intercommunication, the invention of the bicycle and the automobile, the decadence of both social and sacerdotal authority in the community, the breaking up of the old solidarity of the village life and the gathering of strangers in towns and suburbs, the growth of factories that throw men and women isolated from their families and ancestral social surroundings promiscuously into one another's company, and the almost universal emphasis of the most prominent aspects of modern life upon material pleasures and progress—all these have immensely increased this tension, and divorce must now be made easier than before to relieve it. And the whole trend of modern legislation in this respect indicates the psychophysical character of this problem.

And as this sex-love grows universally out of our natural yearning, partly physical and partly mental and emotional, for self-expansion and self-realisation, even so our love for our country and our nation also grows out of the same psychophysical needs. This desire for self-expansion and self-realisation is universal in the race. It finds crude and brutal expression in wild barbarism. It seeks more self-regulated and refined expression in the civilised man. But it is absent, really, from no individual or community. And it is this natural desire which, being denied its legitimate and adequate scope and fulfilment, inflames the patriotic passions of people and drives them to acts of rebellion against constituted authority. This is the history of all revolutions. And in seeking to make a correct diagnosis of revolutionary patriotism and political crimes in any country, we cannot overlook or ignore their universal psychophysical reference.

Civilisation and Crime.

This is indeed why we find so close a relation between criminality and what we call civilisation. It is generally admitted that statistics of certain kinds of crime increase always with the progress of this civilisation. It does not mean that our criminal instincts, instead of being subdued and chastened with our advance from savagery to civilisation, is only strengthened and developed; but only this, namely, that primitive culture grants us far wider latitude for the play and satisfaction of our natural instincts and appetites than what we are permitted to enjoy in more advanced and organised stages of social evolution. Offences against person diminish in direct ratio to our progress in civilisation, because what we call justice in civilised parlance, which means the satisfaction, really, of our natural instinct of revenge against a wrong-doer, is infinitely far less assured in savagery than in civilisation. On the other hand, however, offences against property show a very distinct tendency to increase with the advance of this civilisation, because the growth of private proprietorship upon the necessaries of life, restricts very seriously the field of the satisfaction of men's primary instincts of physical sustenance and self-preservation. Begging is not criminal among us in India; and no man, at least in our primitive village life, ever dreams of handing a famished brother over to the Police for having helped himself to a few edible fruits or roots from his field or orchard under the impulse of hunger. As a result, statistics of theft or burglary or cheating, etc., in India compare very favourably with those of England, for instance, where the sense of private ownership is much stronger and the scope for the satisfaction of a penniless man's hunger and thirst immensely more limited than they are among us. In England itself criminal statistics have shown a very marked tendency to improve since the repeal of the older laws that provided for the most drastic and inhuman punishment for the least encroachment upon the exorbitant claims of the private proprietary of the descendants of the old feudal lords. The more rigid and relentless the restraints that society seeks to impose upon human passions and appetites, the stronger becomes the spirit of social revolt in the individual members of that society, and more numerous becomes the number of habitual criminals there. In fact there are a very large class of what may be called law-made criminals in every civilised community—men and women who would not have been criminals at all if only society had left a little more legitimate room for the play and satisfaction of their natural instincts and appetites.

The Psychophysics of the Swadeshi Movement.

The Swadeshi Movement in Bengal was, however, never studied and appraised properly either by our own leaders or by the Executive Government in the country, in the light of these supremely significant psychophysical facts. The leaders thought that it was simply an expression of the patriotic sentiments of the people which their agitations had evoked. The Government thought that it was merely the outburst of a new spirit of antagonism against their authority. That it was partly both cannot be denied. But the supreme fact was that both this new patriotism and this new antagonism were neither merely intellectual nor moral, but essentially physical and psychophysical. The old patriotism of the Congress was almost entirely intellectual and emotional. It was something which the study and inspiration of English literature and European history had induced in our modern-educated classes. It was essentially imitative and imaginative.

It had little or no reference to the solid realities of our life. The generation to which the early Congress-leaders belonged enjoyed much larger freedom intellectually and morally than those who came after them. It was the period of pure intellection. The articulate classes were dazzled by the new Illumination which the British had brought with them into the country. The Government was exceedingly nervous about the fearful possibilities of any sudden outburst of the ancient "superstitions" and "fanaticism" of the people. The new Illumination was regarded as an effective antidote against these. The new spirit of freedom called into being by English education was, therefore, not only welcomed but openly encouraged by the authorities, especially as it first took the form of a revolt against the current faiths and established social institutions of the people wherein really lay the source of possible danger to the new political order in the country. The spirit of freedom always and everywhere grows out of some sense of painful bondage. And the only real sense of bondage in the generation which was first possessed by the spirit of the new Illumination, had reference to their social and religious life. There was as yet really little or no deep sense of bondage in the community in the political field. The spirit of political freedom was so far not indigenous, but imported; imitative, not natural; imaginative, if not even fanciful, and not real. Indeed, the new political order in the country instead of creating any real sense of bondage, offered a freedom in our religious and social life that had been cruelly denied us by our social and sacerdotal authorities. And the highest political ambition of our English-educated classes was not to supplant, but simply to increasingly participate in the new political life and authority in their country, in common with their new and alien rulers. These were the ideals of the earlier political movements in this country, and they had, therefore, really little or no psychophysical impetus or reference in them.

This psychophysical impetus was, however, a new and supremely significant fact in the Swadeshi Movement. But it was either ignored or misunderstood by the Government of Lord Minto. Not even Lord Morley could properly seize this fact. And they pursued a policy which, by seeking to forcibly repress this new movement, helped only to increase the strength of these psychophysical forces. These forces want exceedingly delicate handling. They may be controlled but can never be crushed. True statesmanship would try to play the Providence in regard to these and seek rather to guide them from within than to oppose them from without. Lord Minto absolutely failed to do it. He and his advisors looked upon the new spirit of self-help and self-assertion in the people and the numerous movements in which it commenced to materialise itself, as a new menace to British rule in India. They failed to see that it was only an attempt on the part of the starved physical and psychophysical impulses of the youths of the land, to find due play and satisfaction through various self-organised and self-regulated activities for the promotion of what they conceived to be the public good. Whatever menace there might have existed in these new movements could have been easily removed by friendly co-operation with their leaders. It might have been fully provided against by benevolent inactivity and wise watchfulness. When any new social or political forces suddenly come into being and commence to show signs of running into harmful excesses, the right thing to do is not to try to crush them out of existence altogether, but only to grant them sufficient scope for their safe and legitimate play and fulfilment. This scope was, however, denied to the new forces which found expression through the manifold activities of the Swadeshi Movement in Bengal. And this denial constitutes the real psychophysical cause of the propaganda of political criminalism in this country.

The Psychophysics of the "Political" Criminal.

Considering the character of those who are suspected of being involved in the propaganda of political criminalism in this country, we must look for the peculiar psycho-physical root and reference of it in the general psychophysics of youth and adolescence. I wonder if it has ever struck anybody that the strength and inspiration of the swadeshi agitation of the last few years came mainly from the opening that it offered to the youths of the country for the play and fulfilment of their natural instincts and energies. The appeal of the new patriotism in the country with its ideal of self-help and self-reliance, was mainly to the natural idealism of youth. So far as the actual political and patriotic activities of the previous generations were concerned, these gave but little room for the play of youthful idealism, and but little scope for the employment of youthful energies. In the activities of the Congress, the youths of the nation had really neither part nor lot, save and except what the young students of the town or city where the annual session of the Congress was held, had in serving the guests of the Reception Committee, as Congress-Volunteers. The pageant of the Congress did offer some scope for the satisfaction of the natural love of youth for self-display. But the show lasted only for three or four days in the year, and those who could directly take part in it, were drawn from the youthful student-population of the particular locality where the session of the Congress was held. The natural idealism and exuberant energies of the general body of the youthful intellectuals of the country were, however, being systematically starved. Our old social life that gave some scope for the play of youthful enthusiasm and energy, through numerous socio-religious ceremonials and shows, had already fallen into decay under the influence of the new education that the British Government had introduced and which undermined our old faiths and practically killed many of our old social and religious institutions. The movement of the intellectual populations from village to city, deprived the new generation of our young men of even the limited opportunities that the village life still offered for the play and fulfilment of youthful instincts and desires. The Swadeshi Agitation offered, for the first time, a new field for the play and satisfaction of the starved instincts and energies of the new generation of our youthful intellectuals. This agitation spread from town to town and even into remote rural areas. It was not confined, like the Congress Agitation, to a particular period of time, but was carried on from day to day. The so-called volunteer movement started as a three days' show by the

Congress, which was confined within the narrow limits of the city where the Congress session was held for any particular year, spread now all over the country and developed into a permanent institution. This so-called National Volunteer Movement offered, for the first time in the history of British India, a splendid field for the satisfaction of the natural idealism of the youths and the employment of the exuberant energies of the rising generation of the country. Few people, whether among our own leaders or among the representatives of the Government, seemed to realise the supreme psychophysical reference of this National Volunteer Movement. On the one side it organised, through the public processions in which these volunteers in their improvised uniforms and their quasi-military organisation and drill, took a prominent part, a new set of public pageants that helped at once to evoke and satisfy the instinctive love of self-display of the youths of the country. It was one of the most attractive features of the Swadeshi Agitation. On the other side, the employment of these new national volunteers in various kinds of public work—as for instance, in keeping order and rendering help to the old and decrepit, during public festivals, when men and women gathered in their thousands and tens of thousands, and in doing other quasi-police duties—offered a new field for the satisfaction of their natural enthusiasm for public service. At the back of all these activities there worked also the universal instinct of self-assertion which gives to the youths of every nation their first sense of strength and power. Youth not only loves self-display and is universally inspired by the spirit of romance and adventure, but it is also somewhat self-assertive and pugnacious. All these characteristics of youth have a distinct and universal psychophysical origin and reference. In dealing with these universal characteristics of youth one must never ignore this fact. The desire for self-display, self-expansion, and self-assertion is as natural and strong in youth as the desire for food and drink and sex-satisfaction is universal, and almost over-powering, in the race. Both are constitutional and instinctive. They may be regulated, but can never be suppressed. Any attempt to suppress these universal human instincts leads only to lawlessness and disorder. Priests and princes have made the attempt in almost every country to suppress these natural instincts of mankind, and having thus sown the wind had always also to reap the whirlwind: and the course of civilisation has, as a result of their folly, been marked by brutal struggles and bloody revolutions.

The Boy-Scout Movement: the only Remedy.

To fight this evil propaganda successfully this psychophysical cause of it must be removed. And it can be very easily removed by the inauguration of a Boy Scout Movement in this country, in all our schools and colleges, exactly along the lines in which it is working with such marvellous results in Great Britain. So far as the youthful intellectuals, who offer the only recruiting ground to the Indian revolutionary, are concerned, this Indian Boy-Scout Movement would at once remove the psychophysical impetus from the revolutionary propaganda; and by meeting in a legitimate and open way the demands of youthful idealism and energy for self-expression and self-fulfilment, it would practically starve the revolutionary movement out to whatever extent it may actually exist among us. This is the only psychophysical remedy for this growing evil. It will require considerable courage to adopt it, I know. But serious diseases always and everywhere call not for timid and tentative but bold and radical treatment. This is as true in politics as it is in clinics.

CALCUTTA:
August and September, 1913.

CHAPTER XIV.

AN INDIAN BOY-SCOUT MOVEMENT.

WANTED AN INDIAN BOY-SCOUT MOVEMENT.

THE President of the last Bengal Provincial Conference, in discussing the problem of political criminalism in the country, asked the Government to organise a Boy-Scout Movement among our youthful students, as a preventive against the seductions of the political revolutionary. The same idea had been put forward by me in the *Hindu Review* last year. It was even noticed by the Anglo-Indian press. The *Indian Daily News* went so far as to admit that there was "something" in it. For loyalty is the very plinth and foundation of this Boy-Scout Movement. But the Boy-Scout of to-day would want to be a Volunteer to-morrow: and what then? That was how the *Daily News* dismissed the idea as impracticable. In discussing Mr. Byomkesh Chakravarty's Presidential Address, the *Englishman* practically raises the same plea. Can we trust these young men to be "loyal to our rule," when they have acquired the strength and the training that comes through the discipline of the Boy-Scout? This seems to the *Englishman* the crux of the whole question.

A FUNDAMENTAL PRE-CONDITION.

In putting forward the suggestion for a Boy-Scout Movement in India, I had, however, fully anticipated and answered all these objections. The Boy-Scout Movement by itself, I know, will not help the solution of this problem. But we never put it forward as an isolated prescription. The fundamental thing is to completely abandon the policy that encourages the Anglo-Indian scribe to identify himself with the Government of India, as against the Indian people who are mere outsiders in it. This "our ruling" must be stopped, if not in fact—for that must take time—but in idea and thought, at once. The Government of India may be manned, as now, by a body of Englishmen for a pretty long time to come. British Ministers may control our foreign policy, and their representative in India may initiate and control the Home Administration until such time when, in the course of natural, peaceful evolution, these rights and functions shall be gradually transferred to us. But while there need be no immediate change in the practical administrative control and direction of the country, there must be a radical change in the spirit and ideal of its Government. This change must be such as will create and encourage the conceit of own-ness in our people in regard to their Government. It must be *our rule, our Government, our officials*, at least in thought and idea, now and immediately, and not of any other class or country. This conceit must be sedulously cultivated. All the recent troubles are really due to the open repudiation of this idea by Lord Curzon. It was he who first openly declared that the Government of India was and would always continue to be British and not Indian, as long as the British were in this country. This was what set up an irreconcilable conflict between patriotism on the one side, and loyalty to the established political order and authority in the country, on the other. This conflict must first of all be removed. This is an essential, a primary condition of the success of anything that the representatives of the Government or the leaders of the people may do to fight and cure the revolutionary propaganda in the country. In suggesting the organisation of a Boy-Scout Movement in this country as an antidote against this revolutionary propaganda, I had made all this absolutely clear. This revolutionary propaganda has, as I pointed out, a twofold origin, one intellectual, the other psychophysical. The strong and widespread conviction among our articulate classes that Indian and British interests, the demands of the new national spirit in India and the requirements of the unity and integrity of the British Empire—are not only unreconciled so far, but are eternally irreconcilable, constitutes the intellectual root and origin of this revolutionary movement. This is the primary cause. The psychophysical causes work and operate upon this intellectual ground, to create the youthful revolutionary. The removal of this conflict, not perhaps in fact, which may not be possible immediately, but in idea, is an absolute condition-precedent of the success of any psychophysical remedy, as for instance, like the organisation of an Indian Boy-Scout Movement, that may be prescribed to prevent or cure this political criminalism among us.

Reconciliation between Nationalism and Imperialism.

The first need of the situation as I have repeatedly urged, therefore, is the declaration of a policy that will offer a permanent reconciliation between Nationalism and Imperialism or internationalism. A nation can never, by mere expansion and conquest, grow into an Empire. The two are distinct categories; they represent two different orders of political entities. An Empire is composed of many nations even as a nation grows out of the combination of many races or communities. The present British Empire is a compound of many nationalities. It is an international relation. For the preservation and growth of this Empire, all conflicts between the different limbs and parts of it must be removed and reconciled. The conflict here is not between any particular part and the whole of which it is a part; but only between one part and another. Our conflict is *not* with the *Empire* but with Great Britain or the British Colonies, that are also *parts* of this whole, and not the whole itself. The evil has come through the usurpation of the rights and functions of the *Whole* by *some* of its parts. This conflict will cease the moment the Whole comes to its own, is freed from this usurpation, and is able, by this freedom, to stand aloof from the partialities of the parts, and thus to mediate between them, and reconcile, in its larger life, the petty conflicts of isolated particularistic interests. The evolution of this true Imperialism must take time. We cannot force it immediately. In the meanwhile, however, a beginning must be made, by the different parts of the existing nucleus of this true Empire, to work up a reasonable reconciliation of these particularistic conflicts. This policy of reconciliation must be initiated and proclaimed in India. We must be assured of the fullest and freest realisation of our own national life. National autonomy must be assured to us. The foundations of it must be laid now, and at once. The gradual development of this autonomy must be openly accepted and avowed as the objective of the policy of the Indian Government. The present rulers of India must make up their mind that India must come, sooner or later, to her own, that she must be a self-governed and self-defended unit of the Empire, and not perpetually continue to be a mere Dependency. This Dependency-idea must be abandoned, killed, coffined, and buried for ever. India's place and function as a co-partner in the coming Federation of the British Empire, equal to the other partners of it in every respect, must be fully and freely conceded, now in idea, ultimately in fact. British policy in India should be framed to help this ultimate ideal. If this is done, then, and only then, will it be possible for the Government to permit the organisation of a Boy-Scout Movement among us. It is only, as part of this larger policy of reconciliation and unity, that it will be possible to use and apply it as an effective cure of, or prophylactic against, the contagion of revolutionary criminalism that seems to be perpetually spreading among our youthful intellectual populations, forming new centres of communication every day.

Before suggesting the organisation of a Boy-Scout Movement as a prophylactic against the revolutionary propaganda, I had, therefore, distinctly asked for the declaration of this policy of reconciliation and compromise. I wrote :—

"And, finally, it would help the present situation more than most people can imagine now, if His Excellency

(Lord Hardinge) could place on record a reasoned statement of British policy in India, pointing out the possible lines of development, worked by the pressure of the actualities of the present situation in the British Empire on the one side, and in world-politics on the other, and frankly and unequivocally indicating the basis upon which there can and must be a complete reconciliation between the fullest self-expansion and self-fulfilment of the composite Indian nation, and the maintenance and consolidation of the present British Empire—a reconciliation that is essential as much for the future of Indian Nationalism itself as it is for British Imperialism. All this will remove, I do not say completely, but without doubt very considerably, the present conviction that Indian and British interests are absolutely irreconcilable, and, consequently, the only hope for India lies in the ultimate severance of her present connection with Great Britain, howsoever it may have to be worked out."

It is only after this is done, and the intellectual cause of the present revolutionary patriotism has been removed, that it will be possible for the Government to permit the organisation of this Indian Boy-Scout Movement. The revolutionary propaganda owns, as I have repeatedly said, a two-fold origin: one intellectual, the other psycho-physical. And as I said—considering the character of those who are generally found guilty of political criminalism among us—we must look for the peculiar psycho-physical root and reference of it, in the general psycho-physics of youth and adolescence. So far as the actual political and patriotic activities of the previous generations were concerned, these gave but little room for the play of youthful idealism, and but little scope for the employment of youthful energies. The natural idealism and exuberant energies of the general body of the youthful intellectuals of the country were thus being systematically starved. The Swadeshi Agitation offered, for the first time, a new field for the play and satisfaction of the starved instincts and energies of the new generation of our youthful intellectuals. The so-called National Volunteer Movement offered, for the first time in the history of British India, a splendid field for the satisfaction of the natural idealism of youth and the employment of the exuberant energies of the rising generations in the service of their country. Few people, whether among our own leaders, or among the representatives of the Government, seemed to have realised the supreme psychophysical character of this National Volunteer Movement. On the one side it organised, through the public processions in which these "Volunteers" in their improvised uniforms and their quasi-military organisation and drill, took a prominent part, a new set of public pageants that helped at once to evoke and satisfy the instinctive love of self-display of the youths of the country. On the other side, the employment of these new National Volunteers in various kinds of self-organised public duties—as for instance, in keeping order during crowded public festivals, when men and women gathered in their thousands and tens of thousands, and specially in rendering help to the old and the decrepit and women and little children, and in doing other quasi-police duties—offered a new field for the satisfaction of their natural enthusiasm for public service. At the back of all these there worked also the universal instinct of self-assertion, which gives to the youths of every nation, their first sense of strength and power. Youth not only loves self-display, and is universally inspired by the spirit of romance and adventure, but it is also somewhat self-assertive and pugnacious. This desire for self-display, self-expansion, and self-assertion is as natural and strong in youth as is the desire for food and drink and sex-satisfaction universal and over-powering in the race. These are instinctive and constitutional. They may be regulated, but can never be suppressed. Any attempt to suppress these universal human instincts inevitably and universally leads only to lawlessness and disorder. The suppression of the Swadeshi Agitation, and especially of this so-called National Volunteer Movement by Lord Minto's Crimes Act, is not a little responsible for the hold that the revolutionary propaganda seems, clearly, to have secured upon the mind and fancy of at least a section of our young men. It is useless to discuss the wisdom of that Act now. Lord Minto having first sanctioned the general policy of his Administration, towards the new Swadeshi and Boycott agitation, was forced later on to adopt these repressive measures, for which the criminal propaganda of a section of the Indian Nationalists found apparent excuse and justification. But these measures have not as yet succeeded in crushing the political criminal out of existence. This is admitted now even by the authors and advocates of those measures themselves.

Political Crimes and Public Sympathy.

In fact, the conviction that the political assassin has come to stay with us is gaining ground in every quarter.

Perhaps we shall never get rid of him. The freest countries have not succeeded in securing absolute safety for their high-placed officials. But it is not the mere presence of the political criminal that makes the Indian situation so serious. The most serious thing here is the wide sympathy which the political criminal gets from his own community. It is positively mischievous to shut one's eyes to this fact and mislead the Government by proclaiming that people at large abhor these crimes. The truth is that they do not. If it were not so, these crimes would not have been possible in this country. We have not as yet developed the real anarchist among us. The political criminal here is not engaged in a deliberate anti-social propaganda. The European anarchist and revolutionary is a deliberate enemy of society. He is disgusted with social inequalities. Envy or greed, envy in regard to the people of wealth and rank, and greed in regard to their earthly possessions, these are frequently the inspiration of the European criminal anarchist. But all anarchists in Europe are not of this criminal type. The philosophical anarchist of the type of Prince Kropotkin of course belongs altogether to a different class. This philosophical anarchism is the logic of the individualistic rationalism of the European thought of the last two centuries. It is, no doubt, the intellectual parent of the criminal anarchist; but the philosophical anarchist is a far superior being. He is a lofty idealist, who has nothing to do personally with the criminal anarchist. This European type has not as yet developed in this country. The political criminal in India is not an enemy of the social order really, but only of the existing political order in the country. His crimes do not, therefore, outrage the conscience of his community. On the contrary, every young man who risks his life in joining this criminal propaganda knows and feels it in his heart of hearts, that whatever fate may befall him, his name will be cherished with secret admiration by his people. And he is absolutely right here. It is notorious that the failure of every political prosecution causes universal rejoicing in the community. This rejoicing is not inspired by any deep and reasonable conviction of the innocence of the parties acquitted. The question of guilt or innocence does not come in here at all. Even those who are convicted do not actually lose this public sympathy. It would, however, be a grievous wrong to convict a whole community of any criminal intent or even of any active sympathy with the political criminal. The feeling is dangerous to the cause of peace and order, but it is not, therefore, really criminal. It is due to a variety of psychological and psychophysical causes. In the first place, it is a very common, if not an absolutely universal human instinct—we may call it a weakness if we like—to feel inwardly and almost unconsciously glad at the discomfiture of a strong man at the hands of his weaker rival or opponent. We all stand, instinctively, in fear of the strong man, unless he happens to be our own friend or ally. And the overthrow of strength by weakness, of the bully by the coward, appeals, vicariously, to our own inner weakness; and we inwardly enjoy the triumph of the weak and the timid over the strong and the brave. Nobody is, however, glad when a weak man is beaten by his stronger brother. No people are ever glad at the discomfiture of the governed at the hands of their own Government. But everybody including even such staunch advocates of law and order as the *Englishman* or the *Pioneer*, and even the respectable *Times* itself—unless he is directly interested in the issues of the struggle—is always glad when any people drive their own Government to bay. The Government may have very good reasons for ruthlessly putting down a popular outburst. The people, by embarrassing their Government, may be only paving the way for their own ruin. The real and ultimate good of the people, even the prospects of their final emancipation, may demand their temporary suppression and subjection. But these are matters for quiet and sober reflection. Our instincts are however rarely or never guided or controlled by balanced judgments. The instinctive life stands on a different plane from the reflective or the rational life. The general mental attitude of people towards the political criminal is a matter of instinct only. It would have certainly been criminal, if there were any large body of conscious and considered opinion at its back. Nine hundred and ninety-nine out of every thousand persons who inwardly rejoice at the acquittal of every political criminal and feel irritated at their prosecution, especially if it shows any excessive and indiscreet zeal on the part of the police to secure conviction, would instinctively shrink from committing any of these deeds themselves, which, when done by others, inwardly pleases them somewhat. This very fact shows that they are, really, not criminals themselves. Nor would it be right to take this shrinking from the actual committal of these crimes, entirely due to mere dread of consequences. This shrinking is not an animal, a mere physical, but a distinctly moral instinct. It is an expression of the inherited humanity of our people. The secret pleasure which they feel at the committal of these outrages by others is, itself, on the contrary, a purely physical or psycho-physical thing. The Penal Code has no cure for it. The disease is not amenable to official threats or police annoyance or surveillance. A whole nation ought not to, and cannot really, be treated as a pack of unruly school-boys, or as a gang of hardened and habitual criminals. To treat them as criminals is the surest way to make them so. The school-boy treatment, on the other hand, only increases existing irritation, and kills the very springs of sobriety and good sense in the community. Abuse inevitably increases that very bitterness and race-antipathy which really lie at the root of the whole problem. Threats and abuse only lead to the concealment of truth. Yet the greatest need of the present situation is that the Government should know the truth about it, without any mental or other reservations; and they should know it not from secret agents of the police or even from their own subordinate officers who may not be always either capable of getting at it themselves or of speaking out unreservedly when they do know it, but from respectable and courageous spokesmen and leaders of the people without any private axe to grind. And having thus known and seized the real truth of the situation that faces them, they must calmly, and without passion or prejudice, consider how best to meet it.

The True Remedy.

It is, really, no use blinking the fact, therefore, that the political criminal does get almost universal public sympathy here, as he does almost all over the world. He would not have got it if only people could view him as an enemy of the future well-being of his own country, as he admittedly is of the present Government. And it rests entirely with the Government and those who claim especial identification with them, to induce this idea in the public mind. The *Englishman* says that he must be assured of the "loyalty" of our young men, before they can be permitted to be organised into Boy-Scout companies. The *Daily News* said that though the *idea* of a Boy-Scout Movement in India, as a prophylactic against the present revolutionary propaganda, was good, that there was "something" in it, yet the thing was hardly thinkable now, for the ample reason that the Boy-Scout of to-day would naturally desire to be a volunteer to-morrow, and what complications would it not create? The *Daily News* had evidently read only the last paragraph of our article on the Psychophysics of Political Criminalism or had simply skipped over what preceded it. For we had very carefully considered and anticipated all these possible objections. The suggestion regarding the organisation of a Boy-Scout Movement was not an isolated and simple prescription. It was joined to other suggestions without which it would not at all serve the ends proposed there. The main objective was to stop or weaken the propaganda of political criminalism in the country. The strength of this propaganda came, as I said, from two causes, one intellectual, and the other psychophysical. Both these causes worked together. The intellectual cause was the deep-rooted and wide-spread conviction among our articulate classes that Indian and British interests are not only unreconciled so far, but are eternally irreconcilable, as long as the two countries are politically bound up together. The interests of India can never be advanced to their fullest legitimate limits as long as the present British connection lasts. This is an almost universal belief. And this conviction, namely, that nationalist aspirations in India are absolutely irreconcilable with the maintenance of the unity and integrity of the present British Empire, lies at the very root and centre of every form and shade of revolutionary patriotism and anti-British sentiment in this country. The entire body of our articulate populations are more or less steeped in this new nationalism. Some are cautious, some are reckless ; some are wise, and some are foolish ; some are diplomatic, some are straightforward ; some are eager to save their skins, and some do not mind risking it ; some are Moderates, and some are Extremists ; but every Indian whose interests have widened beyond the limits of his personal or family life is a nationalist at heart. Every Indian whose vision has been widened and whose sensibilities have been quickened by contact with the outside world wants to be in his own country as the great and puissant peoples of other lands are in their own. And every one of these Indians feels more or less keenly the present dependent position of his country. So far as this desire for national freedom and self-realisation is concerned, the distinction between the Moderate and the Extremist is artificial, arbitrary, and absolutely unreal. The revolutionary Extremist, and the constitutional Congressman are both moved by this one desire. The former seeks national independence, the latter pursues the ideal of colonial self-government; and though the wording of their ideal is different, the substance is the same. The real difference between them is one of temperaments and methods; and not of ultimate ideals and objectives. It is no use shutting our eyes to this fact. It is worse than useless to conceal it from the Government unless the object of this "loyalty" be not to help but only to hoodwink them. Such disclaimers and concealments may serve the private ends of self-seeking politicians, but cannot further the well-being of the country. And psychologically considered, this universal desire of our articulate and intellectual classes for as complete a measure of political freedom as is enjoyed by the Colonials or the Britishers themselves, is the fundamental cause of the present unrest, of which this so-called political criminalism is a troublesome and dangerous symptom. And it is impossible to cure this symptom without removing the conviction that Indian Nationalism and British Imperialism are not only unreconciled with each other just now, but there is no chance of any reasonable reconciliation between them even in the future. This conviction must be sought to be removed, if not previous to, at least simultaneously with, the application of any other remedy that may be prescribed to cure this political criminalism.

Patriotism and Loyalty.

And if this conviction is removed, if the Government enunciate a policy that will fully reconcile nationalist aspirations with the perpetuation of the British connection, then the present conflict, in the thoughts and sentiments of the general body of our youthful intellectuals, between "patriotism" and "loyalty" will also be automatically settled.

But instead of trying to reconcile the patriotism of our people with their fealty to the present Government in the country, the Anglo-Indian publicists seek rather to keep up this unfortunate conflict. They do not seem to understand that wherever any Government sets up any antithesis between patriotism and loyalty, it is not the former that really suffers, but rather, on the contrary, the very attempt to force loyalty above patriotism makes people inwardly more deeply disloyal than ever. The *Englishman* recognises this in Ulster, but would not see that human nature is the same in Ireland as it is in India, and that what is natural and true in Ulster must also be equally natural and true in Bengal. To make the people truly loyal to their rule, the Government must also themselves be openly loyal to the highest ideals and interests of the people. It is only where a Government fail to do so, where they are not able to completely identify themselves with the interests and ambitions of the subject populations, that revolutions burst forth, involving oftentimes both the rulers and the ruled in common ruin. The Indian revolutionary too, whatever may be his strength, is the product of this foolish conflict between patriotism and loyalty which hair-brained publicists and shortsighted politicians have sought to conjure up among us. And this political criminalism can never be successfully fought, until this conflict is satisfactorily settled.

The Boy-Scout Movement would help this settlement very considerably in a two-fold way. In the first place, the very fact that our young men are permitted to put themselves under the *quasi*-military training under which the Boy-Scout is placed would prove that the Government is no longer afraid of the cultivation of the higher military virtues by our people. It is because they are, or supposed to be, so afraid, that even the *Indian Daily News* considers this suggestion, though otherwise reasonable, to be yet impossible in India. The organisation of Indian Boy-Scout companies would practically be a public declaration on the part of the Government that they are completely identified with the people and are, therefore, no longer afraid of the strength or organisation of the people, and are prepared to fully co-operate with them for the preservation of peace and order in the community. It would mean that the Government was convinced of the unity of their interests with those of the governed and feel strong in their strength and safe in the growth of their capacity for self-organisation and self-government. For as long as the Government were not prepared to allow the people an effective and supreme voice in the administration of their own affairs, they could not, possibly, place the powerful weapon of an extensive Boy-Scout organisation in the hands of their subjects. With a large body of national scouts at their back, the leaders of the people would be able to cry "check" on the Government at any moment when the latter's acts and policies ran counter to the wishes of the governed. All this is as plain as day. And the suggestion for a Boy-Scout Movement in India means, therefore, much more than what appears on the face of it. It means the initiation of a real policy of reconciliation between Nationalist aspirations in India and the perpetuation of the British connection with her. Lord Hardinge has already initiated such a policy. But as yet his Lordship has not given any practical shape and form to it. The inauguration of a Boy-Scout Movement among our young men would give this shape and form to his far-reaching statesmanship. It would prove that the implications of the Despatch of 1911 are something more substantial than mere wise and benevolent intention or pre-vision. It would wean away our young men from the seductions of the political revolutionary, and would enable the authorities to use and employ the very class from which the political criminal is now recruited against this revolutionary propaganda.

If we had no Boy-Scouts in India, this demand might have been rejected. But the presence of the Anglo-Indian and European Boy-Scouts among us lends a very ugly interpretation to the refusal of the Government to permit similar organisations among the youths of the nation, and thereby increases and deepens the existing conflict in the country. If the Government cannot gather up sufficient courage to allow the formation of Boy-Scout companies among Indian young men, they should prohibit their organisation among Anglo-Indian and European young men in this country. If we cannot have equal rights, the next best thing is to have equal privations. For the sight of these Anglo-Indian Boy-Scouts must deepen the sense of wrong which the wholesale and indiscriminate suppression of the National Volunteers created in the country.

CALCUTTA: *May*, 1914.

CHAPTER XV.

CRIME AND KARMA.

A Study in Social Unreason.

Modern civilisation, by which we have been taught to understand the civilisation of modern Europe and America, has so far notoriously failed in its understanding and treatment of crime and the criminal classes. And the legalistic, as distinguished from what may be called the naturalistic—the moral, as distinguished from the physiological and psychophysical—view of human impulses and the human character is almost entirely responsible for this failure. Christian morals have always been something superimposed upon man, from outside, by a Power—not himself. This is the legacy that Christian Europe received from the thought and culture of Judaism. The "thou shalt-not" spirit of the Judaistic Law and Commandment has almost completely dominated Christian ethics for the last two thousand years. It has, therefore, always set itself up in more or less open antagonism to the natural instincts of man. This cleavage between the moral and the natural life is almost entirely responsible for the failure of Christianity to deal effectively with crime and criminalism.

Owing to this conflict between man's instincts and what is called his conscience, either fear of punishment or love of reward has been the chief moral incentive in Christendom. Even Jesus Christ did not appeal to anything deeper or higher than this. His Sermon on the Mount, the finest thing in the whole New Testament records, strikes no deeper or higher key: "Blessed are the pure in heart, *for* theirs is the Kingdom of Heaven." "Blessed are they that suffer persecutions for my sake, *for* they shall be rewarded:" This idea of reward runs all through these lofty beatitudes. And wherever there is any idea of rewards, there is, necessarily, an idea of punishment also. "Do this and you will be duly rewarded," carries with it the implication, "refuse to do it, and you shall be punished." Rewards and punishments are almost like shadow and shine, eternally joined together in the same idea or law. The one is unthinkable and incomplete without the other; and both are administered by an outside authority.

Every action, whether physical or mental, carries with it its own consequences; and these consequences may either be pleasant or painful. When the consequence of an act is pleasant, we may call it, in a loose way, our reward; and when painful, we may characterise it, similarly, as punishment. But the real concept rewards and punishments are different from the natural sequences or results of our actions. The concept consequence has no ethical value, the concept reward or punishment has. That is the fundamental difference between them. And this ethical value is derived essentially from the idea of a law that it is our duty to obey. This word duty implies something that is due by one to another. The concept is, thus, fundamentally contractual or covenantal. For all dues are for value received. I received something from you, and, therefore, something is due to you by me. This is the root-idea of duty. And it is, therefore, really based on barter or contract ; and carries with it, consequently, an odour of selfishness, however distilled and superfined it may be. Ethics, based upon this conception of duty—duty to God, duty to society, duty to family, duty to one's own self, in all these various forms into which it was classified by old Christian thinkers—must, by its very nature, be essentially commercial. A culture dominated by this ethical conception can hardly expect to solve the problem of crime or discover or devise any effective and rational method of dealing with criminalism.

This legalistic view of ethics must develop a retributive spirit in dealing with crimes and criminals. And it is absolutely unquestionable that retribution, and not reform, has hitherto been the dominating idea both in the criminal laws and the administration of criminal justice in all European countries. The Church and the State have both worked together to help this retributive idea. The Church proclaimed sacerdotal or ecclesiastical laws for the regulation of the religious life of the people. It did so as an outside authority, owning the seal and sanction of a God who practically rules his world from without. It never was identified with the people as they actually are, with all their strength and weaknesses, and, therefore, had little real sympathy, and no patience, with their failings. It never tried to draw religion out of them but always imposed it upon them from the outside. The Church was the Body of Christ, the God-Man or the Man-God ; but not the Body of the people, *as they are*, with all their hungry appetites and burning passions. It, therefore, took no notice of this common, low, vicious, weak, human nature, but simply proclaimed what men should and what they should not do ; and when they failed to obey, it punished them. Rewards and punishments were all that the Church could offer. Instruction was all that it gave. The State also, followed, naturally in the steps of the Church, and promulgated its laws, leaving each individual citizen free to obey or disobey these laws, and when they were broken, punishment was all that it had to offer to the delinquent. Both the Church and the State have thus been far more eager to uphold their authority by dealing retributive justice to those who violated their laws than to remedy the evils which this disobedience revealed. For nearly two thousand years Christendom has dealt with its criminals in this just, but essentially, heartless way.

Recent investigations into the nature and origin of man's criminal propensities, have, however, commenced to reveal their essential physiological and psychophysical origin and reference. The recognition of heredity as a very powerful factor in the formation of human character, has very largely modified the older and stricter views of individual responsibilities. It is being increasingly recognised that we owe, to a very large extent, the rudimentary elements of our mental and moral, as well as those of our physical, constitution to our parents and forbears, and it is, therefore, as reasonable to hold us personally responsible for our mental or moral tendencies as it would be to do so for our physical deformities or deficiencies. The entire science of eugenics, having for its object, first the investigation of the causes of men's physical, mental, and moral natures, their origin and history, and then the due regulation of their marital relations, with a view to the improvement of their progeny and the preservation of their race—has commenced to work upon this hypothesis, namely, the reality and strength of heredity in the formation of people's physical, mental, and moral life and character. Eugenics may have, possibly, taken a much too exaggerated view of the influence of heredity in the making of man's minds and morals; but making every allowance for these exaggerations, we cannot refuse to admit that heredity does contribute very materially to the formation of our mind and body. Add to this the influences that our early education exert over our mental and moral life, and think how impossible it is for any human individual either to control or evade these early influences. Lastly, think of the general influences that his society, its economic arrangements and political organisation, exercise over him, and how impossible it is for him, individually, to alter or amend these economic and political institutions. And if one will only do this, one will not be long in discovering the actual measure of the responsibility of individual members of society for their own acts. There are economic structures that are bound to foster laziness among certain classes, and envy and greed are inevitably generated in large masses, by other economic structures. The envy of the European proletariat, and the greed of the European capitalists, are two ends of the same stick; and the responsibility for both these must be fixed upon the competitive and capitalistic economic structures of European society. The anti-social acts and tendencies in Europe, that war against the laws and rights of personal property, are very largely due to this envy on the one side and greed on the other, and the conflict between capital and labour, carried on from generation to generation, has been helping to increase these evil tendencies on both sides, through hereditary transmission. The working-man transmits his envy to his children, as the capitalist his greed; and these grow, in this way, in both intensity and volume, from generation to generation. Born in this envy the children of the working classes, particularly of those who stand on the lowest rungs of the economic ladder, are brought up in an atmosphere of intense hatred of the richer classes; and who would have the hardihood to hold these children, when they grow up to manhood or womanhood, responsible for any anti-social thoughts and acts which this hereditary envy and this transmitted sense of social injustice may lead them to? As the economic structures and laws of different communities are fundamentally responsible for a certain class of immoral or criminal or anti-social tendencies in the people, so their social structures and laws are equally responsible for other classes of anti-social and immoral tendencies. The rigidity of the law regarding the marital relation in monogamous communities like those of Europe and America, joined to the almost absolute freedom of social intercourse between the sexes that prevail among them, is very largely, if not entirely, responsible for all sorts of offences against the laws of sex and marriage that are found in those countries. They will eat beef, drink beer, live amidst artistic surroundings—all calculated to appeal to their sense of the beautiful in form, colour, sound and touch, and all of which have, both biologically and psychologically, a secret and powerful reference to the sex-instinct—sit in warm rooms with well-groomed gentlemen and well-dressed ladies, talking either social scandal or, in higher and more educated circles, about art and literature that have oftentimes a reference to the diviner passion—go with one another to the theatre or the music hall, enjoy in one another's company all the amorous displays of the popular stage, drive home at midnight together, in cosy carriages after a champagne supper; dance tango or skate with one another—and then society is shocked if the rising tide of passion breaks cruelly through the bonds of the marital relation. You must reap what you sow. This is really, our law of Karma. But the pity of it is that while society sows the wind, it compels the poor individual to reap the whirlwind. Society makes the criminal all the world over; and yet it is the same society which, like the gentleman who ruins a poor and guileless maiden and then leaves her to her shame and sin to turn judge against her, punishes the individuals for crimes to which it had itself driven them. This is the barest truth about criminal law and the administration of so-called criminal justice almost in every civilised country.

As the very structure of particular societies is almost entirely responsible for certain classes of crimes, which they first help to create in certain sections of their own community, and then turn judge and executor against these criminals; so the physical and mental structure of individuals also are equally responsible for other crimes which they are driven to commit. In both these cases, personal responsibility of the criminal is reduced to a minimum. Some criminal impulses are purely temperamental—the drink-rage, for instance, in some men; or an absolutely uncontrollable anger or sex-impulse in others. These are far more physical and psychophysical in their origin, than really moral. I have known instances of men and women, who instantly lose all control of their limbs, the moment certain parts of their body are tickled. I have heard of a sepoy who was subject to this disease, and one day he actually slapped his officer, during parade, because somehow this particular part of his body had been touched and tickled unwittingly by him. I have seen a very respectable young woman suddenly fall upon a stranger, standing by her side for a similar reason. Neither of these persons were responsible for the assault which they committed. We are all of us, more or less, like this sepoy and this young woman. There are points which no one can touch in us, however unwittingly it may be, without absolutely driving us beyond ourselves, and forcing us to words and deeds which, in our own sober moments, it is absolutely impossible for us to be guilty of. That a large percentage of the crimes that the courts punish or of the vices that society condemns, are really due to these physiological and psychophysical idiosyncrasies, who ever cares to enquire? And what is the actual degree of individual moral responsibility that can be fixed in these cases, who ever cares to ponder? Had this been done, we would have a much saner and more humane method of dealing with crimes and criminals than what our much-vaunted civilisation has as yet discovered or adopted.

The time has come, however, for a complete re-consideration of the whole attitude of modern civilisation, towards crimes and criminals, and especially for a thorough over-hauling of our prison-systems. Modern criminology has done already a great deal, to furnish all the civilised Governments of our day, with the broad generalisation upon which this new prison-reform must be worked up. Broadly speaking, I think it may be safely accepted that the classification of criminals into two broad divisions, namely, those who are criminals by instinct, and those who are criminals through mere force of outer circumstances, is correct. That there are some criminals, whose criminality is deeply ingrained in the very make of their mind and body, some of whom have specific physical defects, in the very structure of their body, and, particularly of their cranium, the receptacle of their brains, can hardly be denied. Lombroso's characterisation of the physical peculiarities of the instinctive criminal, may require more careful examination and analysis than what had been applied to it by himself ; and this examination and analysis may, possibly, disprove the universality of the physical tests which he prescribed ; and there may be, indeed are, criminals of the instinctive class who have not the peculiar structural formations attributed to it by Lombroso. In all these matters, his characterisation of the instinctive criminal may have to be largely amended. But notwithstanding all this, it seems hardly possible to deny the existence of this class of criminals, whom it is impossible or next to impossible, to cure of their anti-social impulses. The State must, in the interest of its own safety and the protection of the life and property of the individuals belonging to it, adopt particular measures for the detention and segregation of these instinctive and incurable cases.

The practical difficulty here would be the detection of these and their differentiation from other and curable cases. Psychometry might perhaps some day help it; but so far it is hardly an established science, and its conclusions cannot, therefore, be absolutely relied upon for the correct determination of the fact, whether a particular criminal is or is not of the instinctive or the circumstantial class. Observation and experiment are the only means available here. And the very first step in modern prison-reform must be to place every offender under careful observation. At present our Penal and Criminal Procedure Codes recognise only two or three classes of criminals, namely, first offenders, class A, and old offenders, class B, to which a third class C, is also added, I think, to designate those who have been repeatedly to prison, and who are generally recognised as incurables. This classification is too wide for purposes of accurate characterisation of the nature of the different individual offenders. It does not at all help the formation of really correct and scientific conclusions regarding the nature of the criminal, whether he belongs to the instinctive or the circumstantial class. A first offender in law may be a very old and practised criminal who has only escaped detection or conviction so long. A good many of the cleverest criminals, the leaders of criminal gangs, very frequently keep themselves beyond the arm of the law. In their case a first conviction can never mean really a first offence. These cleverest criminals are oftentimes free from those physiological or physical defects that, according to Lombroso, marked the instinctive criminal. They supply the brains of the criminal gangs and very frequently use the palpably instinctive criminals, whose very structure betrays their criminal instincts, for the commission of organised criminalities. And the presence of these "gentlemen criminals," so numerous in almost every European country, makes the existing classification into first and old offenders practcially useless for any real scientific investigations into the subject. There are old offenders again, who may be only repeated victims of outer circumstances, and whom these circumstances have driven to criminal associations and acts, which are not due to any inborn criminal instincts in them. In view of these difficulties, therefore, the first step towards a truly rational and scientific study of criminalism, and the adoption of an effective system of prison-administration, would be to abolish these arbitrary and empirical classifications alogether, and take each individual, as soon as he is detected and convicted of any criminal act or intention, upon his own merits, and place him under careful observation for the determination of the inner character, so to say, of his criminality. This is the very first thing that must be done in introducing any rational system of prison-reform, in the light of modern researches in physiology, psychology, and sociology. It would involve a thorough re-casting of our existing Penal Codes and the prevailing methods of the administration of criminal justice in every civilised country. For a really scientific treatment of criminalism the present hide-bound Penal Codes must first of all be thoroughly re-cast. Imprisonment, which means actually the detention of a criminal in a house of correction, must no longer be viewed as a punishment inflicted on the criminal for his crime; but only as a measure of safety for society in the first place, and a means for the determination of the real character of the criminal and the true nature of his crime in the next place. In other words, the old idea of retributive justice must be absolutely abandoned, and it must be supplanted by the new and more rational and moral curative ideal. The object of the detention of the criminal must be, above all else, the curing of his criminal habits or impulses. Even the protection of society itself must be considered as coming not before but only after the interest of the individual convict here. In fact there is no real conflitt or antithesis between these two. The cure of the criminal provides for the safety of society far more effectively than what his punishment or detention would ever expect to achieve. It is only where this cure is impossible that this other negative measure, for ensuring public safety, has to be adopted. And when cure, and not retribution, comes to be recognised as the main and only objective of criminal administration, the present system of specific punishment for specific crimes must be absolutely abandoned; and the period of detention for every criminal will have to be determined, not by the Judge or Magistrate who convicts him, but by the prison authorities who keep him under their observation; for it is only they who are able to know what the real character of the offender is, and how long he has to be detained to effect a reasonably radical cure of his criminal tendencies. In a word, the prisons must be converted into moral hospitals, so to say, and the prison authorities be installed there, after necessary education and equipment, as mind-doctors. The idea would sound strange to many people. It would be difficult of adoption immediately. But this is the only way to which modern physiology, psychology, and the larger conceptions of social well-being, that modern humanitarianism has been developing—all tend, in this matter. And some day society shall adopt these reforms. In the promotion of this larger, more rational, and humanitarian *idealism*, our own culture with its conception of the law of Karma, will render, I believe, very substantial help.

CALCUTTA, *June*, 1914.

CHAPTER XVI.

THE NEW EDUCATION POLICY.

THE EDUCATION AGITATION.

THE Government of India have acted with unpardonable unwisdom in provoking a conflict with the Calcutta University just now.* It has aroused public feeling in this province to a pitch which is only slightly lower than that caused by Lord Curzon's partition scheme. In fact, the issues raised by the Government of India's letter about these University lectureships are far more vital than those raised by that ill-fated measure. Are leaders of political thought and life in the country to be precluded from participating in the education of the youths of their nation on account of their political opinions or activities ?—that is really the fundamental question raised here by the Government of India. Neither Mr. Rasul nor Mr. Suhrawardy,

* The Vice-Chancellor and Syndicate of the Calcutta University appointed three members of the Calcutta Bar, with British University-degrees, to certain lectureships in the University. Technically all such appointments are made subject to the sanction of the Governor-General in Council. The University Executive communicated these appointments to the Government of India, and the lecturers took up their work in anticipation of the formal sanction of the Government. For a long time the Government of India did not take any notice of these appointments, but after more than two years, practically demanded the dismissal of these lecturers, on the ground of their alleged political opinions and associations. This provoked the conflict referred to here.

nor Mr. Jaysawal has been convicted of any political offence, though in few civilised countries even conviction for a political offence, which involved no moral turpitude, would be regarded as a disqualification for any educational office. The only charge against them is that they have been connected with political movements—which means, at its worst, that they have taken part in public protests against certain acts and policies of the Executive Government in India, or that they have been known to hold political opinions that are looked upon with disfavour by the Indian Executive, or have been associated with the so-called "extremist" propaganda. To make this as an offence, justifying the deprivation of any man of his right to have and hold any public office is really to attack the very foundations of civic freedom and to upset all the political values hitherto attached to British rule in India by every one of its apologists and defenders. It is an attack, however insidious it may be, upon the primary rights of citizenship—the right of private judgment and freedom of thought. No self-respecting community can take an assault like this upon their primary rights lying low. No one has any reason to be surprised, therefore, that the Bengalee community have risen up in a strong and united protest against this new education policy of the Government of India.

Opening Old Sores.

And every one who is not a violent revolutionary among us, must deeply regret this unfortunate development. Things were gradually quieting down. The old sores were slowly healing up. The bitterness which the clash and conflict of the past few years had created, was gradually wearing off. And there were signs of a slow return of the people to a more reasonable and generous mood on all sides. We were all striving to work up a reasonable reconciliation between the legitimate demands of Nationalism on the one side, and the real requirements of Imperialism on the other, and were gradually weaning the minds of the rising generations away from all unhealthy and outlandish revolutionary notions. They were gradually coming to recognise the wisdom and truth of Lord Hardinge's Indian policy, and were commencing to lend it their intellectual adherence, as the only rational and safe line of the evolution of modern Indian history and State-craft. But all this has been suddenly and rudely disturbed by this act of the Government of India. And we are once more being borne down by a paralysing sense of utter helplessness to save a situation which seems to be growing more and more hopeless every day.

The present Agitation and the Political Situation.

In fact, in view of the possible recrudescence of the old unrest, which required the presence of the King Emperor himself to pacify, I sometimes feel that it would perhaps have been better to let this action of the Government of India pass unchallenged, than to get up a public protest and agitation against it. This protest has no doubt been headed by men whose sobriety and moderation have never been denied and whose loyalty to the British connection had not been questioned even in the stormy days of the Partition-agitation. There is no danger of any revival of the old unrest personally and directly by these respectable leaders of public opinion. But it should not be forgotten that the Partition agitation was also started and led originally by some of these very leaders themselves. It was they who had originated that movement, which, however, passed rapidly out of their hands and developed tendencies which they were the very first to disclaim and denounce. It is, in fact, the inevitable fate of all so-called "moderate" agitation. It re-acts upon others, and even the most moderate and qualified condemnation of any act or policy of the Government, affecting any vital interests of the governed, inflames the passions of the younger generations. And it is because this new education-policy and the protest that has already been raised against it, are likely to arouse youthful passions in the country, that I so deeply regret this act of unwisdom of the Government of India, and am sometimes even inclined to feel that we would have done well to ignore it altogether. There are circumstances when an experienced physician would rather allow a malady to run its own course and spend itself out in its own way, than cause undesirable excitement or irritation in the patient's system by direct medication. There are occasions when even political wrongs and injustice may have to be suffered in silence. There are very serious considerations that might lead one to hesitate to start a fresh agitation just now in this country. There are, on the other hand, many considerations equally cogent, that demanded a public protest. In view of these conflicting and complex considerations, it was not easy to determine which was the right course. But now that the protest has been made, and the agitation has been started, the issues have passed out of our hands. The Government, and the Government alone, can save the situation by frankly and honourably withdrawing from a position which can be defended neither on considerations of justice nor on grounds of expediency. And the country looks up to Lord Hardinge to do it.

THE VICEROY AND THE NEW POLICY.

For it is generally believed that the Viceroy is not personally responsible for this act of his ministers. And the whole-hearted sympathy of every intelligent and thoughtful Indian politician must go out at this juncture to Lord Hardinge, who has, in one sense, been the first victim of this act. The multitudes, with the lack of discrimination characteristic of the multitudes everywhere, will readily set this new attempt to cripple the intellectual freedom of the Indian populations, to the credit of the Head of the Government. Yet, unless all our readings of His Excellency's policy and statesmanship be absolutely wrong, it is impossible to believe that such wreckless unwisdom as is betrayed by Mr. Sharp's letter to the Calcutta University, could have received Lord Hardinge's support. But few people realise the helplessness of a Viceroy's position, who, though the Head of the State, cannot over-ride the decisions of his own Council, except under very exceptional circumstances and in regard to certain specific matters. The administrative authority in British India is vested, not in the Viceroy, but in the Governor-General-in-Council. Should any vital difference arise between him and his Council, the Governor-General may, of course, offer to resign, but he cannot, except in certain specified cases, over-ride it. The decision of the Government conveyed in Mr. Sharp's letter is not that of the Viceroy, but of the Governor-General-in-Council ; and it is quite possible—in fact, it seems all but certain—that it has not had Lord Hardinge's personal sanction and support. At the same time, one has simply to consider the general situation in the country, and the relative positions of Lord Hardinge and his councillors, to realise how difficult it must have been for his Lordship to even offer a stout opposition to the views put forward by his colleagues. The Delhi outrage has not only affected His Excellency's health, but has even considerably weakened his public policy in the eye of the petty politicians entrusted with the work of administration in India. This outrage, and the persistence of the official idea that there are a class of malevolent irreconcilables in the country who can be crushed by rigorous repressions but can never be conciliated by any concessions short of the actual abdication of the authority of the Government, and lastly, the reports of continued political dacoities from different parts of Bengal—all these are urged as proofs of the complete failure of Lord Hardinge's Indian policy. And all these have, consequently, made his Lordship's position more difficult and delicate than it ever was before. These would try, perhaps, the patience of an angel. Lord Hardinge is only a man. And very few men, indeed, could command sufficient mental strength, after so severe a shock as that which Lord Hardinge received from the assassin's bomb at Delhi, to assert himself against men who claimed longer experience of the country and its people than what he himself had. The situation in Bengal had become impossible. Lord Minto had failed to control it by his policy of right-handed repressions and left-handed concessions. Lord Hardinge offered to try his policy. He had, it was well-known, the support of the British Cabinet. He had the support of the King himself. The Indian Bureaucracy had no faith really in his weak-kneed measures. But they had no option in the matter. And they accepted it as something inevitable. But no one can lend his loyal support to what he accepts only as the inevitable. Lord Hardinge's Indian policy has succeeded as fully as could be expected under the circumstance. But it has not succeeded fully and absolutely. I do not believe that Lord Hardinge himself expected more from it. His Lordship must know that revolutionary patriotism is easier to arouse than to control or correct. The bitterness created in the community by the conflicts of the two previous Administrations, could not be immediately cured by the mere enunciation of a more reasonable and conciliatory policy. It requires the vision of a true statesman to realise the far-reaching trends and aims of a truly statesmanly policy. A statesmanly policy takes a wide and long view of history and socio-political evolution, not only of the particular country for which it is enunciated, but also of its present and future neighbours and allies and opponents. Such a broad and long view of things cannot be taken by the man in the street anywhere. And above all, it requires considerable strength of imagination and very great moral stamina, to forgive and forget a past series of actual wrongs and repressions, out of regard for some distant and possible good. Lord Hardinge could not wipe out the memories of the Minto *régime*. He could not even openly repudiate the acts and politics of his predecessor. He could not repeal all his restrictive Acts and Ordinances. His Lordship could only enunciate a new policy, pregnant with immense future possibilities. He could only hold out, cautiously and tentatively, a promise of reconciliation and progress for the future. But the Indian public is not wholly unfamiliar with the character of politicians' promises. They could not, therefore, become wildly enthusiastic over Lord Hardinge's policy and promises. The return of the country to a normal and healthy mood was bound to be a slow affair. But those who never lent their loyal support to Lord Hardinge's far-seeing policy, was not disposed to give this time to an irritated people to come back to their normal condition. They wanted wonders. They asked for a miracle. The Partition being repealed, all unrest, and especially all underground revolutionary activities, must at once cease. This is what they demanded. It was an impossible demand. It was not satisfied. Revolutionary propaganda continued to be carried on in secret through contraband pamphlets and leaflets. Dacoities did not cease. Even the hand of the political assassin was not stayed. And all these marked, in the eye of the *zubburdust* bureaucrat, the complete failure of Lord Hardinge's policy. All these have somewhat strengthened their position. And they are trying once more to revive the spirit of the Minto *régime*.

And the Viceroy's position is so delicate and difficult, because his Lordship here has to be responsible for the consequences of a course of action which he could not really control, and yet which he cannot openly disclaim. If there is trouble once more in the country, a fresh recrudescence of the old unrest, the blame of it would fall on Lord Hardinge. It would proclaim his failure. It would kill practically all his future prospects. Nor would it make our own lot in any way easier. In the present state of his health, Lord Hardinge cannot be expected to face the anxieties of the situation that Lord Minto had to grapple with. Already the situation is becoming more and more difficult and anxious. The Mahomedans are a fresh cause of anxiety to the Government. They have commenced to assume a bolder and more defiant attitude than had ever been known in the past. The present Moslem unrest is not a mere local outburst of fanaticism. The Moslem mob has been finding educated leaders. The latter have learnt some lessons from the recent agitation in Bengal and the ultimate success of that movement, as proved by the King's visit and the repeal of the Partition. This new phase of the Mahomedan problem in India is a cause of infinitely greater anxiety to the authorities than the Bengal agitation ever was. The Government will have its hands full with this problem for some time to come. And it is no pleasant thing for the Head of the Administration at this time to find himself face to face with a fresh agitation in the most difficult Province in the Indian Empire. His Council may be fiddling, but the Viceroy must feel the gravity of the situation keenly. Peace or unrest matters but little to the nameless councillors who have sucked the official orange dry and have no personal consequences to fear.

Sir Reginald Craddock has no stake in this struggle. His pension is assured. The failure of the Government will not be associated with his name. History will mete out its commendation or condemnation neither to Sir Reginald Craddock nor to Sir Harcourt Butler, nor to Mr. Sharp, nor to any other of their friends and colleagues, but only to Lord Hardinge of Penshurst. And this is the tragedy of the Viceroy's position. And when one realises all this, one cannot refuse to give to Lord Hardinge every sympathy, consideration, and help that one can command, at the present crisis. If we suffer, it would be well and just for us to bear this in mind, that His Excellency too is a victim of the forces that threaten to create all these fresh trouble for us. The thought will sober down public indignation and induce moderation in whatever methods may have to be adopted to fight this new influence in the counsels of the Government. Our indignation at the attitude and action of his councillors should not be permitted to interfere with our sympathy and consideration for the Viceroy.

The Decadence of the Indian Bureaucracy.

Even these councillors themselves deserve our pity rather than our indignation. The wrong that they are doing is due not so much to their moral perversity as to their intellectual incapacity. And even here, they too are victims of circumstances. The larger qualities of statesmanship that characterised the British rulers in the eighteenth and the early nineteenth centuries, when every official had to tackle some original problem of government, have fallen out of cultivation in the Indian Civil Service. The altered circumstances of the country have little or no scope for their cultivation. The present officials spend all their life in working out details and carrying out standing orders. They live all their days in an atmosphere of isolation and unreality. As administrators of a settled country, the responsibilities of their office do not, as a rule, even call for any special watchfulness from these officials. They receive, according to established routine, reports of the condition of the people from their subordinates, and pass these on to their own superiors, without any careful examination or analyses. The country being quiet, there is really no need for such examination or analyses. But this is not the kind of training that brings out the higher capacities of the intellect or the will in any man. The present generation of Indian officials never get the training that moulds the true statesman. They never have the education and the opportunities that make even an all-round man. They live too easy a life. While their responsibilities are comparatively light, their emoluments are large and their honour and rank very high. They are always obeyed but rarely argued with, and never opposed, by those who live and labour about them. They do not get, therefore, that superior and healthy intellectual discipline which ordinary educated people, even in the lower walks of life, get through the constant clash and conflict of their ideas and opinions with those of their equals. They are not called upon to seriously study or analyse any acute economic or political problems. They can neither cultivate, therefore, the imagination of the idealist nor the vision of the statesman.

It is not at all strange, therefore, that Lord Hardinge's councillors have failed to seize the actualities of the present situation in India. They do not at all realise it, therefore, that the supreme need of the hour in India is to keep the people quiet, to give them rest, to allow the public mind to gradually get back its lost equilibrium. As was inevitable in times of unusual excitement, people lost their sense of proportion and their right perspective. But they have, at the same time, gained a lot during these years of stress and strife. A new self-consciousness is the most important of these—and a new sense of power, a new ambition for adequate achievement, a new desire to find their legitimate place among the makers of modern history and humanity; and above all things, they have gained a new sensitiveness and a new idealism. To shape, to direct, to develop and help such promising elements of a nation's rejuvenated life to their true and legitimate fulfilment is an ambition that might lure the gods. It is an achievement for which no labour and no sacrifice would count too hard or too costly. But our sun-dried bureaucrat is no idealist. Without any vision of the future, he is only troubled and irritated by the growing pains of the people, which disturb his peace and interfere with his play. He is angry with the people who have broken into the placid course of his official life and preferment. And his only desire is to crush these disturbers of the peace, even as a man crushes, in the hollow of his hand, the troublesome fly that buzzes about his ears and runs into his nose and thus breaks up his mid-day nap. The act may not be statesmanly, but the attitude is perfectly human. One sees here the incongruity between the little man and his lofty office; and a sense of incongruity may excite one's irascibility or even appeal to one's pity; but it makes no room for indignation.

The Motif of the New Policy.

The whole trouble is due to the pitiful ignorance and incapacity of those who have evidently been seeking to force the hands of the Viceroy in this matter. They have no knowledge of the country, and not the faintest grasp of the real problem before them. We all know what their inner motive is. They are completely upset by the signs of revolutionary unrest about them. They believe, and not without some show of reason either, that this revolutionary spirit has commenced to obsess the minds of a large and growing section of the youthful intellectuals in the country. The Indian student community is very largely and powerfully influenced by this revolutionary propaganda. It is a danger to the State. It is no less a menace even to Society. And they are determined to put this down at any cost. The Indian politicians may not directly preach sedition. They are not, in fact, either openly or secretly associated with this anarchical propaganda. But all the same they are indirectly responsible for all these troubles. They prepare the ground for the growth of revolutionary ideas. The youth of the nation must, therefore, be removed by every possible or impossible means from the sphere of influence of these politicians. The Government, at least, must not encourage or even tolerate their association with the student population of the country. This is, to put in very plain language, the whole case for the educational advisers of Lord

Hardinge. But the moment we see it, in its honest nakedness, we recognise the ignorant fatuity upon which it is based.

THE NEW SITUATION AND THE BUREAUCRATIC SPIRIT.

The main object of this new educational policy is to put down the spirit of revolutionary patriotism that seems to have taken hold of at least a section of our school-and-college-going populations. Up to a certain point, there is perfect agreement in this matter between the responsible leaders of Indian public opinion and the educational advisers of the Indian Government. And the very farthest limit of right reason and true state-craft is also the limit of this agreement. We are as anxious as any Anglo-Indian bureaucrat to cure the rising generations of our country of whatever unhealthy revolutionary opinions and ideals may have possessed their minds. And we are anxious about it, because we know that these imported and undigested notions and ideals spell ruin and disaster to the future of Indian Nationalism. We know that the ideal of isolated and sovereign political independence, which seems to inspire all these revolutionary and anarchical activities is a dangerous and suicidal ideal, from the view-point of Indian Nationalism, in the present condition of the country and the present state of world-politics. To seek to pursue this ideal would only open the way for a fresh Moslem or a new Mongol servitude. And knowing all these fearful possibilities before us, we are as anxious as the most impatient Anglo-Indian bureaucrat, to cure whatever revolutionary spirit may have got entry into our country. This is the farthest limit that reason and state-craft impose upon us in regard to this matter. Neither right reason nor true statesmanship demand, however, that in trying to kill this spirit of revolution and anarchism we must also crush the spirit of patriotism upon which it has grown and with which it has entwined itself; nor that we should undermine the very foundations of that youthful enthusiasm and idealism, which lend to every form of revolutionary patriotism in the world its halo of romance and religion. We recognise these limits; and are always scrupulously anxious, while fighting every form of unhealthy and improvident revolutionary and anarchical waste, to protect and preserve and chasten and strengthen and lead along healthy and reasonable lines the spirit of patriotism and idealism of our younger generations. The educational advisers of the Government are either unable or unwilling to make this discrimination. They are not prepared to make the sacrifices which this discrimination would involve. The growth of any kind of patriotism and public spirit in the country, however sane, chaste and loyal to the British connection these might be, would be bound to demand a radical change in the existing constitution and methods of the Government of the country. They would be bound to curtail the present privileges of the British officialdom in India, and gradually change the autocratic character of the Government itself, and consequently upset all existing official values, whether social or political. The conservative official mind is shocked, therefore, by the very thought of these inevitable changes. It is absolutely wedded to the existing state of things. It cannot bear, therefore, any kind of evolution in the country, however necessary and healthy it may be, which is likely to cause the least disturbance to the existing order. The Indian official is, therefore, not only anxious to kill the spirit of revolution and anarchism in the country, but also to crush out even the very life of that healthy spirit of patriotism of which it is only a parasite. He is anxious to shut up every door and window and even every chink in the walls of our mind, through which outer light might enter and bring the breath of new ideals and inspirations into our souls and quicken our dry bones with new strength and activities. He is afraid of the noble idealism of our youths, and wants to kill it by holding out allurements of office and emoluments to them on the one hand, and threats of perpetual ostracism from the Service of the Government on the other. And this is the real cause of this conflict between the educational advisers of Lord Hardinge and the leaders of thought and public life in the country. And it requires very little imagination and the meagrest acquaintance with the lessons of universal history to foresee the hopelessness of the official cause in this struggle.

Past Education Policy in British India.

The attempt to direct and control the course of public education in the country, mainly and primarily in the interest of the Government, is not at all new. In fact, it is a universal element of state-craft. Every Government has to do it. As long as there is a complete identity of interests between the Government and those whom it governs, this attempt is neither injurious nor unjust. The injury and injustice come in only when there is a conceit of separate interests in the governing classes, who seek, in that case, to curb and cripple the normal course of intellectual and social evolution in the community, out of regard for the prerogatives and privileges of their own body. But whatever the motive or the consequences of it, this attempt is universal. The British Government in India has, from the very beginning, tried, more or less openly, to shape and control the course of public education among us; and the motive has always been to strengthen the foundations of their political authority in the country. In the earlier period of their history, the Government of the East India Company penalised every attempt to educate the people of this country in the literature and science of the West or to preach the Christian religion among them.. Carey was threatened with deportation, because he wanted to open a school in Calcutta and preach the "Gospel" to the Indians. The Government stood then in perpetual fear of the people, and got nervous about anything that might wound the religious susceptibilities of the masses or arouse their fears. This is why the first Missionary College in India had to be located at Serampur, which was then outside British territory, in the possession of the King of Denmark. The subsequent fight between the Anglicists and the Orientalists, was really fought upon the same issue, namely, which system was most calculated to promote the safety of the newly-established foreign Government in the country? And Macaulay won, because his policy was thought to be really and ultimately the better, because by far the safer, of the two. Macaulay's object was to create a body of leaders of public opinion in the country, who would be in perfect sympathy with the ideals and institutions of the ruling race, and who would find, in the honour and emoluments of the service of the new Government, a strong inducement to always stand by that Government and lend their superior moral support to it. Reading Sir John Wood's Despatch between the lines, one cannot fail to discover this inner motive of the educational policy of the Government of the East India Company's Directors, as enunciated in that memorable document. Those were the days when the moral and intellectual cleavage between the people of this country and their foreign rulers was very deep and wide, and when the ruling classes stood in almost constant fear of the superstition and fanaticism of the subject populations. English education and the new Illumination which it brought in its train commenced to undermine these sources of unknown and impalpable dangers, and were consequently publicly encouraged. Every movement of religious and social revolt in the country was then cheerfully encouraged and openly sympathised with by the highest representatives of the Government. All these forged fresh bonds between the rulers and the ruled, had created new interests among the people of the country for the perpetuation of the British authority. But the spirit of freedom which inspired these social and religious revolts was bound to gradually operate in politics also. The spirit of self-assertion against social and sacerdotal authority became gradually manifest against official authority also. The result was a reaction in the education policy of the Government. School text-books that had hitherto been drawing so largely upon English and European sources were directed now to draw upon purely Indian sources. The legendary heroes of Hindustan commenced now to rapidly and rudely replace, in the text-books of the Education Department, the heroes of British, American, French, Italian and Greek history. The result of this official reaction was that it lent indirect but very material support to a movement of social and religious reaction which breathed a very distinct and unmistakable anti-foreign spirit. The Government wanted to recreate, in the rising generations of the country, a proper respect for authority. Obey your conscience as your God—was the older and earlier injunction. Obey your parents, your priests, your society, and your scriptures, and those set in authority over you as representative of the Government : this was the new commandment. People interpret every commandment not as they are meant by those who promulgate it, but as suits their own inclinations or interests best. The new education policy, therefore, failed of its purpose. The very idea was based upon ignorance and folly. You cannot reconcile reverence for Hindu ideals and institutions with genuine respect for the life and character of people whose ways are in every way opposed to these ideals and institutions. As a result of this insensate education policy of the Government (1880-90), there grew up a generation proud not only of the ancient but even of the present-day ideals and institutions of their country, and exceedingly disdainful of all foreign ideals and institutions. The Government had ample evidence of this new development in the country during the Consent-Bill agitation of 1890-91.

A Short-sighted Policy.

It was a very foolish and short-sighted policy, based upon selfishness and promulgated in utter ignorance or disregard of the actualities of the situation which it sought to control. The officials were offended, and possibly also somewhat frightened, by the ways and attitudes of the English-educated classes who refused to render to them the kind of respect that they had been used to receive from the previous generations. Those who had openly encouraged our social and religious revolt, in the name of individual reason and personal freedom, now commenced to condemn the natural expression of our new-born spirit of self-respect and freedom, because it hurt their vanity. These British officials did not see that the spirit of self-assertion in the new generation in India paid really high homage to the character and culture of their own race and country. The conflict so far was only between individuals or between class and class, but not between one culture and civilisation and another. In asserting ourselves against the British official class in India, we never as yet questioned the inherent intellectual and moral superiority of the British nation over our nation. Intellectual and moral slaves of the British people, we only wanted to claim political and social equality with our masters. That was all. This conflict did not touch the foundations of British Rule in India. It created absolutely no desire to cut the British connection. That connection was the sheet anchor of the future hopes and aspirations of the English-educated classes in the country. These educated classes stood apart from the masses. They had nothing, practically, in common with the general populations of the land. They had no faith in popular religion, nor in current social institutions of their country. Their intellectual and spiritual affinities with the British people were, in fact, closer and more vital than with their own countrymen. And in these affinities and the deep and strong loyalty which they always and everywhere create, lay the real strength of the British authority in India. Even ordinary statesmanship, in the interest of the Government itself, would have done nothing to weaken these supreme intellectual and moral bases of British Rule in India. As long as the English-educated classes were loyal to the intellectual and moral ideals and institutions of the British race, as long as they continued to be captivated by the glamour of this foreign culture, so long British authority in India stood upon a rock. But the pettifogging officials had no appreciation of these deeper facts and principles. They were frightened by the apparent spirit of insubordination in the educated youths of the country. It was, clearly, the result of the new education which they were receiving in our public schools and colleges. So they started changing the character of this education. They did not see it, however, that though school text-books and college-curricula might be changed to suit this new reaction in official policy, the general effect of the education that had been received by the people for nearly half a century's time, could not be wiped out by official circulars. The Government failed to take proper note of this very simple fact.

The New Education Policy and the Present Indian Society.

Indeed, if Lord Hardinge's educational advisers had any appreciation of present social conditions and the general intellectual life of our people, they would never have interfered so rudely with the appointments of Messrs. Rasul, Surhawardy and Jaysawal as University lecturers; and would never have set up the crude and confused plea of "pure study" in support of their action. We all understand the motive and meaning of this plea. The Government want to keep the atmosphere of our colleges, schools, and the University which controls them, absolutely free from any sort of political ferment. One can understand this motive, though one may not approve the method adopted here. There was a time, in the days of our youth, forty years ago, when there was absolutely no intellectual community between our schools and colleges on the one side and our homes on the other. There was then an almost impassable gulf between the thoughts and aspirations of the new intellectuals in the country and their parents and elders. Our parents and elders then talked of things which we did not care for, and we thought of things which they did not understand. The school and the college had, in those days, an almost absolute control of our intellectual and moral life. There was then a real school or college atmosphere, all but isolated from that of our homes. But all this is changed to-day. The new thought has permeated the entire community. The parents and elders of to-day were the school boys and college youths of twenty years ago. Our fathers used to talk of their business or social affairs, sometimes of their shāstras and ceremonials among themselves; and we, brought up in the new schools and colleges, had no interest in their conversation and no sympathy with or reverence for their faith or conduct. But we talk of things to-day in which our children are intensely interested. They shut up their books and prick up their ears when we read aloud the daily newspapers, or discuss public questions with friends and neighbours. The influence of our fathers, who did not know English, upon us who were or had been to the new schools and colleges, was almost nil. Their learning was, in our eye, practically mere ignorance, their faith superstition. It is no longer so, as between us and our children. We may have grown cold and calculating with age and experience; they are fervent and improvident. We are cautious, they may be reckless. But whatever difference there may exist between us and our sons in regard to practical affairs, intellectually there is little or no conflict between us. This being so, the home influence is to-day immensely stronger than that of the school and the college. Even our women read the vernacular papers with avidity and discuss the sensations of the day among themselves. And in the face of all this, how can the Government create or maintain an atmosphere of "pure study" in our schools, colleges and universities? The mere attempt would be bound to strengthen those very sentiments which this "pure study" is evidently meant to starve. An "atmosphere of pure study," such as the educational advisers of Lord Hardinge are anxious to create and maintain in our universities, is an absolute impossibility, unless a similar atmosphere of "pure thought and conversation" is simultaneously created and maintained in every educated home in the country, or unless the school-and-college-going populations are kept absolutely confined in their schools and colleges, as juvenile criminals are kept at present in the

Reformatories, and all communications with their parents and relations are entirely cut off for the time they are *in statu pupillari*. No Government, except perhaps in very primitive societies, could do anything like it. Least of all is this possible for a Government like that of the British in India, the representatives of which have such precious little intellectual and moral affinities with the ruled, and which cannot, therefore, control the thought and life of the people from within but must govern them only and always from without. The educational advisers of Lord Hardinge have no appreciation of the enormous difficulties in their way. They do not seem to have any idea of tho endless complexities of the problem before them or of the actualities of our present social and intellectual life, nor even any decent insight into those fundamental psychological facts and laws which control the course of social evolution everywhere. The only thing they seem to know or understand is the growth of revolutionary unrest among the rising generations of the country; and are moved by one supreme motive, namely, to crush and kill this troublesome spirit in them. No Indian statesman nor even any Indian politician or publicist with any appreciation of the trends and tendencies of current world-politics on the one side and of the actualities of the Indian situation on the other, can possibly have any sympathy with the revolutionary ideas that seem to have possessed a section of our young men. There is, therefore, no vital conflict between the ideas of the Government and those of the leaders of public opinion in the country in this matter. But while the advisers of the Government are moved by ignorance and prejudice, the leaders of the people have full knowledge of the situation in the country and are moved by the supreme consideration of the well-being and progress of their nation. The advisers of Lord Hardinge do not understand that the problem before them is more intellectual than political. The Indian revolutionaries as a class are as yet in what may be called the stage of intellection. They have imbibed certain opinions and are moved so far by certain abstract principles of national life and political progress. These are the results of a misreading of European politics and a misinterpretation of Indian history and culture. The disease is intellectual, due to reckless generalisation on the one side and to unwarranted application of the ideals of one people to the interpretation of the needs of a different people on the other. And intellectual problems must be solved by intellectual methods only. What is wanted is a sound political and social philosophy which, while fully and frankly recognising the truth of the fundamental position of Indian Nationalism and the legitimate aspirations of the people to secure their rightful place in modern history and world-politics, will, in the light of these very truths, fight and cure the false generalisations and suicidal ambitions of these youthful revolutionaries. Nothing could be more foolish and unstatesmanly than to try to put down a great intellectual and moral ferment by repressive measure. The real work before the responsible rulers of the country is to convince erring youths of their error, to point out to them the mischief that they are doing to their own cause by ignoring the actualities about them, and not to coerce them into submission to an order of things that, however unreasonably it may be, is revolting to their reason and conscience. It is absolute folly to fight the natural idealism of youth by physical weapons. It is worse than folly to seek to stifle it by material and selfish allurements. No Government can secure either peace for the country subject to their authority or even their own safety, by destroying or undermining the manhood of its people. No administration can manufacture public opinion to order. These are rudimentary truths. Intellectual aberrations in the youths of a nation can be cured only by intellectual freedom, guided and controlled by the higher intellects of the nation itself. The first thing to do is to disabuse the minds of the youthful intellectuals of the country that there is any real and necessary conflict between the highest interests of their nation and those of the Government that holds sway over them. The educational advisers of Lord Hardinge do not seem to have any appreciation of these elementary truths and principles. The step they have taken will be bound to deepen the notion by which large numbers, especially of our young men, are evidently obsessed—that the policy of the Government is to put down, by every means in their power, every form of nationalist activity in the country. It will weaken still further their confidence in the good faith of their rulers. And this is a result which true statesmanship would seek to avoid at all cost. But the educational advisers of Lord Hardinge are not guilty of any statesmanship. This is our misfortune, as well as theirs.

CALCUTTA: *July,* 1913.

CHAPTER XVII.

INDIA AND IMPERIAL PREFERENCE.

A New "Resolution."

It is not easy to understand why the Hon'ble Mr. Chitnavis should have gone out of his way to move a Resolution on Imperial Preference before the Viceregal Council. It shows how little do our "representatives" in the Legislative Councils represent anybody except themselves. Indian public opinion has not as yet devoted any serious thought to this subject. Even the Indian National Congress has not as yet felt called upon to discuss it. There is, absolutely, no body of political or economic thought in the country which has evinced as yet the least little partiality for the programme of the Tariff Reform Party in England. At first sight, it seemed very much likely that the Hon'ble Member had been put up to it, not by his constituency, if he really has any, but by some one like Sir Roper Lethbridge, who has for some time past been telling the British people how India would welcome nothing so much as a preferential tariff, and who thought that their hands might be strengthened by such a move in the Viceregal Council. But if this be the real history of this Resolution, one feels bound to say that it has signally failed of its purpose. Even Mr. Chitnavis could not so completely forget the actual economic condition of British India as to demand this so-called Imperial Preference for its own sake. It is Great Britain that has killed all our ancient industries, and it is she who stands to-day as our most formidable competitor not only in the world-market but even in our home-markets. India wants protection. Mr. Chitnavis would not deny it. And she needs protection not against Germany or Austria or Italy or America but, primarily, against England. To impose a tariff on German or French or Austrian or American imports, while leaving British and Colonial goods to enjoy more or less free access to our markets, might please Sir Roper Lethbridge and his Tory leaders but would in no way profit Indian trade or commerce. On the contrary it might increase the burdens of the Indian consumers by making them practically dependent for a good many things they want upon Great Britain and her Colonies only. It is notorious that German and Austrian goods sell much cheaper here than British goods. A protective and preferential tariff would increase the price of the former without reducing that of the latter. Indeed, protected against German or Austrian or American competitors, by a preferential Indian tariff, British and Colonial producers might be tempted to raise their price and thus increase the burdens of the Indian consumers. I am simply surprised that these plain facts did not strike so experienced a public man as Mr. Chitnavis.

Free Trade *v.* Protection.

It may perhaps be said that this Resolution was simply a cover for putting forth a demand for an all-round protective tariff in India. Such a demand would have, in any case, the support of a large body of articulate public opinion in this country. For it is impossible to deny that there is a very strong protectionist sentiment among us. The entire economics of the Swadeshi-and-Boycott movement was protectionist; though it cannot be said that it has so far been a reasoned and considered national policy. Of course neither Free Trade nor Protection are absolute economic principles. There are circumstances wherein free-trade would be considered mere suicidal folly and protection the only right course. But though under especial conditions protection may be the right economic policy, still it is not the best and the highest, either logically or ideally. But this ideal relation can be realised only under ideal circumstances. The ideal economic arrangement in every community or nation is that each individual shall produce that only which he or she can produce best of all and at the least expenditure of time and energy. Both these conditions must be fulfilled. The commodity must be the best of its kind; the time and energy spent in its production must be the least possible. If *A* can produce a commodity in its highest perfection by spending less time and energy than *B*, *A* should produce it and not *B*, who must find out what he can produce similarly, namely, of the highest quality and at the lowest expense. And *A* and *B* should exchange their goods to their mutual profit. This is the ideal economic arrangement inside every community or nation. This is the truest form of free-trade. Similarly, if each community or nation will produce that only which it can produce best and at the lowest expenditure of time and energy, and then if all the nations will take from one another their respective goods, freely and without any artificial protection or preference, that will be the ideal economic arrangement in international relations. And that arrangement would be based upon absolute Free Trade Principles.

Ideally, therefore, Free Trade is superior to and higher than Protection. Humanity must reach this ideal one day. We enjoy this freedom in our internal trade and commerce. There was a time when even this freedom did not exist, when particular families or tribes or clans or guilds were protected by social or political laws against the trade-competitions of other families, tribes, clans or guilds. Civilisation has outgrown that primitive stage. Now every person is free to produce his best and place it in the open market, at his own price. But this freedom is absent at present in international trade and commerce. But it will come some day, when all the nations shall be as one people, and being co-ordinated with one another inside the organic unity of Universal Humanity, shall fully co-operate with one another for the furtherance of the common weal. We are, however, very far as yet from this millenium. Consequently, just now, neither Free Trade nor Protection can be accepted as a universal and absolute economic good.

The Rationale of Protection.

A tariff is a form of taxation; indirect, therefore insiduous, but taxation it is all the same. And the tax is not paid by the foreign importer but by the people of the country which imposes the tariff. The native consumer pays more for the dutiable articles than he would have done if there were no duties imposed upon them. He buys dearer. Why should he ?—asks the Free-trader. For future profits—the Protectionist answers. This is the whole case, in a nutshell, between Free-trade and Protection. Protection is, thus, only a form of insurance in favour of infant industries or undeveloped resources. I pay more for certain foreign goods to-day, in the hope of making good more than this present loss, by developing my own goods of the same class, in the future, to the same, if not to a superior standard both qualitatively and quantitatively—as that of these foreign goods. So only such industries should be protected as, upon a reasonable calculation, may be considered to have a great future before them. And that future will be determined mainly by two things: first, by the existence of natural facilities in the country for the production of these goods, of a high quality and in large quantities ; and second, by the existence of the right kind of workmanship or large natural aptitudes for it—and sufficient number of workers—for such production, in the community. In other words, whether any industry should or should not be protected will have to be determined (i) by the existence of raw materials in the country needed for it—in sufficient quantity and in accessible localities, or the reasonable probability of producing these materials of the right quality and in adequate quantities, at the same if not lesser cost as they are or can be produced in the countries that are sending out the finished goods made out of these, to the protected country now ; and (ii) by the existence of skilled and cheap labour for the production of those goods among the people themselves. Where these two conditions are present, there is a reasonable assurance of a bright future before any young or undeveloped industry in any country. And it is then only that Protection becomes truly a form of national insurance for a people's industrial and commercial future. Judged by this principle, there are many Indian industries that may reasonably be protected by adequate tariffs. But the tariff must be imposed only upon those imports or exports that threaten to kill or prevent the growth of infant but promising national industries. And the moment we try to apply these principles to the actualities of our own industrial position, we find that our industries need protection against British competitions far more than against those of any other country. Imperial Preference would, therefore, be absolutely useless to us.

Imperial Preference or Economic Dependence ?

In fact, it would be worse than useless. Great Britain exercises absolute political control over us just now, and determines our fiscal policy. Imperial Preference, by killing all competitions between British and non-British goods in our market, would, therefore, almost infinitely increase our economic dependence upon Great Britain. And this combination of political authority and commercial control over us would be a very serious menace to both our political and our economic future as an autonomous State. The right economic policy for us now, therefore, is not to kill non-British exploiters of our markets but rather to encourage and strengthen them. If America, for instance, could be induced to compete with Manchester in our import trade in piece-goods, the latter would either have to submit to a serious diminution of her trade with us, or would have to demand the imposition of an import duty on all piece-goods to equalise her chances with those of her foreign rivals. In the one case our poor people would be able to buy their clothing at much less cost than what they pay now, and in the other our cotton-industry would receive a much-needed protection against unfair foreign competitions. Free-trade is the only remedy we have now —however partial it may be—against the evils of that combination of exploitation and administration which Lord Curzon declared were the dual functions of the Government of India. A well-considered protective tariff upon selected imports would, of course, be the only assurance just now of our industrial future. But we cannot have it. So Free-trade is the next best thing we should try to maintain in our own interest. To advocate so-called Imperial Preference is simply suicidal folly.

CALCUTTA: *April*, 1913.

CHAPTER XVIII.

PAN-ISLAMISM.

An Erroneous Estimate.

It can no longer be denied that Pan-Islamism is gradually coming to be a very important factor in the social and political evolution, in any case of modern India, if not indeed, of the modern world. Yet neither friend nor foe seems so far to very clearly realise either the good or the evil that this new and growing force in modern world-politics may work in the coming centuries. In the consideration of all large world-problems the English-educated Hindu generally takes his cue from his European masters, and he is therefore not prepared to take this Pan-Islamic movement very seriously. He thinks, with Europe, that the days of religious upheavals and fanatical outbursts of ignorant and undisciplined multitudes, as a compelling social or political force, are long gone by. The race now is not with those who command the wildest religious enthusiasm, or possess the highest personal courage, but only with those who own the most up-to-date scientific training and equipment. Japan has, practically, little or no deep religious enthusiasm. The Jap is perhaps the least religious animal in modern civilisation, unless we take his Bushido itself as a form of religion. He is prepared to accept and avow any creed that will be helpful to his earthly national ends. Yet this petty Island Kingdom, devoid of any living enthusiasm for any religious creed or cry, has within a few years won for itself a recognised place in modern world-politics. And it is entirely due to Japan's large scientific acquisitions and perfect military organisation. It will be long, very, very long indeed, before Islam will acquire these, and particularly the former. Islam may count upon her numerical strength, and the strategic advantage which, under certain conditions, the wide distribution of her populations may give her. But these will not ensure her success, and not even her safety, in the event of any open and direct conflict between the forces of Pan-Europeanism on the one side and those of Pan-Islamism on the other. Any outbursts of Moslem fanaticism, such as may very easily be fanned into flame by the Pan-Islamic propaganda, will only help to break up the strength of Islam instead of consolidating it. This is how the ordinary European publicists and politicians feel. This is how even many of my own educated Hindu brethren feel about Pan-Islamism. But the estimate seems to my mind to be entirely erroneous.

Islam as an Aggressive Religious Propaganda.

If Pan-Islamism cherishes the wild dream of once more acting, in the coming centuries, the part that Islam played in the past in shaping the course of historic evolution in the three continents of Asia, Africa and Europe, it is foredoomed no doubt to absolute and ignominous disappointment. History has never been known to repeat itself in this fashion. Islam as an invincible military force has not the ghost of a chance in the modern world. Indeed, I do not believe that any sober and thoughtful Pan-Islamist ever cherishes any such wild idea himself. The inherent aggressive spirit of Islam will seek—in fact, it is already seeking—to realise itself in our age more through friendly proselytisation than through bloody conquests. And in peaceful propagandism Islam has, I think, far greater chance of success than any other great world-religion. Its simple creed has an appeal for primitive and unsophisticated humanity which neither Christianity nor any other system has. "There is no God except God, and Mahomed is His Prophet" is a creed that even a child may grasp. There are no mysteries, no contradictions, no fathomless metaphysics, in this simple declaration of faith. Man's spiritual experiences may rise to much loftier heights or descend to much deeper depths than what this simple creed connotes. Even Islam knows of these higher heights and deeper depths. The lives of Moslem saints bear ample testimony to the deeper notes of the spiritual life. But the rudimentary creed of the Qoran has reduced human religion to what may best be described as its least common multiple. There is no further simplifying it. And this magic simplicity of the creed of Islam is the secret of the success of Moslem propagandism in the modern world, especially among less advanced and less sophisticated tribes, whether in Asia or Africa.

Solidarity of Islam.

It seems, indeed, well nigh impossible to stem the tide of Moslem propagandism either in Asia or Africa. The only competitor in the field is Evangelical Christianity. But Christianity cannot reach primitive intelligence half so near as Islam can. Wherever the Christian missions have attained any large success. it has been due to their political associations and influences rather than to their direct religious message or spiritual ideals. But Islam wins, in any case in our time, without these extraneous helps. On the other hand, Christianity cannot, in our time, use its superior political power or military prowess to force people to accept it. It has to face and fight its rivals with only logic and reason. And so far as the primitive races are concerned this is a very great disadvantage to the Christian missions. And it is just this growing numerical strength of the Moslem populations of the world which constitutes the most serious aspect of the present Pan-Islamic propaganda. And this seriousness comes from the democratic character of Moslem social economy and the strange solidarity of the Moslem communities which it always works up. Islam is the only religious system in the world which has no regular priesthood. In the eye of Āllā every Mussalman is absolutely equal to every other Mussalman. And each individual member of the Islamic fraternity stands in a close, personal, and direct relation to it. And this is the secret of the strange solidarity of Islam. Nor is it a mere matter of subjective sentiment. There are outer and visible symbols. Is it for nothing that Mahomed ordained it that every Moslem, to whatever country or race he might belong, must turn towards the Caaba every time he approaches his God? There is no parallel to it in any other religion or church. There can be no comparison, for instance, in this respect, between the position of Rome in the Catholic world and of Mecca in Islam. The Rome of Islam, if the Caaba may be styled as such, knows no Pope. This Moslem institution exercises no kind of temporal or even religious authority over the Moslem world. In fact, it is not an institution, but, strictly speaking, only an association, an ideal, a pure symbol. It works upon the Moslem populations of the world not by threats of punishment, not through fear, but through love. It works, really, not from without but from within. It leaves every man to pursue his own temporal ends in his own way, and it does not, therefore, prevent even one Moslem fighting another for wealth or woman, for worldly power or position, but simply binds every Moslem with every other Moslem in one ever-present and indissoluble religious bond. In their relations to the Prophet, the Qoran, and the Caaba, all Moslems are eternally united. And one supreme obligation of this relation is that every fighting unit, which means every adult man, in Islam, must leave and dedicate his all, even up to his life, for the protection of the Caaba should it ever be threatened with destruction or pollution by the infidel. And it is just here that the importance and gravity of the Pan-Islamic propaganda lie.

Pan-Islamism and World-Peace.

The success of this Pan-Islamism will never mean another Mussalman irruption upon the civilised world. It will not mean any aggressive movement for the conquest of either Europe or Asia. But it will mean a most determined and united stand of the Moslem populations of the world against the aggressions of Christendom.

These populations are scattered over more than two continents. Practically the whole of Northern and Central Africa, the whole of Western and Central Asia, India, and the North-Eastern Provinces of China are comprised within this Moslem zone. Within this extensive tract we have a huge Moslem population, ignorant and semi-barbarous for the most part no doubt, yet capable of seriously interfering indirectly with the peace and progress of the world. The problem of European Peace, for instance, is no longer a mere European problem but is a huge and complex world-problem. Mr. Norman Angel has completely demonstrated it that modern industrialism has practically removed the ancient motives of international wars among the different European countries. The present Turko-Bulgarian War is the last war of strictly European origin. And even this can hardly be said to have had a truly economic origin. It was moved on the part of the Balkan Allies, at any rate, by a desire for national independence. Neither the Bulgarians nor the Servians nor any other of the smaller States that rose up in arms against the Ottoman Power could forget the wrong that Turkish sovereignty had inflicted upon them. In this respect this latest war was of the old-world type, when nations fought more or less entirely upon sentimental grounds. The modern wars are different. The main motive power in these is economic rather than purely political or patriotic. This motive no longer exists in Europe. The present rivalry between the different European Powers is really of non-European origin. If there is any general European war in our time, it will be caused by the scramble of the European Powers over

Asiatic and African carcasses.* The present incapacity, for purposes of self-defence and self-rule, of the Asiatic and African peoples, constitutes, thus, a very real and serious danger not only to their own independence, but, what is far more serious, even to the general peace and progress of the larger and more advanced humanity of our time. Every Asiatic or African people or country which is striving for its own freedom and consolidation and self-organisation is, whether consciously or unconsciously, fighting, therefore, equally for the future peace and progress of the world.

From this point of view the Pan-Islamic movement is a movement that really makes not for disturbing but rather for ensuring and advancing the peace of the world. No statesman with any vision of the future can, therefore, refuse to sympathise with this movement and wish it god-speed. Those whose imagination cannot soar higher than the vision of a federation of the world, dominated everywhere by the White races only, will naturally smell danger and disaster in the progress of this Pan-Islamic propaganda. And the narrow and selfish vision of these people constitutes, I think, the real danger of this Pan-Islamic movement. With the friendly help and sympathetic direction of the world-powers Pan-Islamism may very easily be a power for good even in the modern world. But it requires very delicate handling. Above all it requires a frank and honest recognition of the legitimate claims of Islam to readjust itself to the needs of the modern thought

---

* The real, as distinguished from the apparent, cause even of the present Pan-European War is the secret ambition of Germany for a world-empire like that of Great Britain rather than the hopeless ambition of securing the Suzerainty of Europe.

and life and organise itself as a self-controlled and autonomous Federation of the Mussalman States of the world. The independence and integrity of Persia, Afghanistan, and the Moslem Principalities of Africa, as well as of the Ottoman Empire, must be maintained. This is the first condition for winning the confidence of Islam, without which this Pan-Islamic force will never be guided and controlled by the leaders of the modern world-politics. The European Concert has unconsciously worked for a similar end in Europe. As a result, the independence and integrity of the different European States, both small and large, have been fully assured. In their own self-interest, the greater Powers have had to do this.* In the interest of European peace itself, a similar assurance is needed for the larger and smaller States of Asia and Africa also. These States must be fully modernised and consolidated and strengthened; for upon their strength and advancement will ultimately depend the peace and progress even of Europe itself.

PAN-ISLAMISM IN INDIA.

Those who think that the recent defeat of Turkey in Europe has killed the backbone of Pan-Islamism, seem to me to lack a thorough grasp of the psychology of this movement. In fact, all the recent troubles of the Ottoman Empire have been a veritable god-send to the Pan-Islamist.

* Even the present war has not falsified this conclusion; and it is obvious that finally, whichever party wins, neither Belgium nor Servia, nor any other smaller States that may be involved in this struggle, will lose their independence. The only State that may be completely wiped out of the map of Europe is Turkey, but even that is a very distant contingency.

He has exploited the sympathy and enthusiasm of the Moslem populations of the world on behalf of Turkey, in the interest of his pet idea. In one sense, the present Pan-Islamic movement may be said to have originated in India. Thirty years ago, Jelaluddin came from Cabul to India, inspired with the vision of an All-World Confederacy of the Princes and Peoples of Islam, that will rejuvenate it and give back to it the position that it once had as a moving and shaping force in human history and civilisation. He passed through India inoculating many a leader of Mahomedan thought in Calcutta and Bombay and other cities with this new virus. As a messenger of this gospel, Jelaluddin went from India to Egypt and Turkey. But the seed that he had sown among us grew in secret for over a quarter of a century. Its only outer manifestation was seen in a new self-consciousness of our Moslem neighbours, a new conceit of separate communal interests, and a new desire to revive, in the name of purity, the old iconoclastic spirit of the Islamic faith and thereby to work a new religious cleavage between the Mahomedans and their Hindu neighbours. The political conflicts between educated Moslems and Hindus were attributed to the natural jealousy of rival aspirants to office and rank, and the religious feuds to a desire to revive the original ideals of Islam and reorganise the old propagandist activities of that faith. But nobody ever suspected these as the slow and silent development of the seed that Jelaluddin had sown in his confidential conferences with the Moslem intellectuals of Calcutta and other places. Mr. Blunt refers to some of these conferences, especially to those held in Calcutta, at most of which the Right Hon. Syed Amirali, then a member of the

Calcutta Bar, was present—in his last work "INDIA UNDER RIPON."

Things, however, commenced to move apace both in and outside India, which soon brought this Pan-Islamic idea to the public view. In India the Indian National Congress at first, and the more virile Swadeshi Movement later on, quickened a self-consciousness in the country, and especially among the Hindu populations. The Swadeshi propaganda developed a particularly pronounced Hindu ideal, which was naturally interpreted by some at least of the Mahomedan leaders in the country as a distinct and real menace to their own political future. Had they thrown themselves heart and soul into this new Nationalist Movement in India, this excessive Hindu emphasis might have been very easily removed. For then the Swadeshi Movement would have developed into a purely economic and political propaganda fully representative of the composite Indian people. But they held aloof. Many of them even set themselves up openly against this movement. The result was that the Hindu influences became predominant and the Hindu note the most pronounced in this new upheaval. It was, perhaps, well that this should have been so. For this Hindu Nationalism will gradually help the evolution of a real Federal Nationalism among us, which seems clearly to be the ideal-end and the ultimate aim of modern historic evolution in India. For the realisation of this Federal Ideal of Nationalism it is necessary that the different Indian communities, representing different world-cultures, must evolve in their own way, along their own line, preserving and developing to the full their respective personalities, be autonomous social units themselves, and then join the others, as members of a great Federation, which will present to the world a new and far more advanced and complex type of Nationality than what the world has so far known. I have always read this as the one eternal aim of historic evolution in India. I do not, therefore, regret this Hindu emphasis of what in the nature of things was bound to be practically a Hindu Movement. I do not regret that our Mahomedan friends practically kept away from it. But what I regret is their spirit of antagonism. What the situation really required of them was the initiation of a real Moslem National Movement, along parallel lines, moved by the same spirit, working for the same ultimate end, but organised in Islamic forms, with the symbols and sacraments familiar to higher Islamic thought and culture. But the Mahomedan leaders already bewitched by the vision of an All-World Islamic Confederacy which Pan-Islamism held out to their view, not only refused to do what was really needed as much in their as in our interest, but secretly commenced to exploit the unrest in the interest of this Pan-Islamism. Lord Minto did not see through the game, and therefore easily played into the hands of the Pan-Islamic leaders.

Pan-Islamism not Religious but Political.

The Turko-Italian conflict of 1911-12 while giving a new impetus to Pan-Islamism, particularly in India, helped also to bring out its true motive and character before all the world. Encouraged by the success of his game of bluff in the matter of the Indian Council Reforms, Syed Amirali now almost openly avowed his allegiance to Pan-Islamism; while his following commenced to exploit the natural sympathy of the Indian Mussalman with the Ottoman Government in their conflict with Italy, in the interest of this propaganda. The bond that binds the followers of Mahomed together is not a political but absolutely and exclusively a religious and spiritual bond. One Moslem prince or community may fight another Moslem prince or community without doing outrage to the Islamic fraternity. In any case they have frequently done so in the past, in this country and elsewhere. Even the Ottoman throne itself is reared upon such a fratricidal feud. If the power of the Mogul had lasted till our day, and Delhi had become the seat of one of the great world-powers, there would have been no religious bar against its declaring war against the Emperor of Turkey himself. The Indian Mussalman was, strictly speaking, under no religious obligation whatever to side with Turkey as against Italy in the last war. The religious obligation would come not merely to side with, but even to fight for Turkey, unto death itself, if the Holy Places of Islam were threatened with possession by the Kaffir, and Turkey stood up for their defence. Neither Tunis nor Tripoli, neither Adrianople nor Stamboul are counted as the Holy Places of Islam. No Mussalman is bound by his religion to defend and keep these temporal and profane cities in the possession of any Moslem potentate. The appeal to the Indian Mussalman both during the Tripoli and the Balkan war, on behalf of Turkey, was not, therefore, really based on religious but only on purely secular and political grounds.

And the politics that worked at the back of these agitations was purely Pan-Islamic.

Out of their Own Mouth.

That I am not misinterpreting the aims and scope of Pan-Islamism is proved by the public confession of faith of a staunch Pan-Islamist, Mr. Zafar Ali Khan, Editor of the *Zamindar*, who has contributed an article on "Indian Mussalmans and Pan-Islamism" to Mr. Jalal Nuri's recent book—"Ittihad-i-Islam," where it appears as a separate chapter. Says Mr. Khan :—

"The talented author of this elegant work has invited me to contribute to it a few pages descriptive of the so-called Pan-Islamic movement from an Indian Moslem's point of view. The invitation, coming as it does from a publicist of such versatile genius as Jalal Nuri, is an honour of which I am deeply sensible ; and in the following lines I propose to discuss 'Pan-Islamism' as it is understood by the Moslems of India who are destined to exercise a great influence on the future of Islam.

"Etymologically the expression Pan-Islamism claims a comparatively recent origin. It was coined by Christian diplomacy to serve as a scurvy pretext for the spoliation of the fast decaying Moslem States. To the man in the street Pan-Islamism was synonymous with a gigantic union of the Moslems of the world having for its cherished object the extermination of Christianity as a living political force. As long as a Morocco, a Tripoli, a Persia, or a Macedonia had to be grabbed, the bogey of Pan-Islamism was a most useful adjunct. It helped the stalwarts of Christendom to constantly confront their fanatical dupes with an imaginary peril, the bare possibility of which was to be removed by depriving the Moslem of his hearth and home. With the dismemberment, absorption, or annexation of almost all the independent Moslem States by the Powers of Europe and with the poor remnants of the integrity of Turkey and Afghanistan trembling in the balance, Christian thinkers have not at present much to say about this over-exploited theme. The time, however, is not far distant when the new life given to the Moslem communities of the world by the terrible events of the past few years may actuate the political theorists of Christian Europe to saddle the Moslems with the revival of the old plot to blow up Europe. Nowhere have these events been followed by an outburst of feeling so genuine in its manifestation and so universal in its character as in India ; and it is no exaggeration to say that the bombardment of Meshed by the Russians, the descent of Italy on Tripoli, the onslaught of the Balkan Allies on Turkey, with all their attendant horrors, have made the Moslems of India a changed people. They are not what they were two years ago.

"Divested of the mischievous conception in which Western Machiavellianism has clothed it and used it as a convenient mode of expression, Pan-Islamism is not a new force, but is as old as Islam itself. The first lesson of Pan-Islamism was given by the Qoran when it said :

'Verily all Moslems are brethren unto each other.'

"The Prophet's definition of Pan-Islamism will never grow old. 'A Moslem's relation to another Moslem,' exclaimed the Sarwar-i-Kainat, 'may be likened to that of the two hands which wash each other.'" The universal brotherhood founded by Islam is a moral binding force which has no equal. Pan-Slavism, Pan-Germanism and many other " isms " of that ilk are only ethnic ebullitions of a territorial character. The brotherhood of Islam, or Pan-Islamism if you will, transcends all considerations of race and class and is of an extra-territorial type in which all the Moslem populations of the world merge their geographical identity and become one nation. During the two months that I have been in Constantinople it has been one of my studied endeavours to bring this cardinal fact home to all the men of light and leading with whom I have come in contact, and it gives me great satisfaction to realise that the six hundred years' intercourse with European civilization has failed to produce any appreciable change in Turkey's conception of Moslem nationality. Just as the Indian Moslems think that they are Moslems first and Indians afterwards, so the scores of Mussalmans of all grades and sections with whom I had occasion to talk on the subject assured me that they were Moslems first and Ottomans afterwards. It is in this conception of the universality of the Moslem brotherhood that lies the chief strength of the Pan-Islamic movement, and the Moslems of India are among the foremost to realize it.

The object of Pan-Islamism, for aught that Christian writers may yet have to say to the contrary, is not to cherish projects of an aggressive nature against Christendom in spite of all that it has done to exterminate Islam, but to act purely on the defensive and to protect what little remains to the Moslems of their once splendid Empire, against further encroachments. In this work of defence Turkey has hitherto been single-handed, but such will no longer be the case. The combined attack of Christian Europe against the integrity of Islam and the covert and overt designs of the Western Powers against the remnant of Turkey have made too deep an impression upon the mind of the Moslems to be easily effaced. They have accordingly made up their mind to stand by Turkey through thick and thin, and mindful of the saying of their blessed Prophet who declared :—"A Moslem is unto another Moslem as a wall which is propped up by its various parts" —they will do all that they can to co-operate with Turkey whose political extinction means their own annihilation. This co-operation need not upset the Christian alarmists. It has nothing in common with the alleged triple alliance negotiated between Japan, China, and Siam, which necessitates, according to the *Berliner Tageblatt*, a probable proposal in the near future on the part of the Russian Tsar, to form a European combination strong enough to crush the yellow races and ensure the perpetual supremacy of the Western Powers in Asia. The co-operation of the Moslems of the world with the Caliphate which has now come to be recognized throughout the Islamic world as a revivified moral force essential to the maintenance of the *status quo* of Islam, will be intellectual and economic in its bearings. Islam is destined to play a great part yet in the political evolution of the world, and those who can think have arrived at the conclusion that the revival of Islam is to be heralded not by the thunder of guns and the flashing of bayonets but by the creation of Universities and the establishment of Banks. This is to be the Pan-Islamism of the future and, Inshaallah, it will achieve its object."

What does it Mean?

It is impossible to read this frank declaration of faith of the Pan-Islamist without being impressed by its essentially political character. The religious reference is feeble and flimsy compared to its pronounced political aims and ends. We all know that it is not merely "the brotherhood of Islam" but every credal and missionary religious fraternity in the world that transcends all "considerations of race and colour." It is the same with Christian and Buddhistic brotherhoods as with Moslem brotherhood. All Christians religiously and spiritually are no less brothers to one another than are all Mussalmans. But though an extra-territorial character may be legitimately claimed for Christian brotherhood as for Moslem brotherhood, it betrays a very sad confusion of thought to claim it for any *nation*, whether Christian or Moslem. The Moslem populations of the world were never, after the first few years of the Caliphate spent in Medina and its neighbourhood, *one* nation. Unity of state-life, based upon unity of territorial possessions, constitutes the very soul and essence of the nation-idea. Even a federal nation fulfils this elementary condition. An Imperial Federation may transcend territorial limitations and be extra-territorial; but even then it must be built and worked upon some unity of state-life and state-organisation. A nation indeed, is not a term of the purely religious life. There is such a thing as Christian or Moslem or Buddhistic or Hindu fraternity, but nothing as a Christian or a Moslem or Buddhist nation meaning *all* Christians or *all* Moslems or *all* Buddhists. There may be such a thing as a Hindu nation, because all Hindus of our time have *one* common territorial abode and are subject to *one* common state-authority and belong to *one* state-organisation. Had China and Japan and Australia and South America been peopled by Hindus, we could never have used the term Hindu nation as we do now. In fact, the writer completely gives the religious plea away when he comes to close quarters, and declares that "the object of Pan-Islamism........is not to cherish projects of an aggressive nature against Christendom ...... but *to act purely on the defensive* and *to protect what little remains to the Moslems of their once splendid Empire against further encroachments.*" The italics are mine; and the words thus italicised bring out the political motive of Pan-Islamism most clearly.

In fact, even an "aggressive propaganda against Christendom" which the Pan-Islamist is so anxious to disclaim, might have been interpreted in a purely religious sense. To convert the Kaffir is as much a duty of the Moslem as to convert the heathen is recognised to be a duty of the Christian. And the Moslemic communities of the world may, with absolute right and justice, combine to build up an international and all-world organisation for this purpose. They may do so for the protection of the socio-religious ideals of the Islamic Church and Moslem culture against the onslaughts of a dominant and all-conquering Christian ethical and social and economic system. Pan-Islamism may very legitimately pursue these ethical and cultural ends. Islam is not an altogether dead force even in the modern world. It is pregnant with large possibilities. The full and free development of these possibilities would be a distinct gain to modern humanity; and perhaps to none would this gain be greater than to Christendom itself. The spirit of Islam is essentially democratic, and its economy is fundamentally socialistic. Islam is, I believe, the only religion that has never advocated monastic ideals or monkish disciplines but that has yet always striven to reach a very lofty attitude of mental and spiritual disattachment towards the things of this world. The religious history of Islam is crowded with noble examples of men and women who never tormented the flesh nor renounced the world on the one side, nor clung to the things of this earth, either to wealth or woman, or to rank or position or even to family and friends, with the infidel tenacity of the ordinary man of the world, on the other. All these are the most precious legacies of Islam. The modern world needs them very badly for its own salvation. With a view to share her glorious moral and spiritual inheritances with the other communities of the world, Islam must be raised out of her present helpless and dependent position. She must first be able to look the modern world horizontally into the face. The preservation of the autonomy and sovereign independence of the existing Mahommedan States, whether in Europe or Asia or Africa, is one of the essential conditions of this. This is, indeed, the first condition. And the next is the modernisation of these independent Moslem States. Popular freedom and democratic political institutions, both of which are in such perfect accord with the spirit of the teachings of the Prophet, must be helped to grow in these free Moslem countries, and they must be equipped, in the fullest possible measure, with every kind of modern knowledge and organisation and scientific appliances for their military protection and economic prosperity. All these are needed as much in the larger interests of Islam itself as in the interests of the larger life of modern humanity. All these are not only absolutely legitimate but exceedingly laudable objects for which all the Islamic communities of the world may, and indeed, should unite. With this moral and spiritual Pan-Islamic propaganda, every one, with a correct appreciation of the course of modern historic evolution, and a vision of that Universal Federation towards which all countries and nations are unmistakably moving—must fully sympathise. They may even be prepared to actively co-operate with Islam in the promotion of these objects, so far as such co-operation may be helpful or practicable. But the unity of Islam is based upon the distinctive character of the socio-religious ideals presented by the Prophet. It is a cultural, which means a moral and spiritual, bond. The true conception of the universal brotherhood of Islam is not merely "extra-territorial," as the present writer contends, but it is also extra-political as well.

A False and Mischievous View.

Yet the ideal of Pan-Islamism presented here is clearly political. Its avowed object is, we are told, "to act on the defensive to protect what little remains to the Moslems of their once splendid Empire." In the earlier centuries of the Hizeera political sovereignty and ascendancy were to some extent essential conditions of the very self-preservation of Islam even as a religious culture and community. It may even be held that in some countries at least, political expansion was forced upon the Moslems by outer circumstances which they neither deliberately sought nor could absolutely control. But that necessity does not exist at all in our time. And to speak of the "splendid Empire" of the Moslems, in the singular number, betrays deliberate forgetfulness or unpardonable ignorance. It may serve the ends of the political Pan-Islamist and for that very reason this false suggestion is exceedingly mischievous. Except in the very infancy of the Caliphate, the Moslems were never under any one single political authority. The Moslem sovereigns never recognised any fraternal obligations with their Moslem neighbours or rivals in fighting them whenever they wanted or dared to do so. They did these things very freely even in the heyday of what this writer calls "their once splendid Empire." This old earth has known other splendid empires, both ancient and mediæval, than that of the Moslems. The Hellenes and the Romans or Italians, and even our own Parsis had splendid empires of their own in the ancient times. The French, and the Moguls in India, had their splendid empires in the middle ages. And what a menace would it be to world-peace and our present world-civilisation if the scattered remnants of these ancient races or nations, now merged peacefully into the various modern nationalities of the world, were to start so many different Pan-Imperial propaganda, for reviving, by their combined effort, the lost glories of their "once splendid Empires!" And this is exactly the irresistible logic of a political Pan-Islamic propaganda such as is preached here. This political Pan-Islamism is a distinct challenge to every non-Moslem state-authority holding sway over any Moslem population. It is a standing menace to the peace of every people composed partly of non-Moslem and partly of Moslem populations.

The Logic of Political Pan-Islamism.

Nor is it easy to see how this Pan-Islamism can hope to secure this end without very seriously weakening the legitimate and natural allegiance of every Pan-Islamist to the non-Moslem Governments under which they may be living, whether in India or Egypt. It is all very well to say that this Pan-Islamism seeks to realise its ends by purely peaceful methods, through the organisation of universities and industries, but we all know that empires are neither built up nor preserved by these innocent weapons. Universities may initiate the Mussalman into the secrets of science, and industries may help him to the acquisition of wealth, but these, of themselves, will not equip him with the modern implements of war or organise invincible Moslem armies, the two things which still determine the fates of empires and kingdoms. The only possible line of work for this political Pan-Islamism must lie, therefore, (i) in creating a Pan-Islamic sentiment among the Moslem populations of the world by appealing to their religious passions; (ii) in helping them to the acquisition of modern scientific knowledge, both for economic and military ends; (iii) in helping the organisation of the modern army and the modern navy fully equipped with all the most advanced instruments and methods of modern warfare with the knowledge and wealth thus acquired, in those independent Moslem States where this can be done safely and freely; (iv) in helping to preserve the independence and integrity of these States until they are fully equipped and organised, by securing on their behalf the moral support of the immense Moslem populations that are subject, for the time being, to the political authority of non-Moslem Governments or peoples ; and (v) in the event of any conflict between these latter and any Moslem State or States, in embarrassing these non-Moslem Governments by the organised passive resistance or open revolt of their Moslem subjects, and aiming ultimately even at their complete overthrow. These are the only conceivable means by which this political Pan-Islamism can hope to "keep to the Moslems the remnants of their once glorious Empire." All these, from the organisation of universities and industries to the incitement of revolts, are parts of an organic whole. By themselves, working separately, none of these have any appreciable worth so far as the object of Pan-Islamism, as enunciated here, is concerned. Thus, the moment we subject it to a searching analysis, we find what a serious menace this political Pan-Islamism, as distinguished from what may be called religious or cultural Pan-Islamism, is to the peace and progress of modern humanity in general and of those countries in particular where there is, as in India, a mixed population of Moslems and non-Moslems.

THE PAN-ISLAMIC PROPAGANDA IN INDIA.

Nor, so far at least as India is concerned, is this menace either very imaginary or very distant. It seems to me that if one were to construct a chronological story of the present cleavage between the Mahomedans and the Hindus and subject the facts and dates thus collected to a critical psychological analysis, it would be found that this Pan-Islamism in one shape or another has been partly responsible for it. Owing to its long contact with Hinduism, Indian Islam had developed a spirit of toleration of other faiths and practices than those of the Qoran, such as was and is unknown to Islam in perhaps any other part of the world. The Mahomedan masses, especially in Bengal, even associated themselves, so far as may be, with the current ceremonialism of their Hindu neighbours. They frequently made pujas to the Hindu's Gods and Goddesses through Hindu priests in Hindu houses, even as Hindus went and made offerings, with due faith and reverence, to Moslem *Peers* or Saints at Moslem dorgas or mausoleums. And all these had practically killed the possibility of any religious feuds between the two communities. But the missionaries of a new Purist Movement in Indian Islam soon revived the old iconoclastic spirit of the Moslem faith, and thus worked up first a religious cleavage, and gradually, as this new enthusiasm grew, a new religious antagonism between these two sections of the Indian community. How far this new Purist Movement in the Mahomedan community in India was inspired, either partly or wholly or directly or indirectly by Pan-Islamism, cannot be said, and perhaps will never be known. But that this propaganda became very active since the early eighties of the last century is well known. Jelaluddin passed through India, early in the eighties, and the attitude of aloofness of the educated Mahomedans of India from the political activities of their Hindu fellow-countrymen was, I think, openly and avowedly taken up gradually immediately after his visit. I still remember the memorable utterance of Sir Syed Ahmed at a reception held in his honour at the house of Babus Pyari Mohan and Hari Mohan Ray, in Amherst Street, when the Syed was on a visit to Calcutta in 1876 or 1877, in which he compared the Hindus and the Mahomedans of Hindusthan, to the two eyes and two hands of a man. It was really the same metaphor which Mahommed had himself used in speaking of the Islamic brotherhood. It is notorious how rapidly this spirit and attitude was changed and the revered Syed openly set himself up as an antagonist to the Indian Nationalist Movement, then represented by the Indian National Congress. We attributed it at the time to the influence of the Anglo-Indian bureaucracy. That influence was no doubt at work, but though it may explain something it cannot explain everything in the history of this conflict between the educated Hindus and educated Mahomedans which grew along with the Congress agitation. The Pan-Islamic spirit was at least partly responsible for it.

Pan-Islamism in India and Indian Nationalism.

The sinister logic of this political Pan-Islamism comes out most prominently, however, in its attitude towards Nationalism. In purely Moslem countries, like, for instance, Persia or Turkey or even Egypt, though perhaps in a lesser degree—Nationalism is practically identical in its ultimate ends and objects with this Pan-Islamism. In fact, so far as these "remnants of the once glorious Empire" of Islam, as Mr. Zafar Ali Khan puts it here, are concerned, perhaps their only chance of life lies in the support that they may get from Pan-Islamism. Both Turkish and Persian Nationalists may naturally think that their only hope of safety lies in the timely development of a world-wide confederacy of the followers of the Prophet, the moral pressure of which, if not its physical strength, might be brought to bear on the policy of their enemies. But in India, Islam, as a political force, stands upon an altogether different footing. Not merely in point of numbers, but equally also in intelligence, education and wealth, the Indian Mahomedans are decidedly behind the Hindu populations of the country. Nationalism in India, even if it works upon its legitimate composite character and constitution, and makes the fullest possible accommodation for the free play and fulfilment of the special character of Islamic culture, as an organic element of Indian, as distinguished from Hindu Nationalism—would never mean for the followers of Islam what Nationalism means in Persia or Turkey for their Persian or Turkish co-religionists. In Persia or Turkey the Mussalmans practically represent the whole nation or state. In India they can never represent more than a part of it. And this fact hurts the conceit of the Moslem leaders of India. The Pan-Islamic idea, wet-nursed, unconsciously, by the short-sighted policy of the Anglo-Indian bureaucracy, and, more particularly, by that of the last two Indian Viceroys, has developed the unhealthy habit in the leaders of the Mahomedan community of India, of nursing in their hearts the memories of their lost political position in the country. They have been distinctly encouraged by foolish Anglo-Indian officials and scribes to cherish the falsehood that the supreme political authority in India passed from the hands of the Mogul directly on to those of the British. They have been led to completely ignore the fact that the insignia of Imperial Rule in India had already slipped away from the enfeebled hands of the Mogul and the Pathan to those of the Shiks on the one side, and of the Mahrattas on the other, when the British stretched out their hands to grasp it. But for the advent and intervention of the British, the supreme political authority in this country would have been held to-day either by the Shiks, or by the Mahrattas, or it would have been divided between these two Hindu Powers. But all this is very conveniently forgotten. And by openly encouraging the Indian Mahomedans to forget or ignore these things, and by pandering to the vanity of the Moslem leaders by giving them preferential treatment in the constitution of the recently "Reformed Councils," the Government have unwittingly helped to strengthen the Pan-Islamic sentiment in this country. And all these have led the Pan-Islamic propaganda in India to openly set itself up as an enemy of Indian Nationalism.

Nor can the Indian Nationalists absolutely absolve themselves of all responsibility for this unfortunate state of things. If the Moslem leaders tried to wipe out the memories of the Shiks and the Mahrattas, the Hindu Nationalist leaders also sought to revive them. It was no doubt a supreme psychological need of the Nationalist propaganda; and so far as these memories were revived to recreate the self-confidence of a people suffering from a state of hopeless and listless inertia, they did only good and no harm. But the effect of this revival did not stop here. It gradually awoke, at least in a section of the Nationalists, the foolish and suicidal ambition of once more re-establishing either a single Hindu State or a confederacy of Hindu States in India. Some people, thus, secretly interpreted Swaraj as a Hindu Raj. And this folly is also to some extent responsible for the antagonism, in any case, of the soberer section of our Moslem fellow-countrymen towards our Nationalist ideals and activities; and thus it lent, unconsciously, considerable support to the Pan-Islamic propaganda among almost all classes of educated Mahomedans.

Is it Confusion of Thought—Or what?

But whatever its historic origin or its psychological justification, the sinister logic of this political Pan-Islamism cannot be disguised and should not be ignored. These implications are very clearly brought out in the very statement regarding the aims and scope of Pan-Islamism, as presented here by Mr. Zafar Ali Khan. And what is most important in this connection is that Mr. Khan here repeats what accredited leaders of the movement like the Rt. Hon. Syed Amir Ali and others have frequently said. I refer to the dictum that the Indian Mussalman is first a Moslem and then an Indian. Either it betrays a most woeful confusion of thought, unworthy of the intellectual leaders of a great world-movement, or it has a very sinister meaning behind it. The term Indian is either a geographical or a political term. It connotes either the place of birth or residence of the human who calls himself by this name; or it connotes his political or state-life and relations. As an Indian, a person is either a native of India, or a subject of the Government of India (like the statutory Indians) or both. This is all that the word Indian means, and absolutely nothing else, neither his race nor his caste nor his creed. On the other hand, the term Mahomedan is a term that connotes only a religious fact, that the person calling himself such belongs to a particular religious communion. It does not connote his geographical habitat or his political associations and obligations. And when a person says, therefore, that he is a Mahomedan first and an Indian next, all that he can mean by it is that his religious associations and obligations must have absolute precedence over his political associations and obligations. In other words, his allegiance to the non-Moslem State of which he may be a subject or a citizen, must give way to his allegiance to the Moslem peoples and princes of the world, when these two come into conflict with each other. This is the necessary logic of that political Pan-Islamism which is evidently represented by Mr. Zafar Ali Khan and Syed Amir Ali and the Moslem League. And as such it is the common enemy of Indian Nationalism in its truest and broadest sense, as well as of the present Government in India.

The True Cure.

And the real cure of this mischievous religio-political movement, so far at any rate as India and Egypt are concerned, must be found in the evolution of a true Nationalist Ideal and the constitution of a Federal Government in India, forming part, as an equal among equals, of the larger Federation of the present British Empire, which has been persistently advocated in these pages.

Calcutta: May, 1913.

INDEX.

(The sign [ ] indicates chapter headings and sub-headings.)

(The sign [ ] indicates chapter headings and sub-headings.)

(*The sign* [ ] *indicates chapter headings and sub-headings.*)

(*The sign* [ ] *indicates chapter headings and sub-headings.*)

(*The sign* [ ] *indicates chapter headings and sub-headings.*)

(*The sign* [ ] *indicates chapter headings and sub-headings.*)

(The sign [ ] indicates chapter headings and sub-headings.)

(The sign [ ] indicates chapter headings and sub-headings.)

(The sign [ ] indicates chapter headings and sub-headings.)

(*The sign* [ ] *indicates chapter headings and sub-headings.*)

(*The sign* [ ] *indicates chapter headings and sub-headings.*)

(The sign [ ] indicates chapter headings and sub-headings.)

(The sign [ ] indicates chapter headings and sub-headings.)

(*The sign* [ ] *indicates chapter headings and sub-headings.*)

(*The sign* [ ] *indicates chapter headings and sub-headings.*)

(The sign [ ] indicates chapter headings and sub-headings.)

(*The sign* [ ] *indicates chapter headings and sub-headings.*)

(The sign [ ] indicates chapter headings and sub-headings.)

(*The sign [ ] indicates chapter headings and sub-headings.*)

(*The sign* [ ] *indicates chapter headings and sub-headings.*)

(The sign [ ] indicates chapter headings and sub-headings.)

(The sign [ ] indicates chapter headings and sub-headings.)

(*The sign* [ ] *indicates chapter headings and sub-headings.*)

(The sign [ ] indicates chapter headings and sub-headings.)

(The sign [ ] indicates chapter headings and sub-headings.)

(The sign [ ] indicates chapter headings and sub-headings.)

FINIS.